A PAINTER'S
JOURNEY

OTHER BOOKS BY BARBARA CARUSO

Wording the Silent Art

A PAINTER'S

1966–1973

JOURNEY

BARBARA CARUSO

THE MERCURY PRESS

The publisher gratefully acknowledges the financial assistance of the Canada Council for the Arts, the Ontario Arts Council, and the Ontario Book Publishing Tax Credit Program. The publisher further acknowledges the financial support of the Government of Canada through the Department of Canadian Heritage's Book Publishing Industry Development Program (BPIDP) for our publishing activities.

Editor: Beverley Daurio
Cover, composition and page design: Beverley Daurio
Cover image: Barbara Caruso, photographed by Nelson Ball (1970)
Back cover photographs by Barbara Caruso (1970)
Printed and bound in Canada
Printed on acid-free paper

1 2 3 4 5   09 08 07 06 05

Library and Archives Canada Cataloguing in Publication
Caruso, Barbara, 1937-
A painter's journey / Barbara Caruso.
ISBN 1-55128-114-7
1. Caruso, Barbara, 1937-   2. Painters—Canada—Biography.
I. Title.
ND249.C32A2 2005   759.11   C2005-905293-7

The Mercury Press
Box 672, Station P, Toronto, Ontario Canada M5S 2Y4
www.themercurypress.ca

Contents

Introduction

I began to write this book forty years ago. I did not know then that I was writing a book; I merely started a journal during a period of frustration. So began this record of my painting, my thoughts about my work and about the people who populated my world at that time. I was not a faithful diarist. There are gaps in this account.

I have followed my journals to tell this story. I have also used my memory, my files and my letters to confirm anecdotes and clarify details. I have tried to retain the voice of my younger self. I am opinionated and critical of others in these writings and I am naive. I do not spare my friends, nor do I spare myself. My journals served many purposes and my reasons for writing evolved as my work progressed.

Painting is a lonely job. Like many artists, I make my work alone in the privacy of my studio. I share that experience here. It is an artist's responsibility to get the work out of the studio and into a public forum where it can be seen. This is not easily accomplished.

From 1966 to 1973 I had five solo exhibitions in private galleries. The difficulties surrounding those shows are described here. The problems I encountered were not uncommon. Other artists will have had similar experiences. But this is my story, and I tell it, without apology, from my own perspective, for that is how I lived it and wrote of it in my journals.

The reader will meet many artists and writers on these pages. Weed Flower Press and Coach House Press figure here insofar as I took part in them. My own small press, Seripress, was begun in these years. The early Canada Council programs of grants for artists and writers play a role. Toronto art dealers, curators and critics visit me, and I them, at a time when Canadian artists were competing for exhibition space with art from the United States. The reader will tour Toronto's galleries seeing the shows as I saw them and together we will see Europe — me, for the first time.

And there is Nelson. From the beginning, Nelson Ball, my poet, is part of this story. He is like a shadow throughout, always present in the background.

It was Nelson who suggested that I transcribe my journals. I thought the idea was preposterous, but I tried — twice. Each time, I found I could not do it; it was too hard. For every disappointment I had written down, I could read ten more between the lines. It took several years for me to realize that if there is a story here, it is about the disappointments, about the joys and frustrations of painting, and about my hopes of finding others who would understand what I had made and why I had made it.

I am grateful to bpNichol (1944–1988) who, for some reason unknown to me, believed that I could write. To Nelson, who believed this book should be published, and I thank Beverley Daurio for making it possible.

We shall tell our story clearly if we treat first what was done first,
if we keep the temporal order of events.

UNKNOWN AUTHOR OF *Ad Herennium*

1966

Kitchener, Ontario

15 June, 1966. Wednesday

Yesterday was bad. Now the feeling is almost past and this book (for hates and impending suicide) seems absurd. I don't doubt that the depression will return.

Jack Cain kept a journal while he was in Vancouver. I have seen it twice in the past month. He carries it with him and shows it to everyone. I begin to think that journals or diaries are kept mainly to be shown. We beg for audience even in our fantasies. Why not in this, too? There are no secret writings, only secret thoughts and those, too, we eventually tell.

17 June, 1966. Friday

Last night, Yvonne Stanton and I drove to Georgetown to Gallery House Sol. Yvonne arranged with John Sommer to have the Printers 14 exhibition at her gallery [Gaslight Gallery in Kitchener] in September, and Mr. Sommer took two of my paintings on consignment.

On the way over, Yvonne proposed that I become her artist — the Gaslight Gallery would give me a show once a year without charging me a fee. For a free show, she said she would raise her commission on sales above the one-third she currently takes. She said she would get other shows for me using her connections. I have discussed this proposal with Nelson only briefly. I don't want to do it.

Yvonne appears to have few connections, no more than I have myself. A show in her gallery is not worth much to me. According to Yvonne, I would have to produce a lot of work to supply all the "little galleries" she spoke of. I don't paint so easily and my work is not popular.

Of course, I want exposure and the smaller galleries serve this purpose, but it's too early for me to tie myself to a gallery. I believe there is a danger of becoming over-exposed in small galleries.

This morning, I read the poems I wrote yesterday. They don't look very good; in fact, all the poems are terrible.

18 June, 1966. Saturday

I worked on cover drawings yesterday — no results yet. I got quite depressed about my lack of facility with these drawings. As for painting, I am impatient to work. I hope my paint arrives soon; as well, I must buy canvas.

Last night, I felt overwhelmingly alone and angry about this isolation. The trip to Georgetown has exaggerated my sense of aloneness; there was talk about painters like Rita Brianski and Libby Altwerger. I'm afraid of being trapped here, and Yvonne's proposal was frightening in that regard.

Last night I dreamed we were in Mexico. Nelson was appalled by the smells as we walked on the street and by the look of the food we saw served in restaurants. But he said he liked being there. I worried about where I could find him some pork and beans and mashed potatoes.

20 June, 1966. Monday

I don't know what to do to alleviate my loneliness. We talked about it over the weekend. Nelson said I should go to Toronto for a few days. (I will, as soon as I have some money to spend.) He said he would go to Toronto himself in a few weeks. He said I should start painting. (I will, as soon as I can buy paint and canvas.) We can't spend money we don't have. This morning, the bill for hospital insurance arrived in the mail; that will use up our money for this month.

21 June, 1966. Tuesday

I'm trying to line up art classes for teaching in the fall. I have two prospects.

I finished reading *Bold Saboteurs* by Chandler Brossard today.

Ray Stanton came by to return the $2 that Yvonne borrowed from me for gas when we went to Georgetown. I asked him to see if she could pay me for the watercolour Helga bought from my show at the gallery. (It would pay for the hospital insurance.)

Nelson phoned me at noon. I like it when he phones. He does well to work at this job. I know he hates it. It isn't "hate," I suppose, but the job seems like a waste of time. He would rather be here writing.

22 June, 1966. Wednesday

It is early, a warm morning, but the apartment stays cool. I have been working on the drawings for the cover of Bill's book [*Ottawa Poems* by William Hawkins (Weed Flower Press)].

Last night, Nelson typed stencils while I worked on the drawings.

23 June, 1966. Thursday

Yesterday, Yvonne came by with a cheque for $23.80, my money for the watercolour that Helga bought. It will help. This morning, I took the cheque to the bank and deposited it in my account, along with the $5.50 for deposit in Nelson's account.

Nelson has finished typing the stencils for Bill's book. I am working with only small success on the cover design. I've put so many hours into this with such puny results.

I am reading Faulkner's *Wild Palms*.

24 June, 1966. Friday

Last night, Nelson and I worked out a weekly budget. We will save from $20 to $26 each week, will spend $15 on groceries, $3.75 for the milkman and the paper-boy, and Nelson will have $6.25 for spending money. It will be a tight squeeze, but we'll try this for a while.

At first, Nelson was annoyed: "Only $6.25! A hell of a way to live." Later, he began to think about what he would do with it, how he would spend it, and he seemed almost enthusiastic about the whole plan. I hope it works.

I put several more hours into that cover design yesterday without good results. I think I'll try the subject with acrylic on paper. I may resolve it that way.

25 June, 1966. Saturday

I did no work on the cover design yesterday. I spent most of my time reading Faulkner's *The Old Man*. I did some housewifery, but otherwise accomplished little.

My paint hasn't arrived yet. The store hasn't called; I'll call on Monday.

Time is uneventful, but pleasant lately. I continue to read the newspaper looking for a part-time job. Maybe I can make up for this summer by teaching art classes this fall.

It is unbearably hot. It will rain soon.

28 June, 1966. Tuesday

My painting from the Ontario Society of Artists exhibition was returned yesterday [*Men and Horses 1* (1965) acrylic on paper]. Shipping cost $11.73 — quite a shock!

I'm painting today.

29 June, 1966. Wednesday

I have finished the cover drawing for Bill Hawkins' book. I think it works at last. I am working now on the title lettering. Lettering! I thought I'd left that behind four years ago.

The paintings (acrylic on paper) I worked on yesterday have both been scrapped. Strangely, it doesn't depress me that neither piece went anywhere.

It's very hot again.

2 July, 1966. Saturday

Yesterday, Nelson was home all day because of the holiday. He spent the morning printing the pages of Bill's book on the Gestetner; I gathered them in the afternoon. We got the job done. The book is going to look good. I think Nelson is pleased with it, too.

We are sticking to our budget. Nelson has been awfully good about it. He is looking forward to his $2 increase as if it were a thousand.

I am reading Norman Mailer's *Advertisements for Myself.*

5 July, 1966. Tuesday

I mailed about a dozen drawings to Carlos Reyes for use in his little magazine, *Potpourri* [Pensa De Lagar/Wine Press, Milwaukee, Oregon]. I will be curious to see what he chooses, if he chooses anything.

I am going to go to Kincardine to work in the store. I will leave around the 20th.

9 July, 1966. Saturday

I'm depressed this morning and I don't know why.

We haven't heard from Bill about the cover for his book. I'm afraid he doesn't like it. I finished the cover for Carlos Reyes' book, *The Windows*, even the lettering. Nelson will take it to the printer today. Me, I go to the laundromat.

11 July, 1966. Monday

Nelson worked on *Weed #5* over the weekend. He has finished the layout and will start to type the stencils tonight. I have read Allen Ginsberg's *Reality Sandwiches*. Now, I'm reading *Kaddish and Other Poems*, also *The Yage Letters* between William Burroughs and Ginsberg. I'm reading Robert Creeley's novel, *The Island*.

12 July, 1966. Tuesday

I feel suspended. I can't work; I read a lot. The weather is oppressively hot, humid, tiring. One would rather lie down on the sidewalk than take another step on the street.

I went to the bank today taking little bits of money for deposit in three different accounts. It's ridiculous, but we have to get some money ahead. Nelson has gotten a $5 raise! He was more pleased about it than he wanted to admit.

I received the entry forms for the Royal Canadian Academy show. I plan to enter two pieces, both *Town Image* pieces. I'll call Yvonne so I can get them out of the gallery. I almost hate to call; I have no ear for her financial problems — we have our own. And she still owes me $100.

14 July, 1966. Thursday

I've been trying to reach Yvonne. This morning, I was told she had gone on holiday for two weeks. I want to get those paintings from the gallery so I can change the matts and backing before I leave for Kincardine. I'll try to get in touch with Ron March.

Nelson picked up the covers from the printer yesterday afternoon and we spent the evening working on Carlos Reyes' book (about 70 copies complete with covers, so far).

I received the new issues of *Art International* and *Canadian Art*. Some exciting things in them. A lot of the sculpture is large and stark; it's confusing me. I wonder how it would feel to be standing near it.

I'm reading *How It Is* by Samuel Beckett again; that is, I'm taking another run at it.

15 July, 1966. Friday

I reached Ron March last night. He came by at noon today, drove me to the gallery and brought me back with the two paintings. He told me that he and Yvonne had spent Monday in Toronto visiting artists in their studios. They were looking for new artists for the gallery. They found no one because all of the artists they saw were already committed to a gallery. Ron said that I was "very well known in Toronto circles." It seems that all of the artists they visited had heard of me. They didn't visit Joe Tatarnic and Dace Birkhans, or Carol Martyn. I don't understand that. I told Yvonne about these three people because they are artists who are *not* committed to a gallery.

I hope Yvonne and Ron will get the gallery rolling again. If they do, I'll have an opportunity to teach some art classes.

I went out for coffee yesterday just to sit and watch people out of the restaurant window. I went to Kresge's and wandered around looking at things with the mad shoppers. I see I can buy three pair of underpants for Nelson for only $1.77. I'll go back tomorrow while they are still there and I still have $1.77.

19 July, 1966. Tuesday

Nelson has finished both of the books. They are packaged now ready to be mailed. There are 178 copies of Bill's *Ottawa Poems* and 131 copies of Carlos Reyes' *The Windows*. Nelson is sending fifty or sixty copies of each book to the bookstores and is mailing notices to the libraries.

I will take the train to Kincardine this evening.

8 August, 1966. Monday

Nelson met me at the train last night. We are going to Yvonne's tonight to talk about art classes at the gallery this fall. Yvonne wants Nelson to organize poetry readings, too.

I received a letter from Joe Tatarnic. It brought me up to date on the Toronto scene. Joe is excited about the large scale paintings he is doing. Sounds good; I'm anxious to see them.

9 August, 1966. Tuesday

We went to Yvonne's last night. Yvonne and her friends, Pete and Ron March, made it an evening of jokes and laughter — they think they are comedians. I felt really impatient with them. However, it was determined that I will teach two night classes a week at the gallery — a painting class on Mondays and a drawing class on Thursdays. I will be paid $15 per class; the courses will be eight weeks long. Nelson is going to try organize a reading for November at the gallery.

11 August, 1966. Thursday

I want to go to Toronto for a day to buy paint. I'm trying to reach Yvonne for more information about the classes — it may take days to reach her. I've tried to call Grant Smith about doing the Saturday morning children's classes again for the Kitchener-Waterloo Art Gallery. No answer — he's probably on holiday.

Nelson has received two manuscripts; one was from David Cull, the other from Seymour Mayne. I think he wants to publish Cull. We will probably be doing another issue of *Weed* soon.

I'm reading *Adventures of a Young Man* by John Dos Passos.

13 August, 1966. Saturday

Last night, Nelson helped me prepare the two paintings, *Town Image #1* and *Town Image #2*, for the Royal Canadian Academy show. In this morning's mail, I received the entry forms for the Watercolour Society's show. I want to send *Town Image #3* and *#4*.

16 August, 1966. Tuesday

Yesterday was a good, good day for both of us. In the afternoon, I worked with brush and ink on paper, making *The Bicycle Rider* — good results at last. It's terrific to see something happen and to be inside it. Nelson worked on poems last night and got somewhere with them. Then we spent a lot of time talking about the drawing and the poems, getting so involved that when we went to bed neither of us could sleep.

Yvonne delivered *Town Image #3* and *#4* and all of the small acrylics that were in the show. She took the sixteen small pieces that I made in 1964 in Mexico. She wants to hang them on the upper floor of the gallery.

Jack Cain called at noon on Sunday to say that he and Harry were driving over to pick us up to go with them to Kleinburg to see the McMichael Estate and its collection of Canadian paintings. Nelson couldn't go; he was working on *Volume 63*, but I went and really enjoyed seeing the place and the paintings. Jack and Harry squabbled a lot on the trip there and back — a bit tedious.

I am writing an introductory letter for each of the night classes. Nelson will print them for me on the Gestetner.

20 August, 1966. Saturday

Last night, we listened to records and talked. Bill Hawkins' song, "It's a dirty shame," recorded by The Esquires, has just been released and Nelson bought a copy. This is what started us listening.

I will go to Toronto next week.

22 August, 1966. Monday

I accomplished no work over the weekend, but Nelson worked on some poems on Sunday, while I did nothing more exciting than the laundry.

I'm having difficulty settling to work. When I think about this next year, I see it as a repetition of this last one — in some respects, that's not a pleasant prospect. The lack of company, the loneliness, is the most difficult thing to endure.

I worry about money. I don't know how we'll pay back Nelson's student loan in less than two years. The thought of staying here for two more years is horrid. The thought of having to put all of my earnings into paying back that loan makes me cringe.

24 August, 1966. Wednesday

I went to Toronto yesterday and really enjoyed the day. I bought eight yards of canvas, 60" wide, and a complete palette of Liquitex acrylic tube colours. It cost me a fortune, $40, but it will be worth it. I didn't buy the paper I wanted — I was out of money.

Joe met me at 3:30 p.m. for coffee. It was good seeing him and it sounds as if he's on to something in his work.

I stopped at the Village Book Store and talked with Marty Ahvenus for a few minutes. The bus left at 5:15 and I got back here at 8 p.m. with all sorts of news to tell Nelson.

This morning's mail brought me a cheque from the Galería San Miguel in Mexico. A man from Texas has bought one of my paintings [*Portrait* (1964) acrylic on paper]. *Other Voices* came for Nelson; he has two poems in this issue.

29 August, 1966. Monday

We were busy over the weekend. Nelson printed *Weed #5* and reprinted copies of *Weed #1*. We gathered, stapled and folded all of them. They only need to be addressed now and mailed.

Last week, I made a painting, acrylic on paper, of *Man on a Bicycle*. I think it is quite successful.

3 September, 1966. Saturday

Yvonne called to say that she will begin advertising the art classes on Tuesday. I finally reached Grant Smith; he will get back to me in mid-September after the gallery committee meets to let me know what the arrangements will be for the children's classes. So, I'm going to have some work after all.

Yesterday, I stretched and primed two large canvases. I wish I knew what to do with them next. I've done nothing worth keeping since *Man on a Bicycle*.

We are getting a little money ahead, but we've made no payments yet on the student loan. That loan is an axe over my head.

6 September, 1966. Tuesday

Nelson did the mock-up for David Cull's book [*3 x 4 Is*] over this weekend, and I wrote a letter to Chris Wells who is doing the cover drawing.

I have done a bicycle rider drawing that I want to make into a large oil painting. Nelson and I have talked a lot about the merit of the "man on a bicycle." I feel clearer about my use of this theme, but I hesitate.

Received a letter from Joe Tatarnic today. He enclosed an invitation for the Printers 14 show at the Gaslight Gallery here.

7 September, 1966. Wednesday

I have begun to work on the large painting of the *Man on a Bicycle*.

8 September, 1966. Thursday

I worked further on *Man on a Bicycle* yesterday. I'm not satisfied with the colour relationships. I want to use the primary colours, red, yellow and blue. At present, the blue areas are pure, the red area is small and low in value. It is the "yellow" areas (now too green) that I want to change to low value yellows, ochres which will have force because of the large size of the areas. I'll try this.

I spoke with Yvonne. She said that she has had a lot of inquiries about the classes. So far, one student has enrolled — a woman who was in my class last year.

Last night, I went to the opening of Printers 14. It is a good show. Jo Manning's and Dace Birkhans' pieces are excellent. Joe's work is good, but not as full or as intense as those two. Libby and Sandra Altwerger's pieces didn't really impress me. John Mattar's work has all sorts of qualities, but somehow I wasn't impressed by it. John Meuller from Doon showed woodcuts, *Homage to a Tree*. They were nice, but struck me as tricky; they are impressions of wood grain. There were two other printers that interested me; one worked with colour and circles, the other used a show-girl figure as subject. I don't remember their names.

John Sommer and his wife were there, and I spoke with Mrs. Sommer. I talked with John Mattar; I haven't seen him since college. I talked with Pete March, with Helga and Yvonne. I was introduced to John Meuller.

9 September, 1966. Friday

Last night, Nelson printed the two letters for the night classes for me. This morning, I sent a copy of both to the art supply store here, and one to my one enrolled student. We spent the rest of last evening addressing copies of *Weed #5* — that job's not finished yet.

Nelson has been reading *Psychotherapy East and West* by Alan Watts with great interest. I have started Watts' *Way of Zen*.

12 September, 1966. Monday

Yvonne called with seven more names of people who have enrolled in the classes.

I mailed my entry forms for the Canadian Society of Painters in Watercolour show today. I will ship the crates this week.

Over the weekend, I finished my painting [*Man on a Bicycle*. oil on canvas]. Nelson pored over the Weed Flower Press account books. He has sent out statements. Maybe he will receive a flood of money now.

14 September, 1966. Wednesday

I began a painting yesterday [*Landscape*. oil on canvas]. I'm pleased with it so far. It's small (about 24" x 36") and I'm using tape to hold the edges of some areas. This is the first time I've used tape, so in that respect, this is an experiment.

15 September, 1966. Thursday

I was so keyed-up yesterday after Yvonne's phone call that I couldn't start to work until 2 p.m. I was in a bit of a panic about the art classes which begin next week.

But I worked the afternoon and again last night, and I stripped the tape off my painting. So far, I'm pleased with the results.

I'm slow to begin work this morning. It is cold in here. The sun is shining, but it must be windy outside because I can feel a breeze on my legs which is coming through the closed door. I can hear the wind groaning in the hallway.

16 September, 1966. Friday
I set down a compositional drawing for a large painting this morning. I still feel doubtful about it, but I may go ahead with it. I may be able to resolve it with paint, rather than hover over the sketch for too long.

Nelson seems to have caught a cold.

19 September, 1966. Monday
Nelson spent the weekend in bed with a fever and is home today because of his cold.

There was lots of mail this morning and it was fun to be able to open it as soon as it arrived. There were two letters from Steve Buri — he sent poems for *Weed.* There was an interesting note from Mr. Scott about *Volume 63, #5.* These were all for Nelson, of course, but he let me read them.

I spent the weekend working on the large painting [*Large Landscape.* oil on canvas]. I used tape again. This one has come off reasonably well; I'm quite excited about it. I'm not sure where I am going with these last few paintings, but I like what I see.

My classes begin tonight.

20 September, 1966. Tuesday
I'm very pleased with the painting class. Eight people came, and one more will be coming next week. They seem an enthusiastic group, willing to work and work quickly. I had the "beginners" make a colour chart last night while the others made drawings from a still life. Next week, I'll have everyone work from still life; I plan to set up two of them.

I had coffee with Yvonne after the class, so I was late getting home. She paid me $120. I'll go to the bank today. Yvonne has asked for three or four pieces of work for her December group show. I'll try to have them for her.

I didn't do much yesterday; I was too anxious about the class. I didn't sleep well last night; I was awake until 4 a.m. I have a cold this morning.

There was a letter from Margaret Randall in this morning's mail addressed to both of us. I read it and learned that my drawings will appear in *El Corno Emplumado #20,* which is *on the way.* She sent three poems to Nelson for *Weed.* I got a letter from Carol Martyn, too. She sounds busy and enthused. She has entered the Winnipeg show. I guess I'll miss that one. I didn't know it was coming up so soon.

21 September, 1966. Wednesday

Last night, Nelson worked on the layout for *Weed #6.* I did some drawing. I have a compositional drawing and I have decided to work it into a large ink drawing before going on to a painting. It is structural, like the last two paintings, and it deals with wall and roof lines — squares, rectangles and triangles.

I want to understand my choices. I believe it's important to question one's "intuition" to become aware of its limitations. I have worked on three paintings, moving from one to the next, without much concern about "content." That doesn't mean the paintings have no content; rather, it means that I have no words to describe it. "This is not a description, it is what occurs." *That* is my content. My paintings work; they satisfy me, at least, but *what am I doing?*

I'm reading the chemistry section in Mayer's book again [Ralph Mayer's *The Artist's Handbook of Materials and Techniques*].

22 September, 1966. Thursday

First drawing class tonight.

26 September, 1966. Monday

It was Thursday or Friday that I worked all day on brush and ink drawings from the compositional sketch I had made. I worked on three pieces; one was 18" x 24" and the others were smaller. I was disappointed and depressed by the results and I've done no real work on them since.

Thursday night's drawing class went well. It is an interesting group. They all said that they would like the classes to continue longer than the eight weeks scheduled and most said they want to paint eventually.

27 September, 1966. Tuesday

The painting class went well last night. I'm pleased by the work the group is doing and surprised by the originality everyone is showing.

My own work is halted. I don't know what I'm doing.

I can't help thinking about Jack Bechtel today. It is hard to believe that he's dead. Jack was my first art instructor; he taught the beginners' class in 1954, my first year at Doon [Doon Summer School of Fine Arts]. I had been painting on my own for two years by then and he treated me as if I were special. He's much too young to die.

28 September, 1966. Wednesday

In this morning's mail, I received notice that one of my paintings has been accepted for the Royal Canadian Academy show. I'm pleased, but not particularly excited about it.

4 October, 1966. Tuesday

I have not been painting for the past two weeks. This makes me feel very restless, but still I don't paint.

The last three paintings, *Man on a Bicycle* and the two landscapes, still look good to me. (I wonder if this is true, or if I am only defending what I have done.) But I'm unable to continue. If I'm being defensive about these paintings, then I may be limiting myself by them. My inability to carry on may be caused by this limit. (Is this true?) I have sketches I could work into paintings, but the doubts I have about them are preventing me.

20 October, 1966. Thursday

I went to Toronto on Tuesday for no particular reason except to *go*. I wandered around by myself, visiting some galleries.

I was impressed by Dennis Burton's show at the Isaacs Gallery. Two pieces in particular impressed me. One was a drawing; it was made so the viewer was looking up a girl's skirt, but it was the combination and balance of drawing and hand lettering that impressed me. The lettering was a "chunk" that formed a strong overlapping area. Another drawing used white gouache to create the bulk and sensuousness of flesh — a chunk of white on the page. I didn't like *Leda and the Swan*, but I was interested in how it was painted.

Isaacs was also showing a sculptor I'd not seen or heard of before, Archie Miller. He was working with the human form on the surface plane of a cube or box (concrete on stainless steel). I thought some of these were very good, but others looked like restatements of the good pieces and so seemed weak and repetitious. I saw a couple of montages by Greg Curnoe that didn't reach me at all and a work by Ted Bieler that I thought was good, but unexciting.

Gallery Moos was showing Ulysse Comptois. The paintings struck me as sloppy and I had difficulty overcoming this initial impression. As well, I thought they were derivative of op art. Now, I wonder if that sloppiness was what was important and I missed it, or misinterpreted it. The sculptures in the show were phallic and fun things. They were like brightly coloured toys and I liked that about them. They looked too heavy and clumsy to be toys, but I think that things that are fun (and even phallic) should be played with. I touched some pieces; I was teased by their appearance.

I went to the print gallery on Yorkville and to Gallery Dresdenere, but saw nothing that interested me.

I went into the Scientology store on Yonge Street and bought two books, so I could learn something about this mad science. I've read both books now and found nothing.

Stopped at the Village Book Store, saw Marty and bought the *Artaud Anthology*. So far, I've read only a few letters, some prose and a couple of poems, but it interests me greatly.

24 October, 1966. Monday

I worked on the *Tightrope Walker* (acrylic on paper) today. I'm not happy with it. Maybe I said all that can be said (or needs to be said) in the first piece I did. I will set all four pieces aside for a while.

31 October, 1966. Monday

Steve Buri was here on Saturday. Steve and Nelson talked about poetry, and Steve talked about himself and his work. On Saturday night, Steve and I went out for a drink. Conversation went much as it would have a year ago. I'm surprised that Steve continues to underestimate Nelson.

I am still struggling to paint. My last effort was a still life, acrylic on paper. The objects are flat shapes of colour and each object has its word (bottle, jug, orange, orange, orange) on it, the letters applied with rubber stamps using acrylic paint [*Still Life*. 24" x 19"]. I think it is reasonably successful, but I don't know if it means anything or will lead anywhere.

Perhaps I'm wrong to expect a painting to *lead* somewhere. It *does* happen, but because it is not happening now, I wonder if I'm condemning my own work prematurely. Must it happen? Is an isolated statement, a fragment, so to speak, not valid? Is it a lesser statement and is that why I'm unhappy? There is no point trying to convince myself that my work is good, that I am *on*, because I *am* unhappy with my work right now. This is something I *feel* and no amount of rationalizing can change the feeling.

Last week, Al Strong bought two of the watercolours I made in Mexico.

1 November, 1966. Tuesday

Last night, before going to teach my class, Nelson and I talked about my frustration with my work. He said that much of my frustration is *that* frustration that I feel about my work no matter how well it is going, but that there is a despondency at present that should not exist. He suggested that if I made about twenty drawings in a week, I might work out of this by finding that I had done ten good pieces of work. I argued against this "exercise," but today I think I should try it.

2 November, 1966. Wednesday
Yesterday, I worked on drawings. I did five pieces and only one has anything going for it. The one piece that I think is successful implies introspection. Using rubber stamps, I put X Y Z inside the figure and A B C D outside of it [*A B C D*. ink on paper]. This idea came from something Virginia Woolf describes in *To the Lighthouse*.

3 November, 1966. Thursday
It is disturbing to realize that I have felt unhappy about my painting since I began to write in this book. Looking back, I remember the depression that prompted this writing. It began just after my show at the Gaslight Gallery [May 4-28] for which I had done so much work. I had spent six months solidly working for that show. Did I believe the work was sound then? I remember that I was up and down about it as I worked, but in spite of my doubts, *I knew I was working*.

Today (I will only speak for today), I feel reasonably good about the drawings I've been doing. True, I've done about a dozen drawings and I only feel really good about two of them. It seems that when each drawing is finished, I am stopped by it. I am looking for some direction from it. I believe each work has some merit, even if it is slight. I'm anxious to work with paint, but I have been unable to face a large canvas — I feel too far away from it.

We have paid down $200 on the student loan; $800 more to go.

4 November, 1966. Friday
Yesterday, I did no drawing, but went out for a while. I spent a couple of hours at the Providence Bookstore looking at art books and reading. I looked through a book on Sumerian art; I sat down and read a great chunk of Hans Richter's *Dada: Art and Anti-art*.

9 November, 1966. Wednesday
I'm painting today. Yesterday, I began a large canvas, *The Chairs*. The work goes slowly because of the complicated pattern involved in the composition. The painting depends on this pattern.

I picked up the entry forms for Perspective '67 at the K-W Art Gallery yesterday. I had a talk with Bert Henderson [curator]. He told me that he and a professor at Waterloo are collaborating on a book about drawing for engineers. He said he was using Paul Klee's books and Fred Hagan's methods to create a program to teach drawing skills to non-artists, that is, to engineers. I begin to see what he is teaching at the university.

11 November, 1966. Friday
I'm a little disturbed about last night's drawing class. Al Strong (he's a student) began to question me about the finicky paintings that are hanging in the gallery. I feel like a coward, because I avoided answering. He persisted, deliberately quizzed me about my thoughts on the work. I don't believe I should comment on a show at the gallery — that's not why I'm there. I got very uncomfortable because I didn't like the work, but didn't want to say so.

14 November, 1966. Monday
I spent most of today working on *The Chairs*. It is almost complete. At one point, I brought the painting into the kitchen and stood it on the floor (leaning against the table). The foreground figure (seen from the back) appears to be outside of the painting, a spectator like myself. I am confused by this; I don't know if that's a good effect or not.

Nelson went to Toronto on Saturday and returned on Sunday. He took some books to sell to Marty and bought as many again — mostly poetry. He stayed at Victor Coleman's where he said there was a party of sorts on Saturday night. It was a strange collection of people — Victor and Elizabeth, Victor's mother, Robert Creeley and his wife Bobbie, Roy Kiyooka, and others he didn't name — about ten or twelve people. Nelson said Creeley seemed completely bored and Roy Kiyooka spent the evening stretched out on the couch, saying nothing. Only Bobbie Creeley was keeping conversation alive. I suspect that Nelson just faded into the woodwork, because he told me he spent the evening reading Victor's poetry books and magazines.

15 November, 1966. Tuesday
I was not satisfied with my painting yesterday. Last night, I showed it to Nelson and we talked about it. He suggested that I could simplify the foreground figure even further. I have done so, and now I know it is finished [*The Chairs*. 36" x 48" oil on canvas].

6 December, 1966. Tuesday
Since last writing here, I have worked on three more paintings. They developed out of the ink drawings that I was doing. The drawings use a checkerboard pattern. The paintings use a coloured checkerboard pattern — many colours, warm and cool, that lead the eye to "dance" over the pattern. There is a featureless figure in

the foreground of each painting — a spectator. Within each painting, there are objects — a table, white chairs, a jug and bottle, oranges and a female figure. The foreground figure is always grey; it is a spectator, or it's the shadow of a man beside the spectator, or the shadow of the viewer. The patterned area, the "floor," is not a regular checkerboard. Being irregular, I believe it will slow down the viewer, making the eye play with the possibilities of that surface. The objects can be identified by their contour only. I have applied flat areas of colour, making no attempt to model the objects.

The use of the female nude has made me think up a little theory; that is, that man sees woman as an extension of himself. All of the objects in the painting, including the nude, are extensions of the man — the grey man in the foreground, or the viewer, or even me (gender is arbitrary here).

The first painting remains tentative. I think the second [*Figure and Still Life.* 36" x 36" oil on canvas] is quite successful and the third [*Figure and Chairs.* 48" x 48" oil on canvas], still unfinished, is the most exciting.

One of Nelson's poems will appear in an article by James Reaney in the Christmas edition of *The Globe and Mail.* I think he's pretty proud about this — he was all smiles when he read the letter that asked for his permission to use it.

The Gaslight Gallery will close as a gallery at the end of December. I've been told that the art classes can continue in the space. I hope so; otherwise, I'm out of a job.

9 December, 1966. Friday

I'm arranging to go to Toronto next week. I'm trying to reach Joe and Dace to see if I can stay with them.

I am having second thoughts about my recent paintings. I am wondering if they are evasions. When this thought first occurred to me it was pretty shattering. I have to believe that this question is a constructive one; I must think it through.

Bert Henderson saw my painting, *Man on a Bicycle* (the acrylic on paper), at the opening at the Gaslight on Wednesday night and he told me he liked it. I was surprised to have so direct and positive a comment from him.

19 December, 1966. Monday

I went to Toronto last week. On arriving, I went to Marty's, the Village Book Store on Gerrard Street, where I ran into Bill Hawkins. Bill was in town for a few days; he said he was indulging himself by seeing movies non-stop — morning, afternoon and night — and he was loving it. I went to Metro Central Library where I saw Joe and he gave me the keys to the apartment. I ran into Dennis McDermott who I hadn't seen since 1963. We went for coffee and had supper together.

On Tuesday, I went gallery hopping. I was most impressed by Graham Coughtry's show at the Isaacs Gallery. At Gallery Moos, I saw a show of 20th century art; I was particularly interested by the Kandinskys and the portraits by Francis Bacon. At Laing Gallery, I saw two paintings by Roy Kiyooka that I thought were great. I visited three other galleries but was not impressed by anything in particular. At 6 p.m., I met Jack Cain for dinner.

On Wednesday, I went to the Mirvish Village on Markham Street where I saw two really good shows — one by Frank Stella, the other by Josef Albers — at the David Mirvish Gallery. The Pollock Gallery had a show of prints by a woman, one of the people who had been in the Printers 14 show here. The work seemed technically fine, but not very exciting.

That evening, we went to Chinatown for a great meal — Joe and Dace, Joe's cousin Bill and a friend, Mary, from the library, and Barbara Sourbrai, who arrived after the meal, but stayed the evening.

On Thursday, I had lunch with Jack at the International Restaurant at College and Spadina, then went on to the Art Gallery of Ontario where I looked at the collection. There was a special show of "toys" in the sculpture court— artists had been asked to make toys for children as a Christmas exhibit. I could identify the painters and sculptors who had made some of the toys by their appearance. I watched a group of children playing with them; they were having a grand time. Then I went to Markham Street to see Carol Martyn at her studio.

Carol's work has changed since I last saw it in Mexico. It is greatly improved, cleaner and fresher. She is working with acrylic paint now and uses tape to get clean boundaries on shapes. I was glad to see her new work at last, and to have a good talk with her.

That night, Joe, Dace and I went to see Fellini's film, *8½*. On our way out of the theatre, we met Dennis McDermott and Susan, Jack and his friend, and Mary from the library and her friend. We had a jolly time gathered together there in the foyer.

I spent Friday morning talking with Joe. My bus to Kitchener left at 1:15 p.m.; I dropped in to see Marty for a few minutes before leaving. I was back here early enough to wash all the dishes Nelson had left piled in the sink before he got home.

28 December, 1966. Wednesday
One of my paintings has been accepted for exhibit in the 7th Annual Exhibition at Rodman Hall in St. Catharines (*Figure and Still Life*. 36" x 36" oil on canvas). I received the entry forms for the Ontario Society of Artists show and for the Canadian Society of Graphic Artists show. I plan to enter both of them.

30 December, 1966. Friday
Confusion regarding the art classes. I can't reach Dave about using the gallery space now that the gallery is closed.

Yvonne told me that she and Ray will not be buying the two paintings they so "definitely" wanted. Also, she told me that Pete and Ron March will not buy the acrylic on paper painting they wanted because they can't afford the $50.

1967

5 January, 1967. Thursday
I have thoughts.

10 January, 1967. Tuesday
I'm taking enrollment for the art classes now. I reached Dave and we agreed on the rent for the gallery space. The phone calls for enrollment have been a distraction, so I've made no attempt to work. I've done nothing since *The House that Jack Built* [24" x 19" ink on paper]. I will be sending out work at the end of this month; I'm busy preparing the work for shipment. I'm doing a lot of reading.

Yvonne said she will send me the $100 this month.

13 February, 1967. Monday
Nelson has begun to type the stencils for *Weed #7*. He will be about a month late with this issue.

There is $199.33 left to pay on Nelson's student loan.

My entry to the Ontario Society of Artists show was rejected; my entries to the Canadian Society of Graphic Artists show were rejected.

9 March, 1967. Thursday
I have neglected this little book. Two entries back, I was taking enrollment for classes. This week, the night classes end — the eight weeks are finished.

On Tuesday, March 7, I paid down the $199.33 on Nelson's student loan. Paid in full. We are free of debt.

Nelson has finished printing *Weed #8* as well as *Weed #7*. I am gathering the pages today. My supplies are low; I'm planning a trip to Toronto soon.

I have sent my entries for Perspective '67 and mailed an application to the Ontario Centennial Art Program. I will try London this year.

I haven't done much work for the past two weeks. Before that, I was working on drawings. I'm uneasy, restless and discontented.

We hope to move back to Toronto by the fall.

12 March, 1967. Sunday

David McFadden visited us this morning as he promised he would. He arrived at 9 a.m. and he brought in the sun, or as Nelson said, he reminded us that the sun was out there and that was good.

13 March, 1967. Monday

Yesterday, I reread Paul Klee's *Pedagogical Sketchbook*. I was startled again by the similarity between his ideas and my own. Was I taught these ideas at some point? If so, I'm pleased that I learned them so well. Not only have I learned them, but I have been teaching them. This gives me some confidence.

14 March, 1967. Tuesday

The Open Letter from Vancouver arrived in today's mail. Nelson has four poems in this issue and Ted Whittaker has made some favourable comments on them. Nelson will be pleased when he sees it.

17 March, 1967. Friday

Several things are in the wind. I will be shipping two paintings to London by next week for the Western Art League show. Also, I want to enter two pieces in the (Centennial) sale show at the Art Institute of Ontario. I ordered lumber today for the crating. Next month, I will put three works in the local Artists Mart.

Yesterday, Nelson brought home all my work from the Gaslight Gallery. When he brought in the paintings, it was like seeing old friends again.

We still plan to move back to Toronto by September. I don't know how we will afford it; we've been checking the Toronto papers for flats and apartments and the rents seem awfully high.

I have been doing drawings toward the cover of Steve Buri's book, *Elephant Girl*.

21 March, 1967. Tuesday

Yesterday, I received a rejection from Perspective '67. However much I had expected a rejection, I was unprepared for it when it came. I called Nelson just to tell him about it and an hour later he came home to spend the rest of the day with me.

Then last night, we framed my entry for the Western Art League show in London. Even Nelson seemed depressed by the hopelessness of entering this show.

As a result, I was bouncing around being cheerful. It is unlikely that I'll be accepted.

23 March, 1967. Thursday
I wrote letters yesterday and read *The End of the Road* by John Barth. I haven't done much work of any sort lately.

Steve Buri sent me some exhibition catalogues. They are elaborate efforts, just like books. I'm reading the Mondrian.

27 March, 1967. Monday
Yesterday, David W. Harris and Nelson Jones were here. They had driven from Toronto, specifically to meet Nelson. It was as if Harris were checking him out; he behaved as if he were conducting an examination. Harris did most of the talking. Jones said very little. Nelson reacted to Harris and withdrew into silence — even more than usual. I knew that Nelson was simply not going to talk, so I thought I should. I asked Harris, who is a concrete and sound poet, if he knew about Hugo Ball's poetry and sound performances. He said he'd never heard of him, so I told him Ball was among the Dada artists in Zurich in 1916. To this, he said: "Well, if you're way back there..." He seemed disgusted with me.

30 March, 1967. Thursday
David McFadden returned the mock-up for his book, *The Poem Poem*. He included his idea for the cover. He wants to use a drawing by Leonardo da Vinci. As it is, it's incomplete.

Yvonne told me that the Beans are interested in buying my large painting for $250. She said they will surely take it by September. She has not contacted the other couple yet, but she is very sure of making the sale.

31 March, 1967. Friday
Nelson is willing to let me work on the cover for David McFadden's book to try tie it together. I'll work on that today. I'm still working on the cover for Steve's book.

3 April, 1967. Monday
I finished McFadden's cover, also Steve's. Nelson has sent them off for the authors' approvals.

Spent most of the day out just wandering around, in and out of department stores and drinking coffee. I tried to buy a rubber stamp set with letters of the alphabet that are bigger than the one I have, but I couldn't find one.

4 April, 1967. Tuesday
I received the rejection from London this morning.

I have no heart to send my entries to the Art Institute of Ontario.

12 April, 1967. Wednesday
I painted yesterday, acrylic on paper. Interesting results.

This morning's mail brought John Newlove's mock-up for his book, *What They Say*. Newlove enclosed a photocopy of a drawing by Claude Breeze for the cover. I'll have to mount it and do the lettering before it can go to the printer.

Barry Lord called Nelson last night. He approved Nelson's choice of poems for his book, *Subject/Object*.

15 April, 1967. Saturday
I'm going to withdraw my entries for the Art Institute show. The other night, while we were moving paintings, one of the entries fell over and was damaged. I don't want to send a substitute, so I've decided to withdraw both paintings. Nelson is encouraging me to enter, but I think that's because he feels guilty. He was helping me move the paintings. I asked him to move a chair away from the stack of paintings, but he said it wouldn't matter. Then the painting fell forward hitting the back of the chair which put a right-angled tear through the canvas at the top right corner. If the chair had been only inches further away, the painting would have fallen flat on its face, probably without damage. I don't have a way to repair a right-angled tear; it would have to be patched from the back and I don't even want to try it. Of course, it was an accident, but I anticipated it and Nelson didn't listen.

23 May, 1967. Tuesday
Nelson's two-week holiday from his job ended today. He has done a lot of work: he printed the Newlove and the McFadden books, and has begun to print Steve's.

We spent three days in Ottawa where we stayed with Bill and Sheila Hawkins. It rained every day that we were there and it was cold, cold, cold. We went to Le Hibou, a coffee house where Bill gives poetry readings and performs music. Bruce Cockburn, who is living at Bill's place, also performs there. We came home with terrible colds.

I have sent some paintings to Hawkins. He believes he can get them into the Lofthouse Gallery in Ottawa. I'm not so sure about that, but I'll let him try.

24 May, 1967. Wednesday
Yesterday afternoon, I worked on a group of small paintings, acrylic on paper, using only black, greys and white. I made fourteen pieces quite spontaneously, putting

down a series of ideas that I had been thinking about, but had hesitated to make into a painting. After spending time over them, I organized them into a group of twelve pieces (each 9" x 12") and gave them the title, *It Grew into a Man*. So far, I'm pleased with them.

Today, I worked on a larger piece (acrylic on paper) after one of the small pieces, using a full range of colour.

25 August, 1967. Friday
Such a long time since my last entry.

I went to Kincardine to work in the store for six weeks, returning on August 14th. Then last week, we went to Toronto to find a place to live. We stayed with Joe and Dace, who will soon be moving to another place, too. We walked and walked and walked, looking at whatever seemed likely, and on Monday we found a place on Markham Street. The rent is $105 a month; that's a lot for us, but we have worked out a survival budget, at least, in theory. Neither of us has a job, so we'll have to hold our breath for a bit. We will move next week.

The apartment has two rooms, a kitchenette and a bathroom. We will use one of the rooms for a studio, the other as a bed-sitting room. We will both use the studio; me, for painting in the daytime, Nelson, for writing in the evenings. It should work.

We saw Victor Coleman in Toronto, and we went to see Stan Bevington at his Coach House — big printing press, and an intense monkish atmosphere. We saw David W. Harris at his tiny apartment furnished with little more than a cot, two chairs and his IBM typewriter. He asked me to do a cover for *LUV #6*. He gave me the manuscript so I could read it; the cover will be printed offset. I worked up the cover and have already sent it to him.

Nelson phoned Bill Hawkins tonight to find out what had happened with my paintings. They are at the Lofthouse Gallery; the owner took them in, said he will keep one or two hanging, changing them periodically. Good news, I suppose.

Last night we had dinner with Mr. Birney. He took us out for a Chinese meal, then we went on to his place on campus where he played some records for us — one of them was percussion only, another was a reading of Beowulf. Then Mr. Birney put on a recording of music that was composed from Beowulf, and he read the text himself— rich rolling sounds, sometimes with sharp edges. Mr. Birney was so animated; it was wonderful. Beowulf is middle English, I think; it sounds like German and I didn't understand a word of it.

Mr. Birney (he would like me to call him Earle) first came to see us in June. He is to be writer-in-residence at U of W this year, and he was looking for people to take part in a workshop he plans to do. This will be for the students, but he wanted some off-campus people if he could find them. Nelson was an obvious choice, but to my surprise, he also wanted me to participate. (He saw my poems in *Weed*, saw that I lived in Kitchener, too, but didn't know who I was.) We have seen Mr. Birney quite a lot, and after we move to Toronto, we will see him there, too.

Toronto

6 September, 1967. Wednesday.
We are moved now and reasonably settled in. The move was difficult; it took two trips with a truck. David McFadden helped us load the truck, rode with us to Toronto and helped unload. He rode back to Kitchener with Nelson, helped load the truck again, then went on home to Hamilton. David chose one of my paintings [*Townscape* (1965) oil on canvas] in trade for his help.

7 September, 1967. Thursday
Nelson has a line on a job at the University of Toronto Library that he *wants*.

People! Suddenly, we are seeing so many people. We went with Victor Coleman to Coach House Press one evening to see the presses at work. We had a surprise visit from Steve Buri. I've been in touch with Carol Martyn and Joe Tatarnic. Joe will be dropping by this afternoon.

20 September, 1967. Wednesday
Time has flown by. Nelson begins work today — his first day at U of T Library in the cataloguing department. I've gotten my first positive results on art classes. I will teach an evening class at Northern Secondary School on Thursdays for 22 weeks.

25 September, 1967. Monday
Jim Gordaneer came by today at noon to see me and to look at my work. I had asked him if I could use his name as a reference on an application for a Canada Council short-term grant. (Jim Scott has agreed to be the other reference.) Jim was generous with his comments on my work. He was most interested by the series of small acrylics on paper, *It Grew into a Man #1-12*.

4 October, 1967. Wednesday
I've mailed my application for a short-term grant. There's not much hope for it. Nelson is writing a letter to the Canada Council about a grant for Weed Flower Press. Earle Birney encouraged him to do this; there is much more hope for that.

I am teaching Saturday morning children's art classes (5-7 years) for the Art Gallery of Ontario. The classes are held at OCA [Ontario College of Art]. Jim

Williamson hired me on as an "assistant instructor." (I taught with Jim at the gallery while I was a student at OCA.) He has hired two people to do this class at assistant's pay. He said that since I am the senior person, I will be in charge — I will be a full instructor at assistant's pay. This, to save the gallery's money. I took it; I needed the job. The adult classes at Northern Secondary School begin tomorrow night.

Bill Hawkins and his friends Penelope Schafer and Elizabeth were here on Monday afternoon. (Bill is a madman.) Victor Coleman was here for an hour or so that evening. He is going to Vancouver. Steve Buri came by; he will leave Toronto for Winnipeg. Jack Cain came over last night.

I made two paintings (acrylic on paper) last week and another this morning [*Red Circle.* 19" x 24"]. I haven't made up my mind about it yet. This afternoon, I went for a walk along Bloor Street. Found a Coles bookstore where I bought a new writing book, a couple of erasers and a mapping pen. I will see Carol Martyn tonight at her studio.

5 October, 1967. Thursday

Carol talked about her friend Milly Ristvedt last night; she thinks I should meet her. Milly is willing to talk about her work. She has been pretty successful over this past year or so — she got into the Winnipeg show (so did Carol), has gotten a Canada Council grant, and now she will be having a one-man show at the Carmen Lamanna Gallery in January. I have not been greatly impressed by her work. I have seen only four paintings; I liked one of them, thought it the best of the four.

After about an hour at Carol's, her friend Gerald arrived. He and Carol began to talk about people, paintings and the art scene. It was as if they were sparring with each other; I didn't participate, but I suspect they both enjoyed having me as an audience. Carol seems to be competitive and is full of value judgements. She is critical of social attitudes, but she has her share of prejudices, too. Gerald is an angry, cool person. He is no longer painting. He is hung-up about the "injustice" of the art world, about those who have success and don't deserve it.

I'm not immune to such ideas, but I see them as hang-ups, totally irrelevant to painting. They can become blinding — no good to anyone at all.

6 October, 1967. Friday

The class at Northern went well enough last night — eighteen people showed up. I was to see Mr. Sullivan before starting the class and it took me half an hour to find him. The business about keeping a register and recording attendance is going to be a nuisance — there are pages of instructions on how it must be done. I didn't get away until after 10 p.m.; I will have to go in early next week to get that register in order.

I have a cold so I stayed in bed most of today. I was awakened at 3 p.m. when a bus ran into a car just outside [corner of Markham and Harbord]. I looked out the window to see hysterical men and weeping women — no one was hurt. The car appeared to have been thrown about ten feet from the point of impact and the back window was shattered. Such a crowd gathered! An ambulance arrived, but no one would go with them.

8 October, 1967. Sunday

The children's class went reasonably well yesterday morning. I taught the class alone again. The (other) assistant hasn't shown up yet.

Steve Buri was here when I got back from class. He left last night for Winnipeg. He seemed reluctant to be leaving Toronto.

Last night, Marty Ahvenus and Harry Howith spent the evening here. A strange team. I like Marty, but Howith is a bit much.

Today, Earle Birney and a friend arrived around noon. Mr. Birney wanted to take us out for lunch, but Nelson declined — we both still have colds and were tired. Mr. Birney is going to support Nelson for a Canada Council bursary for the press, and he gave Nelson some advice on how to proceed, because there is no application form for this kind of grant. Coach House Press and blewointmentpress have already received grants. Mr. Birney thinks Nelson has a good chance.

Nelson has been writing; he is working on some poems right now. Me, I am reading John Canaday's *Mainstreams of Modern Art* again, this time, cover to cover. Recently, I read the autobiography of Malcolm X and *Beautiful Losers* by Leonard Cohen. Also, *Winnie the Pooh* by A. A. Milne — nice book.

9 October, 1967. Monday

This has been an exciting day. I have been making sketches toward paintings, or rather, making notes and drawings about working with the square. I compare "moment" to square or cube (each face of a cube is a square). I investigate the "moment" of seeing, where moment equals square. Anyway, the results are quite exciting; I may get some paintings out if it. I am trying to write down my ideas, but I haven't been very successful at that yet.

10 October, 1967. Tuesday

The search into colour and shape is pretty exciting. I have the beginnings toward a painting. I'm anxious to get something down, to make it permanent. I'm going to stretch a canvas today.

11 October, 1967. Wednesday

I stretched and primed a canvas yesterday (34" x 38"). I am painting today.

12 October, 1967. Thursday

I have been painting. I worked further on the painting I began yesterday [*Investigating the square*. acrylic on canvas]. I am pleased with it. I have begun another — a small one, more or less as an experiment with colour as mass.

Last night, I tried to work out theoretically what I've been doing with paint. I think I need to describe verbally the ideas I'm working with. Value judgements aside, I'm excited about the possibilities in what I'm doing. Perhaps when I have taken the time to consider "value judgement," it will no longer be relevant. At any rate, I want to pursue this course, because I believe in its *value*.

I have a class at Northern tonight. I have to go early to straighten out that damn register.

13 October, 1967. Friday

I'm feeling pleased about these last two canvases. I continue to make notes on them (my verbal approach) to clarify my thinking. The notes are really very elementary. The notes fill out as I develop new compositions. The certainty I feel is a pleasant change; it is more or less the satisfaction one feels when one is making progress, however small.

I need supplies — my paint is low, no stretchers left and very little canvas. I want to buy a staple gun.

Last night, Mr. Sullivan told me that the Board of Education is slow to process pay cheques (some of the teachers are complaining). I won't receive my October cheque until mid-November. He added, "But they're good for it." I should hope so.

14 October, 1967. Saturday

The children's class was alright this morning — the children, that is, not the assistant, Gloria. She finally showed up and she was harder to work with than the children. I mentioned this to Jim Williamson after class. I felt badly complaining about her, but if I hadn't said anything, I know I would be kicking myself now. Unfortunately, I'm not really an "instructor"; I'm an "assistant" too, so I'm in a tricky position.

I went into the AGO before coming home. I saw the Henry Moore show. A couple of the large sculptures really impressed me, but it was the small maquettes, the drawings and the lithographs that interested me most. In Saturday's *Telegram*, Barry Hale called them "stagey." Maybe so, but it hardly matters.

The Centennial show was still up, so I looked at it again. I found new interest in many things — in Kiyooka, whose work is clean and cool. I saw evidence of overpainting, a new decision, on his painting and I admire it all the more for that. He's full of questions, too.

17 October, 1967. Tuesday

Nelson has mailed his letter to Canada Council requesting a press grant. He has Earle Birney's support, also Jim Scott's. He has written Al Purdy for a reference. He is working now on a financial report, which is required by the Council.

I did some writing yesterday (I don't think I should call them poems). I worked further on them last night and I'll try to continue today. Nelson looked at them for me. His criticism is helpful, but I get belligerent about it. I can't carry a poem to completion. His comments frustrate me because I'm helpless to proceed. I'm not a writer.

I'm reading Joseph Conrad's *Heart of Darkness*. I've been reading some of Mr. Birney's poems.

18 October, 1967. Wednesday

Last night, we went out to vote. (Provincial election — the Conservatives have been returned, perhaps a little weakened.) The voting station was in a back porch of a house on Bathurst Street — a tiny space. The cardboard voting booth, the pretense at privacy, the frank seriousness of the people issuing ballots, made the whole ritual a little farcical. Yet, all the players, Nelson and I included, played our parts with the greatest respect.

I stretched and primed a large canvas yesterday. Nelson worked on that financial report last night.

19 October, 1967. Thursday

I'm ready for my class tonight. I want to be early again to straighten out that register. I'm reading Conrad's *Almayer's Folly* now. He writes with calipers.

Nelson was very tired when he came in at 5 p.m. yesterday. It was after 7 p.m. before he could collect himself to work further on the Weed Flower Press financial report.

Barrie Nichol will come by this evening to meet Nelson. I hope he arrives before I leave for the evening class. We've never met him and I'm curious, too.

20 October, 1967. Friday

Yesterday, Nelson was back home by 10:30 a.m. The heat at the library was turned off and everyone working on the fourth floor was sent home. I talked to Jack Cain last night and he said that everyone on the third floor was sent home at noon. They are losing a lot of hours at the library because of the ancient heating system.

In the afternoon, I went to Curry's to buy supplies. I spent almost $40 — twice the amount I had intended. I hope I get paid soon. I need canvas and material for stretchers.

I saw Jack Chambers' show at the Isaacs Gallery. (I want to see the book of this work that Coach House Press has done.) Chambers' work has always seemed complicated to me, but yesterday, I was impressed by its *simplicity*. He worked with silver paint on the images and put colour shapes, like options, adjacent to them. It's a beautifully open idea. The silver is surprisingly warm.

The show at Carmen Lamanna's was by a Quebec woman — Voyer, I think. They were well handled, expressionistic things, but were unexciting for this very reason. Their forms suggested the patterns on the African spears and tools that I've seen at the ROM.

I went up to the Picture Loan Society on Charles Street to talk with Cecil Troy. He told me a great deal about the gallery scene, the changes that have taken place over the past two years. He suggested I try the Jerrold Morris Gallery; said to skip the Picture Loan; suggested the Pollock Gallery, but warned me about Pollock's poor business practices. He said I could try the Adams and Yves Gallery. Albert White, he said, seems unable to sell non-objective work, although he hangs it — a lot of his non-figurative painters have moved out. He called Isaacs a "closed club" that operates out of the Pilot Tavern. Carmen Lamanna, he said, is getting more respect now — Dorothy Cameron's reputation has been hard for him to compete with over the past two years — but he doesn't make sales. Cecil was a well of useful information, generously given.

Barrie (bp) Nichol came by last night. He had some *little* supper with us (there was barely enough food for two). He's an interesting person, a big guy; he reminds me of a farm boy. He has a tic — he blinks his eyes. He has a soft voice and speaks quietly, but quickly. He was still here when I left for my class. We'll probably see him again.

21 October, 1967. Saturday

This morning's class went well enough. I stepped on Gloria right off the bat, so most things were kept in control. The children worked with pastels; the medium was a little too quick for them and impatience came early, but the results were generally good.

Nelson has been working on the mock-up for Carol Bergé's book, *Poems Made of Skin*. I think he's disappointed in the progress he made (or didn't make) on it today. We had to go out to the grocery store, and it broke up his day.

I have finished reading Conrad's *Lagoon*. Nelson brought me a book from the library, Josef Albers' *Despite Straight Lines*. I've been through it once. I want to read it again before he has to return it on Monday.

23 October, 1967. Monday

I am looking at today's painting. The canvas is small, black, brown, mauve. There are two mauve squares, one within the other. The first is true colour; the other is no-colour. The black is no-colour, too. There is a vertical white line; it runs down, like a raindrop on a window. It is immediate, as if it just happened the moment one looked.

24 October, 1967. Tuesday

I worked most of the day on the large canvas. I am working again with a brown, to be read as red. The painting contains a large square that is defined by the canvas' edge on two sides. It is as if suspended by the top left corner. The canvas is on a stretcher that is 1¾" deep.

25 October, 1967. Wednesday

I worked most of the day on the large canvas. I think it is finished now. I will stretch a new canvas tomorrow, the very last I can get out of the material I have.

I saw Carol in her studio last night. She was stretching a large canvas when I arrived. We talked, each of us, about the ideas we were involved with in our work. I know she imitates a great deal, for I have seen her working with an art magazine open at a painting that she is following, modifying it to suit herself. I became aware that she was telling me that her work was the "legacy" that she would leave. Then she told me how she began painting. She was in her 40s; her lover died and she was beside herself with grief. To get out, she took some art classes (night classes, like I'm teaching). She went to the south of France, hoping to paint for a few weeks in a historically creative atmosphere, but found that she could do nothing. Then, she began going to San Miguel de Allende where she met James Pinto. I was moved by this story.

1 November, 1967. Wednesday

I have not begun work on the new canvas. It is a new shape, a long, or tall, rectangle — I haven't decided yet how I will work. The stretcher is 1¾" deep.

Yesterday, I stretched five small canvases, each 12" x 12" — deep stretchers — that I want to bring together as one work. I am making compositional sketches toward this. I've made about fifteen sketches and it's still unresolved. I will work on these small pieces before I work on the large canvas.

2 November, 1967. Thursday

Yesterday, I worked further on sketches for the five small canvases (one work) and seemed to get nowhere. I wanted a composition that would make use of the horizontal and vertical lines formed when the four canvases are brought together as a 24" x 24" square — the fifth piece to hang beside it at the top right, separated from it by an inch or so of wall space. I felt that none of the drawings would work on these small box-like panels. The deep stretcher would give another dimension to the whole. The surface of the painting is flat (two dimensions); here, the third dimension is *real* (not an illusion), due to the deep stretcher. In spite of my indecision, I began to paint and in five hours of work, it resolved itself. I'm more than pleased with the result.

Last night, Sarah Miller called to ask if we would help her out at Coach House. We went down and helped her glue covers on Roy Kiyooka's book, *Nevertheless these Eyes.* After the job was done, we talked a while. Sarah was full of newsy bits; she said Victor will be back from Vancouver on Thursday — she's very happy about that.

I put together the four pieces of my painting today. They seem to be alright. I want to see it hung.

Nelson received a letter from the Canada Council today telling him how to proceed with an application for a grant for Weed Flower Press. I received my first cheque from the AGO for teaching the children's classes — $37.50. That won't go far.

3 November, 1967. Friday

Phone calls today; I did little else. Al Strong called from Waterloo to say that he will be returning my paintings that were in Earl Putnam's Artists Mart and then shown again at Doon. He said one of the pieces sold and I should receive the cheque by tomorrow. Bill Hawkins called; he's in town only for today, so I'm to give Nelson his number.

Barbara Sourbrai called and we had a *very long* talk. We talked about the night classes at Northern Secondary School (she is teaching there, too). She told me that the students drop out and the classes dwindle in December. In January, the enrollment is checked and if there are less than ten people still coming to the class, the class will be dropped and we lose our jobs.

Barbara is teaching a children's class at a YMCA. It has been a craft class and she is doing a more creative painting and drawing course. The "craft" course involves things like making paper moccasins decorated by gluing on macaroni that has been dyed with food colouring. She has two volunteer "assistants" who she is keeping out of her way by sending them off to a back room to dye the macaroni.

We laughed about this, but I wonder if she'll get away with it. She's going to come by to see my new paintings.

7 November, 1967. Tuesday

Al Strong delivered the four paintings today and assured me that one had been sold [*Men and Horses #1* (1965) acrylic on paper]. I have not received payment yet.

We have hung two of my new paintings on the walls. The five-part painting did not hang well because of my poor carpentry, so only the fifth piece is on the wall.

We spent last evening at Coach House Press. We helped gather the pages of Michael Ondaatje's book, *The Dainty Monsters*. Those guys compete with each other to see who will finish collating their stacks of pages first. At one point, tempers flared, but Stan quietly calmed things down. Sarah finished first, but that didn't seem to matter — the competition was really between the boys. Nelson and I finished last.

8 November, 1967. Wednesday

Barbara Sourbrai was here last night. She arrived at 9 p.m. and left well after midnight. An interesting talk, but it was a bit too long.

12 November, 1967. Sunday

Nelson spent this whole week at home. He has done a lot of work over the past few days. He is ready to print *Weed #12* and Bill Bissett's book, *Lebanon Voices*.

I have done no painting with Nelson here — the place just isn't big enough for both of us at the same time, but I set up the cover for Bissett's book, and designed a cover for the new magazine, *Hyphid*. Both covers will go to the printer this week.

I'm concerned about money. Nelson will lose some pay because of this week's illness; I haven't received a cheque yet from the Board of Education; no payment has arrived for the painting sold at Waterloo and no news from the Canada Council about my application.

13 November, 1967. Monday

Nelson has gone to work at the library this morning.

I did some drawing yesterday to no real purpose. I have a new canvas stretched (48" x 48"), the only thing I accomplished last week. So now, I have two canvases ready.

I have been reading William Carlos Williams' *I Wanted to Write a Poem*. Recently, Nelson bought a bunch of new books; I hardly knew where to begin.

14 November, 1967. Tuesday
I painted yesterday. I worked on the tall canvas (55" x 33"). I used last week's sketches as a guide, but the work really formed while I painted. The ground is a black, a blue-black. The shapes on it are grey, grey-mauves and blue-greys. The movement from colour to colour is slow, but dramatic, I think. I like what I see.

I have to think about the surface I'm getting. I have applied paint with a brush on this painting, too, and that leaves strokes on the surface, the evidence of my hand. I like this, but I want to think about it. I've gotten a soft, matt surface, but I'm undecided about whether this surface lies quietly enough, or if it interferes with the colour activity.

Victor Coleman is back from Vancouver. He stopped by last night to give Nelson a copy of his new book, *One/Eye/Love*.

Last night, Nelson and I got into a hassle over the cover for the Carol Bergé book. It is a brush drawing by d.a. levy, a "portrait" of Carol, and I'm to set the title/author lettering in place. *I'd never seen the thing as a face before!* I saw it as an abstract drawing, not a very good one, because it doesn't hold together (for me). Now I have to reconsider the whole thing. I've some thoughts about it this morning, but last night I was just blank.

15 November, 1967. Wednesday
I'm polishing our winter boots. It has begun to snow and it's very cold out there.

I worked further on the tall painting yesterday. I reworked four of the areas and I like the outcome. I'm quite satisfied with it now. [*Vertical painting*. acrylic on canvas]

16 November, 1967. Thursday
Yesterday, I worked on the 48" x 48" canvas. I spent 6½ hours on it and today, I'm pretty happy with it. It is the most exciting piece, so far. It has a black ground with four square areas of mauve-grey that vary from dark to light. (I call the shapes "square," but they are always a little wider than high.) The four areas are placed toward the top right of the canvas, making the black ground a band along the left side and the bottom, as well as between the four squares. The darkest square is at the top right corner and two of its sides are defined by the painting's edge; the square below it is less dark, and the square to the left is lighter still. These two squares have one of their sides defined by the edge of the painting. The fourth square, below the square at the left, is the lightest and it is the only one totally contained within the painting. I have painted a light grey contour line around this square and the others to solidify "position." The lines are horizontal and vertical,

but for one, which is a diagonal. This diagonal commits each square to a specific position and it limits the illusion of space. So, I am using a diagonal to limit the appearance of three-dimensional space. This morning, while I was looking at it, I realized that nothing could be added, or taken away, without destroying the whole thing. I like that.

Carol phoned. I went up to her studio to see what she has been doing and later she came here to see my work. She seemed impressed with my latest paintings; she said some generous things. She seems to be on to something in her work; she has two paintings going, but neither is finished. She is involved with what she calls "ambiguous statement" and is quite excited about it.

I'm out of stretchers *and* out of paint. I'll have to stock up. The cheque for *Men and Horses #1* arrived yesterday ($60). I'll give Nelson $30 and spend the rest on supplies.

17 November, 1967. Friday

I got my cheque from the Board of Education today — $76.30. I did the class at Northern last night; eight people were there, but I marked ten present on the register.

Nelson has finished his application to the Canada Council for a press grant.

20 November, 1967. Monday

I got a letter from the Canada Council saying "sorry to inform you..." Sometimes I think I won't be able to stand another rejection, but each time I get one — I live. Well, forget it.

I phoned around about lumber today and learned that the places here don't cut wood until it's been paid for. They will deliver without charge if the order is over $10. An order under $10, will be delivered for a $1 charge. I went out to the bank, planning to go to the lumber yard and on to buy canvas. I went to the post office, too, and when I finished there, I was out of time. I'll go tomorrow.

When I got back here, I called Carol. I told her about the Canada Council rejection. She was sympathetic, but then she told me her own bad news. She is about to be laid off from her part-time job at Air Canada. She is over 50 years old now and believes she will have a hard time finding other work. Pretty bleak.

21 November, 1967. Tuesday

Jim Gordaneer came to see my new work. He was enthusiastic about it, particularly the most recent piece. He said it was "better than Ad Reinhardt," because it did more! I was really pleased by his response, but I can't help wondering if he even likes Reinhardt's paintings.

Jim told me he has done a drawing that will appear on the cover of *Quarry*. Bill Muysson is in Kingston now and he's involved with the magazine.

I bought lumber for stretchers and a supply of canvas today. I brought the canvas home; the lumber will be delivered tomorrow.

23 November, 1967. Thursday
The lumber was delivered yesterday — clear white pine, 1x2 dressed. I taped the pieces together and laid them on the floor to warm up and dry out. I hope to prevent warping.

I have been thinking about what I will do now that I have new supplies. I think about moving away from blacks into more colour. Actually, I'd like to extend black into colour; I'm not through with it. I know I'll continue working with the square; I have only begun with it. Earlier, I was not able to sustain an idea for more than five or six paintings. Then, I had to make a dramatic change. I can't anticipate what my next painting will be, but I believe I have much to pursue from these last pieces. I feel that my work up to this date is strongly related to what I'm doing now, no matter how many corners I've turned to get to this point.

24 November, 1967. Friday
This morning I made a stretcher, 40" x 42", and stretched the new heavier canvas on it. I haven't primed it yet. I have vague thoughts about what I will do with it. Made a few sketches, but I'm pleased with none of them. I'm not just looking for a "variation," or a "possibility," but something more. I don't know how to say what I mean by that.

There were only seven people at last night's class. I stretched them into ten for the register.

26 November, 1967. Sunday
Nelson printed all of *Weed #12* and one page of *Lebanon Voices* yesterday afternoon. We went out for supper and to a movie and when we got back, I gathered all the pages of *Weed*. That much is done.

27 November, 1967. Monday
I built a stretcher and stretched another canvas this morning. I will prime this one and the one I did on Friday. I have been doing housewifery these past few days.

The mock-up for the Carol Bergé book has been lost in the mail. The post office here says it has to be traced from New York. Nelson will ask Carol to trace it. I expect he will just do it over again. Carol is very upset. She's afraid Nelson will abandon the project. He will write and reassure her.

29 November, 1967. Wednesday

I'm trying to work toward a painting, but my sketches aren't getting me there. I think I'll try some drawings, try to resolve a few things. I want to overcome the appearance of "space" (or, a third dimension). I am looking for limited space, or shallow space, maybe even a square that "floats." I want to explore this somehow.

1 December, 1967. Friday

Nine people came to class last night; I put eleven on the register. The class began working with colour last night — I believe I should have started them earlier, but my class is well ahead of the others already. Next week will be the last class until the new year.

4 December, 1967. Monday

Nelson was home for lunch today. He is working at the main library this week doing a training program, and he is close enough to come home at noon. There was a strange letter from the Canada Council in this morning's mail. The letter (from Naim Kattan) completely dismisses Nelson's application for a press grant. It says that he can apply for an individual writers' grant. The *Aid to Artists* booklet is enclosed. It's as if he (Kattan) didn't read the application.

6 December, 1967. Wednesday

I am working on a painting today. I began it yesterday. I used a roller for the first time to apply paint and ran into difficulties.

The canvas (40" x 42") is smaller than the last one I did. I am working again with four squares and I am using line again to control the appearance of advancing or receding shapes.

9 December, 1967. Saturday

I finished my painting on Thursday. I am pleased with it. Already I am thinking about another painting.

Barbara Sourbrai came by on Wednesday and again she stayed too long. She has loaned me a biography of Stanley Spencer. An interesting life; his work is fascinating. The book hints at things that are not told about his ideas and his relationships; it makes one want to know more.

I saw Carol on Friday afternoon. I was surprised to find that she was working with squares. Our talk was a bit frustrating. It was as if neither of us could understand what the other was saying.

We had the photographers in the children's classes this morning, this time making a film. Only thirteen kids showed up so it was easier to work with them.

I am going to Kincardine for a few days.

18 December, 1967. Monday

I got back from Kincardine on Thursday. I did the children's class on Saturday morning. The photographers were there again. We were told there would be a meeting after class, but it turned out to be a wine and cheese party — Jim and all the instructors. Some fun, although everyone seemed pretty rigid. Ann definitely didn't like it when "the girls" were told to clean up the dishes at the end, but we did it.

I am reading *The Autobiography of William Carlos Williams*.

20 December, 1967. Wednesday

I have spent the morning on a painting that, so far, is a complete bust. What I was after just didn't happen. I'll have to begin again, or continue as if beginning again. I can overpaint what I've done, but it's a real disappointment to find I've done nothing for all the time and work.

21 December, 1967. Thursday

Yesterday's failure is still with me. I go over *everything* in my mind about what I'm doing and I arrive only at more doubts.

I'm going to have to photograph my work. Slides have become important. They are being used for entry into shows and to initially show one's work at the galleries.

Bill Hawkins is in town; we saw him last night. Victor and Sarah are going to move to Vancouver.

22 December, 1967. Friday

Yesterday turned out better than I thought it could. I began work just after 1 p.m. and painted until 4:30. The changes I made changed the original idea I had for the work without changing the structure, the composition. I changed the colour to blues and wound up repainting the entire surface. I worked slowly, considering each move and had a joyous headache when I was finished.

The blues are like an ocean, but the shapes are straight, strong, and architectural. The composition is asymmetrical, but it is also formal. There is an "order of nature" here.

Last night, I sat in front of my painting reading Victor Coleman's "October Fragments," poems (in manuscript) that Victor wrote while he was in Vancouver. It was a good experience; I was drawing a comparison between Victor's poems and my blue painting [*Blue painting (cobalt)*. acrylic on canvas].

26 December, 1967. Tuesday

Yesterday was Christmas day. Nelson typed stencils last night, finishing after midnight. He is working on poems today.

We went out for a walk in the snow last evening. It was cold and windy — really blowing — but we enjoyed it.

1968

2 January, 1968. Tuesday

Victor and Sarah were here last week. Victor saw my blue painting and seemed to like it. I was really pleased by his response. He spoke of the form being a vehicle for the "thing said" (in this case, the colour) and he related it to his poems. The things he said so easily, I couldn't have begun to put into words.

David Rosenberg and his girlfriend, Kati Hewko, joined us. Kati immediately responded to the paintings hung in the room, by saying "Albers. Josef Albers." She is a strange girl. Later, in a moment of anger, she walked out on David — just got up and walked out the door. In fact, she walked out on all of us, but the gesture was intended for David who only shrugged his shoulders. I was surprised at both of them, but Victor and Sarah behaved as if they were used to it.

On Saturday, I went into the David Mirvish Gallery to ask if I could read the Barnett Newman letter in their issue of *Art International*. The receptionist there, Nancy Scott, (she has seen me in there often) began talking with me and suggested I bring in slides of my work for them to see. David Mirvish walked in as I was about to leave, and Miss Scott told him that I was going to bring in slides of my paintings. He was polite; he showed mild interest, but it was not discouraging. Now I *have to* get some slides as soon as possible.

4 January, 1968. Thursday

Stan Bevington came for a visit last night. He was wearing a tweed cap, the kind of cap I haven't seen in years — the kind that has a dome fastener on the peak of the cap. Stan's cap was brand new and he seemed proud of it. He showed us the dome, wore it fastened, and kept the cap on the whole time. Stan talked about printing. He suggested that Nelson could put a motor on his Gestetner. Nelson is still using the old hand-cranked Gestetner he bought in Kitchener for $30 and he would like to have an electric one to speed up the printing jobs and reduce the effort.

I stretched and primed a canvas today. I am working on sketches. I have subscribed to *Art in America* and more recently, to a new magazine, *Avant Garde*. I'm reading Ouspensky's *In Search of the Miraculous*; it's clearer than Gurdjieff's *All and Everything*.

The night classes begin again tonight; the children's classes begin again on Saturday.

5 January, 1968. Friday

I have two promising sketches worked out for paintings. I will prime the smaller canvas today.

Nelson and I will go to Victor and Sarah's for dinner tonight. Sarah doesn't seem to mind cooking.

8 January, 1968. Monday

Nelson is home today with a cold. He is spending his time with the books that Victor gave him — books that Victor didn't want to carry out to Vancouver. Nelson has given him $30 so far for the lot, but thinks he should send him more when he has it.

11 January, 1968. Thursday

Victor and Sarah were here last night. Sarah brought some clothes she doesn't want to take with her. I think I can use them. She didn't want anything for them, but I put $10 in her mailbox this morning. They are going to leave us their rug. It is too big for these rooms, so we'll store it.

15 January, 1968. Monday

Nelson was sent home from work today because of the drifting snow. Employers were asked to dismiss staff at odd hours to avoid rush hour at 5 p.m.

Nelson came in at one o'clock. I had begun to work on a painting by then, so he left me to work alone in the front room. I worked through to 6 p.m. I was working with blues again, and I ran out of cobalt blue. Nelson went out to buy some for me, but he found the art store closed. I worked on, using ultramarine blue in my intermixtures. I was forced into new colour with this painting; I am pleased with my results [*Blue painting (ultramarine)*. 40" x 42" acrylic on canvas].

16 January, 1968. Tuesday

I went out to buy supplies and found the art store still closed. The streets were treacherous; I could hardly walk in all the snow, so I came back empty-handed.

Yesterday's painting is holding up well for me. I set down some sketches last night for the next painting. These last two paintings are reaching somewhere. Each is an "object." The whole canvas is the object; it does not depict, it just *is*. It has order; the order is irregular, but quiet.

I wish I could be more verbal about this. However, I sometimes feel that verbal descriptions of paintings don't just describe, they are meant to *justify*. This is somehow irrelevant to the work. I become less and less willing to talk about my work.

21 January, 1968. Sunday

David McFadden was here this morning. We haven't seen him since he helped us move in September. It was pleasant, but early. While we sat and talked, I watched David look at the paintings hanging in the room. Suddenly, he said to me, "I can see that you've suffered." Surprised, I asked him why he would say that and he answered, "Your paintings are black and blue." He wasn't joking; that's McFadden.

We photographed my paintings today. I have little hope that the slides will turn out. I'll probably miss entering the Canadian Biennial jury show; I won't have the slides in time.

29 January, 1968. Monday

We did a lot of work over the weekend. Today, Nelson is mailing *Hyphid* and *Weed #12*. Yesterday, he printed 70 more copies of Bissett's *Lebanon Voices* as well as most of the reprint of Newlove's *What They Say*. He has two sheets of Newlove to finish tonight. I will gather. I gathered *Lebanon Voices* last night.

I talked with Joe Tatarnic this morning. He's done some painting, but is still working full-time. He has slides of his work, but he hasn't shown them to anyone yet. Carol has slides of her recent work ready to send to Ottawa.

I got a phone call Friday night from Gloria, saying she was sick and wouldn't be in for the Saturday morning class. I called Jim Williamson to ask if he would change the program to a simpler medium (he had scheduled a painting class) so I could handle the class alone. It worked out, but he seemed pretty annoyed with Gloria. This is nothing. A week ago, there was a real charade at the end of the class. Gloria and a naughty little boy got into a tussle, and the little devil actually had Gloria chasing him around a table. He was loving it. I was horrified, so let out, "That's enough!" and brought them both to a halt.

31 January, 1968. Wednesday

I worked on a large canvas today. The painting is square and two squares, one inside the other, are positioned along the same diagonal as the square canvas. This gives three squares, three colours in a static (or stable) composition. The diagonal (not drawn) holds the shapes; the colours hold the surface. The blues move from a blue-mauve to a rich blue-green, low and greyed. The colour is in flux. [*Blue diagonal.* 48" x 48" acrylic on canvas]

2 February, 1968. Friday

I'm pleased with the last painting. I plan to put together more stretchers today so I can go on. Going on gets more and more difficult. Finding the next painting is not easy; it's not easy to distinguish it from the "possibility" or mere "variation."

Most of the slides we took did not turn out. I was disappointed because it means I can't enter the Canadian Biennial in Ottawa.

Last night's class was wild. I did not lose my class, but someone else did. The remaining students from that class came into my class. I met Mr. Sullivan on the bus on the way to Northern and he told me I would be moving into the large still-life room. Seven of my people showed up plus six from the other class. I registered ten of mine, plus six — sixteen present. Mr. Sullivan was very discrete; he didn't come into my room to count heads.

The six new people have done no colour problems, have not made a colour chart and the colours they are working with are limiting. By comparison, my own people are pretty independent. They recognized this, too. My people were a bit arrogant about being able to work on their own while I spent my time with the new people. One new woman has just enrolled in the class, too. I'll have to start from scratch with her. At least, the attendance problem is over.

5 February, 1968. Monday

Over the weekend, Nelson finished the reprints of both Newlove's and David Cull's books — they are gathered, stapled and folded — and he began typing stencils for the Bergé book, *Poems Made of Skin.* The cover is ready for it.

Yesterday, Earle Birney called Nelson about his application to the Canada Council for a press grant. He explained the situation at the Canada Council. There has been a change in administration; Naim Kattan is the new head of the writers' program. Kattan is going by the book; there will be no more press grants. Nelson's application got caught in the middle of this change; there is nothing to be done about it. Birney told Nelson to write directly to Peter Dwyer, but I know Nelson won't do that.

David Rosenberg and Kati were here Saturday night. A good visit; saner than last time.

Today, I made a 40" x 42" stretcher and I stripped down two of my paintings from Kitchener so I can use the stretchers again.

We expect a visit from Jack Cain tonight.

6 February, 1968. Tuesday

Jack stayed late last night. There was some talk about the library, but we spent most of the evening exploring a dream that Jack had. He had written down the dream and brought it with him.

I stretched and primed a canvas today. I've been working on sketches for it, but it's still unsettled.

9 February, 1968. Friday

The class last night was a lot of work. There were seventeen people and another new student will begin next week. There could be nineteen students next week, or twenty-two if everyone showed up at the same time. They really keep me going.

I haven't painted this week; I'm hung up. I'm reading Roland Penrose's book, *Picasso: His Life and Work.*

12 February, 1968. Monday

Today, I took apart the five small paintings (each 12" x 12") and reworked four of them. I did not rework the fifth piece that has hung independent of the four that were attached. The outcome is two new paintings and a fun thing.

I worked from some of the "moment" ideas that I worked out with construction paper some months ago. One little painting has a black ground with a tilted yellow-orange square askew, but contained, at the top left corner. This works nicely alone. Another uses two of the canvases. One of them is grey only; the other has a blue ground and a black square at the centre. I want to hang these side by side, or one above the other as one work in two parts. With the fourth little canvas, I opened it and cut the corner away from the stretcher, turned the corner piece outside in and reattached it. This made a canvas with a square piece missing at one corner. I tried to paint another square at the centre, but I was using a wet roller, and the edges of that shape bled. I lost faith in it, so I painted a green and yellow fish in the centre, added blue wavelets and hung the piece on the diamond in the bathroom.

14 February, 1968. Wednesday

Barbara Sourbrai called yesterday. She didn't seem to know what had happened to the art classes at Northern, just that her classes were exploding with new students, too. She told me she lost her YMCA children's class — said they *fired* her. She's disgusted, mad as hell about having lost to the dyed macaroni.

Today, I went to the Jerrold Morris Gallery to see Robert Hedrick's show. It's a good show. A couple of pieces appear to be earlier than the rest of the work. One piece suggested Kenneth Noland to me because it's a long horizontal, but the comparison ends there. Hedrick was in the gallery. I overheard him speaking with a man about the work. He spoke about colour, about the light spectrum, colour-space, controlling space, the colour of infinite space, floating space, etc. Some of these are ideas I'm working with, but not with Hedrick's certainty.

I asked Hedrick a couple of questions about the Bauhaus. He suggested some books. I asked if he stains the canvas. He said yes, in some areas. He said he uses no ground at all; he neither sizes nor primes the canvas.

18 February, 1968. Sunday
Kati and David came by Saturday night with two people from New York, Dennis Williams and his wife.

I saw Carol in her studio today. She is working on a new canvas. We talked about the Hedrick show at the Morris Gallery; we got different things from it. We talked a bit about the light spectrum, but that didn't seem to get anywhere.

21 February, 1968. Wednesday
I went out today carrying my six little slides and wandered around, eventually arriving at the Mirvish Gallery. Nancy looked at them and showed them to the guy — I think his name is Allie or something [Alkis Klonaridis]. He looked over the slides twice, then asked how long I had been working in that manner. I said for about a year. I told him I had been painting since I was 15, but I didn't say how old I was. (Nelson said that was a mistake because people always think I am much younger than I am.) He went on to say he liked what he saw and that he thought my work was "certainly competent." He suggested I show the slides to some of the other galleries — Lamanna, 123, Pollock and Moos. I left shortly after. Nancy said that she would try arrange for "one of them" to come down to see my work. She will call me tomorrow. I fairly ran down the street.

25 February, 1968. Sunday
I was pretty excited about what happened at the Mirvish Gallery. Nancy Scott called the next day to say that Alkis would come Tuesday at 2:30 p.m. to look at my work. I'm not quite sure why he is coming. He has probably done all he can do by looking at the slides and directing me to other galleries.

On Friday night, I went with Carol to the opening of the Guggenheim collection at the AGO. The people! It's a good show; I'll go back to see it again.

26 February, 1968. Monday
I stretched another canvas today. I'm working on sketches — a few things happening. I want to involve a diagonal, but I'm afraid it will be too strong. I don't

want overlapping areas. Still, I'm curious. I'm uncertain about working without a ground. I've always put gesso on canvas.

2 March, 1968. Saturday
Alkis from Mirvish Gallery canceled Tuesday's visit. The shipment for the Stella show arrived at the gallery that day. I've heard nothing since then; it's hard to say when (or if) I will hear.

3 March, 1968. Sunday
Nelson is away.

I primed my canvas and stretched another this afternoon. I didn't prime the second one, but read instead. With Nelson away and the prospect of Alkis looking at my work, I feel suspended.

I went up to Carol's studio tonight. She has a big blue painting going. It looks good, well conceived. This and her red painting work well. She came back here and we had coffee and much talk.

7 March, 1968. Thursday
I'm in a bind about my work. I haven't been able to go ahead since I prepared the last two canvases. I have sketches, ideas ready to go, but I'm overwhelmed with uncertainty. As meaningful as my work is to me, a fear of meaninglessness is heavy on me now. Any justification at this point is simply that. I can't seem to make myself move on with it. I'm afraid I am working toward a void.

11 March, 1968. Monday
Morning. I just looked at the last entry. I was really down — I remember — but I did get to that canvas.

Yesterday, we finished photographing my paintings again.

Jim Lowell, the bookseller from Cleveland, Ohio, appeared at our door yesterday. He'd come to pick up the books that Victor left here for him and, I suspect, to meet Nelson. He stayed about an hour — a fairly silent hour.

13 March, 1968. Wednesday
I'm pretty excited about my last two paintings. The first piece led to another piece of work that further defines the context of the first. At present, I feel anywhere but in a void; rather, I feel I have new scope.

The first painting works with blues and blue-greys [*Blue Canvas*. 38" x 48" acrylic on canvas]. The new painting works with reds. The colour change and the change in composition occurred together. The size of the painting allows the "square" to move to a rectangle without loss of order. I was skeptical that it could come off, but I'm pleased with the result.

I am to call the Mirvish Gallery again tomorrow.

14 March, 1968. Thursday

Alkis Klonaridis has just left. I showed him ten pieces of work. He chose those that he felt were most successful. The two most recent pieces seemed less successful to him than the previous works. He said that the new pieces were less unified than the others, although he thought the move toward colour (red) was good.

He said I should show my work around, perhaps put a few pieces out on consignment (he suggested Carmen Lamanna and Pollock, again), but he felt I should hold off with a show for a year or so. He made a few suggestions about how I might work larger in so small a space.

I'm left with much to think about. He wants to come again when I have new work and said that if I wanted a reference for a Canada Council grant, he would give me one.

19 March, 1968. Tuesday

Today, I went to the Carmen Lamanna Gallery with my slides. I hardly know what to think of what happened.

Lamanna looked at my slides. He went over them four times, then said almost nothing.

Well, he did say he liked them. He told me that the gallery was booked two seasons ahead, but he took my name, address, etc. and said he would come to see my work when he found time. (I doubt that he'll call.) I asked if I could bring him slides of new work when I had it, and he said that I could.

All of this took quite a long time, for Lamanna left long silences between his thoughts and he mumbles when he speaks. He seemed somehow interested, but he was so non-committal that I don't know if I was being encouraged or put down by what he said.

I'm not sure what to do next. I suppose I should approach another gallery for an opinion, at least.

5 April, 1968. Friday

I went to the Pollock Gallery with my slides today. Even before he looked at them, Mr. Pollock told me that he was in the process of dropping a number of artists he was showing and would not be taking on anyone new. But he looked, and seemed quite enthusiastic about my work. He said he would like to see what I do over the summer (that is, come back with new work in the fall). He said he might be able to use my work in a group show.

I'm no further ahead really, but at least he knows that I exist.

I reworked the red painting this week. I changed the colour to blues, blue-greys and mauves; I also changed the composition. I have another large canvas ready. I'm working on sketches for it now.

10 April, 1968. Wednesday

I have been working on the large canvas this week. I am working without a ground on this one and I've had a lot of trouble with bleeding edges. I like the matt surface one gets on the raw canvas, but the canvas just drinks the paint. I'm working with blues and mauves. The colours are richer and more intense than the earlier blue-greys. [*Large blue.* 48" x 48" acrylic on canvas]

I received the entry forms for the Colour and Form Society show this morning. Carol and I are both thinking of entering.

10 May, 1968. Friday

Jim Williamson phoned to tell me that tomorrow's class will be on colour [theory]. I will use colour slides and chips. The children's show is scheduled for the 15th and 16th of June and he wants me to help hang it.

I want to call Wally French [sculptor]. He's teaching the AGO children's classes, too. He told me he would like to see what I'm doing.

Nelson is beginning to work on the second issue of *Hyphid*. The Bergé book is finished and sent out, but strangely, no word yet from Carol.

14 May, 1968. Tuesday

Wally French came at noon today. I was impressed by the way he looked at my work and by what he said. He asked questions and made comments in a direct manner. He preferred the two black/grey paintings that involve line; these, he said, had something in common with his own work. He looked at the earlier work on the slides and we talked about what led me into the work I am doing now. Then, we talked about teaching. He said he would put my name in at Stratford for his classes (he is moving to New York) and suggested I try OCA. He said he would try drop my name where he could. When he was leaving, he said he liked my work. I believe him. It was a good visit.

17 May, 1968. Friday

Yesterday, Jim Williamson called to give me three classes for the summer. I will instruct two of them and assist Jim with the third. The classes will be on Tuesdays and Wednesdays for seven weeks over July and August. I was pleased; the summer won't be as lean as I thought it would be.

I stretched two canvases yesterday. I'll prime them today.

22 May, 1968. Wednesday

Yesterday afternoon, I went over to Yonge Street to the Isaacs Gallery and the Carmen Lamanna Gallery. At Isaacs, I saw the show of four sculptures by Arthur (Mike) Handy. I was particularly impressed by two of them. I went into Lamanna and saw the Royden Rabinowitch show. (Royden is the twin brother of David, who shows at the Pollock Gallery.) The work is strange and, to me, confusing — both David and Royden make sculpture that is very low to the floor. I am bothered by it because I think I should lie down on the floor to see it. I don't do that, of course, and because I don't, I believe I'm missing something. I talked with Lamanna; as usual, he was dolefully gracious.

I went next door for a coffee and found both Rabinowitch brothers were in there. I spoke to them, was asked to join them. Talk was about the London group of artists and the Toronto gallery scene. They had a great deal of advice for me.

They are an interesting pair. They are young (25), tough and full of boyish energy. They are very self-confident; have a lot of push. They told me they were planning to blow Carmen's mind. Lamanna says he doesn't have storage space in the gallery for Royden's work, so they are going to put it up on the roof.

28 May, 1968. Tuesday

I have two new paintings. The first is an extension of the earlier two that use four square areas that press to the right [*Blue #1*. 40" x 43½" acrylic on canvas]. The second painting has four squares and there is a ¼" line around all the areas and around the outer edge of the painting. The line defines area as area on the two-dimensional plane. There is no illusory space here. [*Blue #2*. 40" x 43½" acrylic on canvas.]

Ray Souster brought Nelson the remaining pages of *New Wave Canada* on Friday night. I began to gather pages last night. It will probably take the whole summer to collate the thing. At least, I'm started.

15 June, 1968. Saturday

It's a long time since I've written here and so many things have happened. It's as if the world were splitting up. The shooting and death of Robert Kennedy — so soon after the assassination of Martin Luther King [April 4, 1968]. Suspicions of conspiracies — white man's madness.

I helped hang the children's show at the AGO yesterday. Spent most of the day there. The show is on today and tomorrow. There will be a good turnout.

I've been working this week using construction paper. I have some things I hope to take into paintings. I have a large canvas ready.

Last week, Jim Lowell showed up and stayed most of the afternoon. Later, Doug Fetherling came by. He's very young, tall and he has very long hair. He's self-conscious, for all his bravado; when Nelson opened the door, he introduced himself as "the Right Reverend Doug Fetherling."

I saw Carol last night. I went up to her studio, then she came back here for coffee.

Bill Hawkins just called. He and Sheila will be over this afternoon. He is returning my paintings from the Lofthouse Gallery.

24 November, 1968. Sunday
I've just told Nelson that I'm about to make an entry. He said, "What for?" I said, "Posterity." He said "Oh, shit." So there it is.

I've read through the last few entries. Impossible to bring this up to date.

We have moved —

1970

10 August, 1970. Monday
I'm at it again.

It's a long while since I kept a journal. There's little satisfaction in writing letters these days — I've no one to write who will respond. I'm much alone with only myself for company; this should keep me from talking to myself.

I feel I should write several pages for a first entry. One should get off to a good airy start. I have the example of Mark Twain whose books I've been reading, as well as Paul Klee who rewrote his journals four times. The first is a lesson in extravagance; the second, in restraint.

I'll start with yesterday. We went to the AGO. I went alone, but Nelson met me there later. The show was Realism(e)s, a survey show collected from Montreal by Mario Amaya. It was mixed, a small collection that didn't quite live up to its name.

Last week, we went to the ROM. We spent a leisurely time in the south wing of the first floor looking at English and French furnishings, glassware, pottery and china. We saw the 15th-century Hall and Chamber. Saw some knives and forks that made me think of Chaucer. We toured the mineralogy rooms. Fantastic images and colours. We've only gone to the Museum together once before. Nelson grows impatient too soon for me, but this time, we were more attuned — we both enjoyed it.

Nelson is still cataloguing Marty's poetry books at the Village Book Store. He has been working there after work at the library and in the evenings. He says he will be home late all this week.

I have not been painting for the past week. The weather has been too hot. I have one more painting I want to make to complete this group of works, then I'll likely move on to making silkscreen prints.

This entry is a pale effort, but the die is cast.

11 August, 1970. Tuesday

Last night, we put two of my paintings onto stretchers. They are both 48" x 48". They look good. I have no titles for any of this work yet.

I called Jim Williamson today and learned that the Saturday morning children's classes are on for the fall although Jim doesn't know yet how much space he'll have at the college. He said that there's a letter in the mail confirming my post. He has me down to teach painting and colour to students up to 18 years. It sounds good.

I wrote a letter to Milly Ristvedt.

I talked with Alkis at the Mirvish Gallery today. He said to see him again in September and he'll come to see my new work.

I'm working on the cover for Victor Coleman's book, *Old Friends' Ghosts*.

Later: I've just finished reading my last journal. I'm surprised I could read it through. I'm aware of things that are not written down, as well as the words on the page. The record of my work astounded me. I am myself still. I still have vain hopes of having my work seen. I am like the ball on a string (a bat-ball) forever bouncing back for another whack from the paddle that takes me nowhere. It's two years later and I'm still canvassing the same galleries, asking the same people to look at my work.

The final entry was made a couple of months after we moved to this place on Bathurst Street from that little apartment on Markham Street — we moved in September. We have two rooms here, but the front room is big enough to use as my painting studio and as a living space (we turn the couch into a bed at night). The smaller room (which would normally be used as a bedroom) is where Nelson works on Weed Flower Press (he has an electric Gestetner now) and where he writes. We have a real kitchen here with enough room for a table. I am renting a small room in the Mirvish Village on Markham Street that I use as a print studio.

I begin to think I complain too much about a lack of "recognition." I'm probably better off than I think and just as well off as most of the painters I know. But it's not easy.

In 1968, a new gallery called Collector's Cabinet opened on Yonge Street. The couple who ran it came to see my work and took one piece for a group show. When I went to the gallery to see the show hung, I found my painting on the second floor attributed to another artist! I told them about it, of course, and they changed the card. The gallery closed a few months later.

Last year, Carol and I put work into Aggregation [gallery] on Jarvis Street. They took some of my small works, the paintings on paper (1966-68). The gallery was begun as a collective by a group of recent graduates from OCA for the purpose of showing their own work. It's run now by two of them, Dave Tuck and Lynne Wynick. They offered me a one-man show.

So I've had a show at Aggregation this year (April 14-25). It got two good reviews (one by Kay Kritzwiser in *The Globe and Mail*, the other by Barry Lord in *The Toronto Star*). I will probably show again at Aggregation in 1971.

All the work in my show was made here, after we moved. I showed nine paintings, five of them made up of two, three or four canvases hung together. The smallest work (*Small Diagonal*) was two square canvases, each 30" x 30", hung side by side as one work; the largest (*Big Silence*) was made up of four square canvases, with about an inch of wall space between them to make a square painting eight feet by eight feet. I have come to think of this work and all the paintings I made in 1967-8 as the "grey work."

Now I am working with colour in a new way. I began this group of paintings last year and I am about to finish it. I want one more painting.

Alkis told me today that he would look. Call again, he said, in September. Then he said, "The important thing is that you work, that you make the paintings, and that you show." I could have fallen to my knees and wept in exasperation. *That's what I've been doing!*

13 August, 1970. Thursday

Yesterday, I called Alan Toff, as he asked, to see if he was able to keep the appointment with me at the gallery. He said he could, so we met at Aggregation at 3 p.m. He looked at all of the paintings from the show, but for two pieces, and also all of the earlier small acrylic paintings on paper. He seemed impressed; he chose his favourites from both bodies of work. He said that I can count on being included in the show he is doing at Scarborough College next April. I am to get in touch with him again in October.

The gallery looked good in spite of all the crafts that are in it right now. Things were nicely set up. Dave and Lynne were gracious and friendly toward Toff and introduced us to their new receptionist, Loretta. I was quite flattered by her; she was open with her admiration of my work and said she had wanted to meet me.

Last night, Jim Lowell called Nelson. Nelson is going to print Jim's next catalogue (Asphodel Book Shop). I'll do the cover. The catalogue is to be ready by the end of September.

14 August, 1970. Friday

Dave Tuck called yesterday. He suggested raising some of the prices on my work because he thinks they now seem too low. (He priced them, insisting on low prices.) With no sales from those prices, I hardly think a higher price will make any difference. I said okay.

I plan to stretch a large piece of canvas this weekend. I am thinking about a title for this work. I want to use the overall title, *Colour Lock Series*. I could use the title *Colour Lock* on all the paintings and number them in the order that I made them. I'll work it out.

I worked on Victor's cover yesterday. The lettering looks sloppy now that it's finished, so I will reset it. The drawing has an active line that tends to juggle the lettering. Every imperfection is exaggerated. Nothing to do but do it over again.

I'm reading Mark Twain's *Literary Essays*. I'm really enjoying his books.

15 August, 1970. Saturday

Nelson was up and away early this morning. He has gone to Coach House Press for the sale of David Rosenberg's books. Then he is going directly to Marty's to work on the poetry catalogue; I won't see him until late this afternoon.

George Bowering is in town. We will probably see him and Victor soon. Victor will have to see the cover for his book. I reset the lettering yesterday.

We've heard that John Newlove is in town working as an editor at McClelland & Stewart.

I've begun Mark Twain's last book, *Christian Science*. Twain is easy reading; one can move swiftly through his prose. I've been reading a lot through this hot weather.

17 August, 1970. Monday

Yesterday, I photographed the last three paintings [*Colour Lock #12, #13* and *#14*. each 48" x 48" acrylic on canvas], then covered them. I am sending slides and photographs to Dennis Young, curator of contemporary art at the AGO.

Nelson will work again tonight at Marty's, so this day will be long.

I am reading Francesco Carletti's *My Voyage around the World*. The book is a translation of the manuscript. The trip was from 1594 to 1606.

18 August, 1970. Tuesday

Last night, we stretched the large piece of canvas on the easel-boards. The painting will be five feet by ten feet. Yesterday, I worked further on the sketches for this painting, indicating the colours I am going to make. I will work with a red, a blue, and a low yellow (not toward green) at the centre, then a green and a purple at the ends which will be held down by a grey and a grey-yellow-green. The colours in these positions should read in a double arc.

I plan to begin with the red and the blue areas. They will be the most intense colours. I will determine the relationships of the other colours from them. Anyway, that's my plan. I'm going to size the canvas today.

I believe that colour controls colour. Over this past year, I've worked with colour with a new awareness. Itten's *The Art of Color* and Albers' *Interaction of Color* opened it up for me. Even Goethe's colour theory helped to put things in place. Years ago, I studied Ostwald's and Munsell's systems of colour, but they don't deal with "colour effect" in the way Itten and Albers do. Now that I've worked with colour relationships, the "locking" of colour to colour by the effect that one colour has on the other, or that two colours have on a third and the third colour has on the first, etc., I think that colour is never singular. Even a single colour plays off the "white" of the canvas, or a painting that has only one colour plays off the white of the wall and one sees "effect." I've known this all along, but never as thoroughly as I know it now. I've been watching it happen with every colour I've laid on canvas over the past year.

21 August, 1970. Friday

Nelson left for Cleveland this morning. He will be on the bus from 9:40 a.m. until 5:30 p.m. I expect him back on Sunday. Last night, it was 9:30 p.m. before Nelson got home from Marty's, so we ate out at the Indian restaurant, the Mohol, on Bloor Street.

I began working on the big canvas yesterday. I laid the tape for two of the colour areas. I had trouble getting the shapes the way I want them. Each shape is a loose-edged square, approximately 30" x 30". I mixed all seven colours and saw them dry on my test sheet. Two still aren't right; I'll adjust them. Then I worked two areas, the red shape and the blue shape. Strong. I'll work further today.

Dave Tuck called again from Aggregation. Now he wants to raise the prices on the small acrylics on paper. I said okay.

My slides and photos were returned from the AGO with a note from Dennis Young. I am to call him after Labour Day.

22 August, 1970. Saturday

The big painting is coming along beautifully. Yesterday, I worked three more areas. I'm really excited about how they work. I remixed the colour for the grey area at the top left (it is beside the red shape). I adjusted the grey-yellow-green, too. It's at the top right beside the blue. I'm particularly excited about the large yellow area. It's a rectangle, approximately 30" x 60". I lowered the yellow by adding purple. The yellow greyed beautifully and did not move toward green. The yellow shape is below the red and blue shapes at the centre of the canvas.

I went out last night to see if Carol was at her studio. Her light was off, so I went for a coffee. Jenny, the young waitress, was just off work so she sat down with me and we talked. She is 22, full of energy and seems a bit erratic. She says she likes to talk on an "emotional level." To her, that involves describing her dreams and her feelings about things. She said she took part in a "sensitivity group" last year at Ryerson and she really enjoyed it. She expressed a fear that people might consider her "weird" or "abnormal," but I feel that she is deliberately trying to appear just that way. It is as if she is challenging the people she meets. I don't see anything wrong with this; I think she is trying to assert herself and it doesn't really matter if she does it in a self-indulgent way. She will seem less deliberate as she becomes more sure of herself.

23 August, 1970. Sunday

I expect Nelson back around four o'clock this afternoon.

Yesterday's work completed the big painting. I applied the last two areas of colour, a green shape at the bottom left and a purple shape at the bottom right. I'm really pleased with it [*Colour Lock #15*. 60" x 120" acrylic on canvas].

25 August, 1970. Tuesday

I spent most of yesterday reading. I went out for a walk through the Mirvish Village. The David Mirvish Gallery, renovated and expanded, is being painted white.

Carol called last night to say she would be at her studio and would drop in for a coffee. Then she called again to cancel. She's really not feeling well yet. Carol thinks she may have asthma.

I finished reading a book of short stories by Twain. I've begun his *Joan of Arc*; it's in two volumes.

26 August, 1970. Wednesday

I got a call from the St. James Town YMCA yesterday. A Reg Bundy has taken over Peckham's job. I will see him this afternoon about art classes for the fall.

28 August, 1970. Friday

I saw Reg Bundy on Wednesday. I said I could teach a drawing class again this year, or a drawing and painting class if that was what he wanted. Nothing is decided. I did not hesitate to tell him how poor I thought the facilities were there. I've no idea if he will improve them. He said he will call me.

Yesterday was slow and lazy; I was very tired. I'm reading *Innocents Abroad* — two volumes.

Last night, Nelson started work on the layouts for both catalogues — Marty's poetry catalogue and Jim Lowell's Asphodel catalogue. I must begin work on the cover for the Asphodel.

We will see David Rosenberg and Arlette on Monday. Nelson invited them for dinner.

31 August, 1970. Monday

I saw Carol yesterday. She seems little better. She is upset about having lost the fire escape entrance to her studio, which is next door to the David Mirvish Gallery. She arrived at her studio to find the fire escape gone — nothing had been said to her about it. Mirvish simply took it down. The fire escape was not only the entrance to her second floor studio, it is how she gets her paintings in and out of the building. Now she will have to bring them down an inside staircase and she doesn't think it is wide enough for her large paintings. No one knows what Mirvish is doing, but the newly expanded gallery has priority. Carol thinks she will be evicted.

David and Arlette are coming for dinner tonight, if they remember.

1 September, 1970. Tuesday

Milly Ristvedt called at noon yesterday (she was in town only for the day) and came over for the afternoon. She told me she's painting up a storm; she has made fifteen new paintings in the past three or four months. She said that she's working on three different series at once. She is happy (and pretty excited) about the results, but wasn't specific about any of the paintings. She won't be showing at Carmen Lamanna's gallery this year, but she will show at the Waddington Gallery in Montreal. Henry Saxe will have a show of his sculpture with Lamanna in October; she said I'll see both of them in town then.

Milly looked at my big painting. I think she liked it, although she was critical about the grey shape's relationship to the red shape. She said that the grey shape couldn't reach the grey-yellow-green shape through the primaries (red and blue). I have given this much thought and I don't agree with her objection. It appears that she is reading the colours from top left to top right. There is no need to do that; rather, let the colour direct the eye. The eye travels on the intense colours (green, red, blue and purple) in an arc, and the grey reaches the grey-yellow-green through the large greyed yellow shape when the eye travels on another (inverted) arc.

Milly said that Lamanna or Isaacs should see this new work. She seems to think they would take it. (She's optimistic.) She said that I should be more aggressive.

David and Arlette came for dinner last night. Actually, they forgot, only remembered at the last minute, so arrived a little late. The meal was kind of dull (I tried, but I'm no cook). David seemed worn out. His parents are with them for these last few days before they leave for Europe and he's probably feeling crowded. It was a nice enough evening, but everyone was a little tired.

2 September, 1970. Wednesday
Prompted by Milly's visit, I called Carmen Lamanna yesterday. He told me to come in at 1 p.m. I went over with my slides. He took a long time looking at them. He was impressed enough to say that he would try to come and see the work, but he set no date. He will call.

He suggested that I bring in some good slides when I have them (my slides are really poor) and he will keep them on file to show to people who are interested. He said he does this for some artists he doesn't represent. He told me about how he works with his artists. For an exhibition, he (the gallery) prints the announcement, pays for an ad in *The Globe and Mail* and for one in *Artscanada*. "That's all," he said. If the artists want ads in the American art magazines, they pay for them themselves. He seemed puzzled by the fact that most of his artists do. So, I learn from this that it is the artists who are advertising Lamanna's gallery in the American magazines instead of the other way around.

bpNichol stopped by briefly last night. Then I went over to see Carol. She has begun a new painting. Her last three are good; she should be happy with them, but she still maintains that she doesn't know what she is doing. She came back here with me to see my big painting. We talked. She still coughs a lot and doesn't seem well.

John Newlove called last night just at a moment when Nelson had gone out to buy cigarettes. I spoke with him only for as long as it took Nelson to get back.

Nelson will see him next week. He's going to give Nelson a poem to print at the front of Jim Lowell's Asphodel catalogue.

We will visit Robert Downing tonight.

3 September, 1970. Thursday

We saw Robert Downing and his wife, Sally, last night. Sally is a delicate girl who makes fine photographs. We spent time looking at slides and photos of each other's work. I took my slides and Nelson took some Weed Flower Press books. We saw some of Sally's work, colour photos of flowers and some black and white photos of microscopic, cellular images. We saw slides of Downing's show at Whitechapel in England. Downing talked about teaching and about sculpture. I really enjoyed the evening.

7 September, 1970. Monday

Nelson spent most of the weekend typing the stencils for the two catalogues. Yesterday afternoon he went out to see John Newlove. He enjoyed the visit; he talked about it most of the evening. I am nervous about seeing Newlove again.

While Nelson was out, I worked on the Asphodel cover and it came together at last. In fact, it opened up some possibilities that I pushed into drawings last night. I'm not sure what I've got yet. I am working intuitively, arbitrarily juxtaposing the square shape. The spaces between the squares are active and irregular, separating the orderly figure. The square has soft corners. I used a felt tip pen for the cover drawing, allowing the corners of each square to burst slightly. Then I tried drawing with graphite. The graphite shape is not as soft, but it is flexible, controllable.

Yesterday, we looked at the mock-up for the book of poems and prints that we worked on last winter. It still seems a good idea. We talked about pursuing it and doing an edition of 25 or 50 copies [*Points of Attention*].

Today, I spent over five hours making drawings. They are exciting things to look at, but I'm strung out and confused by them. I don't know where I'm headed with them. I'm chasing something. I'll just have to chase.

9 September, 1970. Wednesday

I called Mr. Sullivan at Northern Secondary School today about the night classes. I will teach two classes a week (Tuesday and Thursday) this year. I called Dennis Young at the AGO. He will come to see my work next Wednesday at 1:30 p.m.

I finished reading *The Good Soldier* by Ford Madox Ford.

10 September, 1970. Thursday

I made more drawings yesterday. Then last night, I got involved making "word-poem-drawings." I used the one-inch letter stencils (Gothic and Roman), making tonal drawings with graphite that form a word that pictures its meaning. I'm going to do a few more today. I'm loaded with ideas; it's great fun.

15 September, 1970. Tuesday

Last night we folded the pages for the Asphodel catalogue. Nelson will trim them today, then put on the covers. It will be ready for Jim by the weekend.

Carol called. She told me the new David Mirvish Gallery will have a "grand opening" on Saturday night.

16 September, 1970. Wednesday

Last night, Nelson went to Coach House Press to trim the pages of Jim's catalogue. I stayed here and folded the covers. (I finished this morning.) Nelson returned with the galley proofs for his own book, *The Pre-Linguistic Heights*. Stan told him the book would be done by next month. We will both see Stan soon to discuss the book's design.

I expect Dennis Young today.

17 September, 1970. Thursday

Dennis Young came, as arranged, yesterday. He is a young man, tall, good-looking, but he appears at first to have a forbidding arrogance. I was scared of him. I showed him my paintings and as he looked he talked a lot, seemed highly critical, asking a lot of questions about how (and why) I made them. I thought the whole interview was a wipe-out. I answered his questions and countered most of his criticism with those justifications I believe in — I had nothing to lose. He stayed for an hour and a half. Before he left, I asked if he would support me for a Canada Council grant. He said, "by all means." I even said that I would want a *favourable* letter of reference and he said, "without doubt." I was so surprised. And pleased.

Jim Lowell phoned Nelson last night. He will arrive in town on Friday night. He'll come here for dinner on Saturday and the Newloves will come over in the evening. John wants to meet Jim and asked Nelson to arrange it.

Earle Birney was here last night. We have not seen him in almost two years. He phoned from Pete's Restaurant just around the corner on Bloor and while he was phoning, someone stole his wallet! (He lost $100.) He reported the theft before he got here, but has no hope of the wallet being recovered. It's terrible — such bad luck!

He described his past year, both in and out of Toronto. It was incredible. He told us he was in an accident, in a taxi on Yonge Street, last January. His jaw was broken and he needed dental and plastic surgery. He spent January through March recuperating. In April, he did a reading tour in the US. In May and June, he had to be treated for a mastoid infection, caused by an error made by the dentist after the accident. He spent the summer in British Columbia where he did a lot of writing. But now, he is no sooner back in Toronto and he gets robbed! He said that Toronto is a Hoodoo for him this year.

18 September, 1970. Friday
I wrote the Canada Council for application forms yesterday. I have Alan Toff and Dennis Young for references so far. Barry Lord is at the National Gallery in Ottawa now, so I'll get in touch with him.

Roy Kiyooka's book, *Stoned Gloves*, is out from Coach House. It's a beautiful book. It will serve as a catalogue for an exhibition of Kyiooka's photographs that will open soon in Edmonton. The show will tour for two years.

Yesterday, I spent time at my print studio on Markham Street cleaning screens for my silkscreen equipment. I brought back some of the drawing paper I keep over there. I want to do more graphite drawings using stencils. I also want to begin sketches toward the print for Nelson's *The Pre-Linguistic Heights*.

Nelson spent last evening gluing covers on the Asphodel catalogue. I read. I finished Rachel Carson's *Silent Spring*.

19 September, 1970. Saturday
I worked on graphite drawings yesterday. I have cut some new shapes to use as stencils. I'm packing and stacking shapes on the page. In two of the drawings I used letters as shapes — difficult to make that work, but I like the possibilities it opens up. I worked as well on the drawing for the print for *The Pre-Linguistic Heights*. I have determined the size of the print and the shapes that will be involved, but not the colours. I'm still thinking about that.

Received confirmation in yesterday's mail about the classes at St. James Town. I will teach Wednesday evenings if the class gets enough enrollment (minimum: twelve students). I doubt it will get off the ground. I have to be there on the 24th to take enrollment.

Jim Lowell called. We expect him for dinner. The Newloves will come for the evening.

20 September, 1970. Sunday

I could not have predicted last night. As much as I expected Newlove's ridicule, I would not have believed he could be so low.

Jim came in the late afternoon. We had a nice visit and dinner. He was pleased with the catalogue (and the cover). Newlove arrived at about 8:30 with Susan and another couple. They had all been drinking. The talk was crude, a stupid attempt to be witty. I could see that both Jim and Nelson were turned off by them. Newlove tried to take a couple of shots at me about the paintings in the room. Then he went to work on Nelson and his socks. Nelson was visibly annoyed. Then Newlove took another shot at me and it hit home. He knew it. That sneering little smile — he looked so satisfied. Jim saw it happen and knew. When talk went on, I got up and walked back to the kitchen. I could not go back into the front room, so I went out. Outside, I felt sick with anger and I was angry at myself. *What am I doing out here on the street? That son of a bitch has driven me out of my own place!*

I walked over to Markham Street and watched the people going in and out of the Mirvish Gallery. It was the "grand opening." The people were all in formal dress; the women wore evening gowns. I phoned Nelson to say I would be in my print studio and to come there when the people had gone. Apparently things were going from bad to worse at the apartment. Nelson came over to the studio to see if I was okay. He said the other couple had already left. When he got back, the Newloves had gone. He came back and got me and when we returned, dear Jim was tidying, emptying the ashtrays. We talked for a bit, obliquely, all clearly disgusted. Newlove had wanted to meet Jim, and this is what he did. He won't come here again.

22 September, 1970. Tuesday

I received instructions about the Saturday morning children's classes from the AGO in yesterday's mail. Barbara Hall called at noon. She is excited about the classes. She will be teaching 8-10-year-olds all year. I'm scheduled for 11-18-year-olds on rotation. It should be an interesting year.

Nelson and I both received invitations to the Oberon Press book launch in Ottawa. *The Cosmic Chef* will be among the books launched. Nelson replied, affirming for both of us. The launch will take place in October over the weekend the League of Canadian Poets meets in Ottawa and we are going to that.

I got a reply from Kim Ondaatje. I'm a member now of CAR (Canadian Artists Representation). I'll write a letter to the Benson Commission in support of the Nancy Poole tax reform proposal.

I worked at my Markham Street studio cleaning screens.

I'd like to forget Newlove. I can't help wondering where the poems come from. I guess it's possible to be a good poet and, at the same time, a rotten human being.

24 September, 1970. Thursday

Yesterday, Lynne from Aggregation called to tell me about OISE (Ontario Institute for Studies in Education). OISE plans to form a collection of art and they will look at work at the gallery. Lynne asked me for some of the new work. I agreed to give them a slide of one of the Colour Lock paintings, and if there is interest shown in it, to give them that one painting for their next group show. As well, I'll give them four or five of the new graphite drawings for that show. Last night, Lynne and Dave came over to pick up the slide and to talk this over. (My show of Colour Lock paintings is scheduled for February; I don't want too much of the work to go out now.)

The Canada Council application forms came. It's discouraging just to read them. It's like getting down on both knees.

25 September, 1970. Friday

I went to St. James Town last night to take registration for my class. It was a waste of time. Only five people enrolled in the drawing course and three in the mixed media course. I met Colette Gagnon, who will teach mixed media; she will also be teaching the Saturday morning classes for the AGO this year. The YMCA office will continue to take enrollment until next Wednesday. They'll let me know if the class is on or off.

I will see Carol's nephew, Peter Martyn, tonight. He's a photographer. I'll find out if he can take slides of the new paintings.

27 September, 1970. Sunday

The children's classes began yesterday. Big enrollment; the classes are huge. I did a class, drawing from the model, with one of the 11-13-year-old groups. I was disappointed with the set up. We had a meeting after class. The space at the college and the storage will be even more restricted this year. It seems, too, that the promise of working with 14-18-year-olds (on rotation) was empty. The guys will work with the older classes; "the girls," as usual, will teach the youngest ones. I felt ready to scream "discrimination." I spoke with Barbara Hall; she's disappointed, too.

Peter Martyn came on Friday. He will make three sets of original slides of the eleven paintings for $75.

28 September, 1970. Monday

Victor Coleman called about the design for Nelson's book, *The Pre-Linguistic Heights.* Yesterday, we went to Coach House to meet with him about it. The number of changes he proposed was staggering — I wondered if we were talking about the same book. The most radical change was in the shape of the book — from a square book, 6½" x 6½" to a 5½" x 7" book. Victor suggested a square be drawn on each page and a square outline appear on the title page. We vetoed that. He showed us some paper he thought should be used for the wrapper. It was polished one side and so light it kept rolling up in his hands. We talked him out of using it. We looked at paper for text and at cover stock and made a choice. The "special edition" will have my print tipped in as a frontispiece (with tissue) so the page facing the title will be left clear for it. The whole edition will be printed the same way; the "special edition" will be made special by the inclusion of the print. Victor said something about jacking up the price of a book by throwing in some art work. (I was mildly offended by that.)

Last night, Nelson and I went over the details of that meeting. Nelson seems more settled about it now. Nelson wants a white book, white and grey — with colour added by my print reproduced on the cover. He wants a nice book, one that we could not produce ourselves.

Jim Spence came by yesterday. We found him hovering on the sidewalk when we got back from Coach House. He came in for coffee and some talk. He is going to register for my Thursday night class at Northern. It will be good to have him in the class again.

bpNichol came by just after Mr. Spence left. He seemed spaced out, but it's always good to see him. He read to us from the manuscript he's working on, "The Life and Loves of Captain George." It will be a marathon to read when he's done with it; it's packed.

I chose three of my graphite drawings to have framed by Aggregation. I showed them to Nelson, then together we chose two more to be framed and brought back home [*Graphite Drawing(s), Series 1.* 18" x 24"].

29 September, 1970. Tuesday

I worked on the print for Nelson's book yesterday. I used acrylic to work out the areas and I have a better idea of the shape and colour for it now. I should be able to prepare the screen for it soon.

Carol and I went to the opening of Robert Sinclair's show at Aggregation. Sinclair's work is landscape oriented, lean and spare. The watercolours were the most immediate pieces; the drawings and pastels were almost as good. The paintings were generally small scale, but I thought the largest paintings were difficult.

They had demanding space problems; I wondered if that was accidental because they seemed unresolved. I talked with Sinclair. At first, he seemed uncomfortable — kept looking away from me. I learned that he was not particularly involved with space problems. It was an interesting discussion and I think he even enjoyed it. Later, I learned from Lynne that she had "warned" Sinclair about me.

30 September, 1970. Wednesday
I worked on drawings yesterday. I made five new ones. I was surprised by the number, but once I started, they just poured out.

I went to the Mirvish Gallery. It's the first time I've been in since they reopened. All my hostility toward the overflow of American art that is burying us disappeared. It's a beautiful show. There is a huge Bush (Canadian), a Larry Poons, a Noland (grey!), a Stella, a Morris Louis, a Frankenthaler, a Motherwell and a Hans Hofmann (beautiful). There's also a Darby Bannard and a piece by the Californian, Davis — I was least interested by these. There are floor sculptures by Anthony Caro, Robert Murray (Canadian) and Michael Steiner. I'm glad I didn't have to go to New York to see this show. I may wish there were more space for Canadians in this town, but I'm really excited by this work and glad to be able to see it.

I surprised myself by speaking to some brash kids in the gallery (probably art students) about the Motherwell painting. One of the girls in the group was showing an open interest in the painting, but she was getting so much bull from the two boys she was with that I had to say something. I interrupted when I heard one boy dismiss the Motherwell as "just a wash." (He wanted to know the price of the painting, but Alkis wouldn't answer him or show him the list.) I have to laugh at myself now. I wasn't angry, just impatient with the one boy. I told him to "be quiet" so I could answer the girl's question. Imagine. But I don't like to see someone spoil another person's pleasure like that.

I have to call St. James Town to see if I have a class tonight.

1 October, 1970. Thursday
The class at St. James Town has sixteen people registered. Thirteen of them showed up last night. There were materials, drawing boards and easels for only seven people. I took in some paper and pencils so we could get started. Bundy promises there will be more easels by next week. They are a good group; it will be a good class if Bundy comes across.

Peter Martyn came and photographed my paintings last night. Nelson helped him move the paintings and the job was done by the time I got back from the class.

I have done some sketches toward new paintings.

2 October, 1970. Friday

I read Paul Klee's *On Modern Art* yesterday — twice. It's very fine, precise, a beautiful thing. I'm reminded of the diary excerpts by John McCracken that I read last week. It's exciting to find such fine thinking written down.

I'm thinking toward new paintings.

5 October, 1970. Monday

Klee's thoughts on line and tonal value prompted me to think about my drawings. As a result, on Friday I worked further, making ten new pieces. I went over these later, eliminating one piece. These drawings are an extension of the first drawings. On Sunday, I worked further, dealing deliberately with "weight" and "measure" [*Series 1*. 9" x 12"].

7 October, 1970. Wednesday

The class last night at Northern was full. Twenty-five people registered and twenty-four of them showed up. Most of them showed quite a bit of facility in drawing. It should be a good class.

8 October, 1970. Thursday

Barry Lord called from Ottawa last night to say that he will support me for a Canada Council grant. Peter Martyn will deliver my slides tonight so I'll be able to take them to Ottawa.

I did the St. James Town class last night. The easels and drawing boards were there. Bundy came in and stayed for a while. I don't know what he thought; I didn't have a chance to talk with him; I was busy getting three new people started.

13 October, 1970. Tuesday

First, I'll return to last Thursday. The second class at Northern had twenty-five people registered and all of them were there. When I got home, Peter Martyn and Sara were here. Peter brought two good sets of slides (originals) and two sets that were duplicates. I may be a bit restricted. The slides look good, but they should be masked and remounted.

We went to Ottawa Friday night, arriving very late at the hotel. At breakfast, Saturday morning, the coffee shop was full of poets. They were greeting each other and table hopping even before they'd had coffee. Mike Ondaatje, Douglas Barbour and Stephen Scobie sat near us. Mr. Birney was there; Francis Sparshott and Don Gutteridge I knew. Most, I didn't recognize.

Nelson didn't go out to Carleton University until noon. Instead, we went for a walk along the Sparks Street Mall. I called Barry Lord and arranged to leave my slides at the National Gallery for him. I had lunch at the gallery then looked at the contemporary art on the fifth floor. I saw a Dan Flavin fluorescent light work installed alone in a room — I'd never seen one of his works before. I saw one of Frank Stella's black paintings, an Olitski, a Karel Appel and George Segal's *Garage*. Saw a piece by a British artist that was simply a cord stretched taut diagonally across a small room from a corner of the ceiling to the opposite corner on the floor. It managed to occupy and define the space of the room. One felt as if one were inside a cube. I thought it was brilliant. A couple, who were coming out of the room just as I went in, said to me, "There's nothing in there." Then I went down to the fourth floor and saw the exhibition by Joaquin Torrès-Garcia (works from 1890 to 1949).

I met Nelson at the hotel and he told me about the League's business meeting at the university. There had been talk about Americans teaching in Canadian universities, about Canada's limited distribution of Canadian literature and about the Canada Council and the Governor General's Award in terms of their policies regarding Americans and landed immigrants. There had been a big argument between Michael Yates and Dorothy Livesay. Yates, it seems, has insulted Livesay, and she wants an apology. It had been a hot afternoon.

We went, then, to the Oberon Press book launch party. Evidence of the afternoon's heated talks met us at the door. Just inside, Dorothy Livesay was talking to two people. She was loud and excited; the argument about Yates seemed to preoccupy everyone in the room. I met a few new people — Steve McCaffery and Andreas Schroeder, the poet who recently did an issue of a magazine on phony German poets. I spoke with George Jonas briefly, also John Robert Colombo. Talked with Mr. Birney and with Mike Ondaatje again. It was a close-packed, stand-up-and-be-squashed party.

A bus arrived at 7:30 p.m. to take everyone out to the university for a steak dinner at the cafeteria. Douglas Lochhead was there greeting people. Nelson and I were late getting in, but he shepherded us through. Then, everyone went on to the reading.

Thirty poets read. It was mixed, but I enjoyed all of it. I really liked Dennis Lee's poems, and Mike Ondaatje's. Readings are performances; they are great to watch. I met Angela Bowering, there with George, and Lionel Kearns — *By the Light of the Silvery McLune*.

On Sunday, Nelson went to Carleton again. I wandered around the Arts Centre — its three roof levels are gardened. I could see William Ronald's mural through the windows. Then I went back to the National Gallery. I saw the camels this time. Saw a Robert Murray, a Tousignant, an Intersystems piece, a large three-part work by Walt Redinger, a Curnoe. On the second floor (Flemish, British and

French collections), I met Lionel Kearns. He said he had had enough of meetings and was seeing the gallery instead.

Nelson and I decided to have a Chinese dinner. On the way out of the hotel, we met Douglas Barbour and Stephen Scobie; they came with us and we all ate together, then went to the final party where Nelson and I stayed for only about an hour. We went to Le Hibou, but didn't go in; we had expected Bruce Cockburn to be performing there, but he wasn't. We left Ottawa on Monday, arriving in Toronto late in the afternoon. We ate at the Mohol Restaurant on Bloor and came home.

14 October, 1970. Wednesday
Slept late yesterday. I read Gore Vidal's *Myra Breckinridge*. There were twenty people in the class at Northern last night.

18 October, 1970. Sunday
Nelson took a day and a half off work this week. He has begun to print the pages of Marty's catalogue. On Thursday afternoon, I gathered the first four sheets; Friday morning, I gathered four more. This is going to be a long slow job. I will gather four sheets at a time, then gather those gatherings.

On Friday, we went together to the galleries. At the Dunkelman Gallery, we saw Jim Dine's show — paintings of heart shapes with coats hung on the canvases. I particularly liked some of the smaller pieces. Jared Sable looked at my slides. He said I can call in another month to arrange for him to come to the studio. He delivered this message to me in a strange way. Although I was standing right in front of him, he turned to Nelson when he finished looking at the slides and said, "Tell her to call in another month..." When we were outside again, I remarked on this to Nelson. He thought it was strange, too. I guess I should show my slides to dealers by myself. That way, they'll have to talk to me.

We went to the Jerrold Morris Gallery and saw Kazuo Nakamura's show. Very exciting work, but difficult — an evolutionary involvement. Morris glanced at my slides, then went into a great long spiel about the economy and politics. We went into Gallery Moos where there was a mixed show of international work. No one there was free to look at slides. Then Nelson went to Marty's and I went on to Isaacs' and Lamanna's.

Isaacs looked at my slides. I could tell he wasn't impressed, but he was nice about it. The gallery was hung with collages by Dennis Burton. They needed more time than I was able to give them. Lamanna looked at the slides; he said they were good enough for him to keep on file. He talked with me for about an hour. The outcome? He won't give me a show. I still don't know what to think about what he said.

Lamanna came to the studio one evening about a year and a half ago. He stayed fairly long, looking at paintings, even at the books and book covers. He seemed to like what he saw. He asked to see what I did in another year. The Colour Lock paintings are what I have done, so I have felt justified in asking for another studio visit. On Friday, he said that he would not come to the studio again because, if he did, he knew he would like the work, but he would still have to turn me down and he didn't like doing that — it makes him feel bad. He asked me not to show him any more of my work.

On Saturday, I saw Darby Bannard's show at the Mirvish Gallery and Thelma Van Alstyne at Pollock's.

Aggregation called to tell me that OISE has bought my painting, *Small Diagonals*. They bought a number of pieces (one of Carol's). This will be good for everyone.

Pierre Laporte is dead, killed by the FLQ. The War Measures Act has been in effect for several days and the safety of James Cross is unknown. The situation is bad; we have taken a big step backwards.

22 October, 1970. Thursday

I met Carol shortly after noon yesterday and we took a cab over to Aggregation. I took in five more drawings to be mounted, covered and shown unframed. (I can't afford more frames right now.) Carol signed her two drawings and we both took a last look at our paintings, sold to OISE. Then we had lunch at Grumbles.

I went back to the gallery to talk with Lynne. They have priced my framed drawings at $60. Less their commission of one-third, that gives me $40. When I remove the cost of the frame, I have $28.50 for the drawing. I told Lynne that their price was too low and I would like them to raise it. I want about $50 for the drawing, so with their commission and the cost of the frame, the drawings should be priced at $90 framed. An unframed drawing would be priced at $75 and the buyer pays for the frame when it is added. She told me that they priced my drawings low because there weren't as many lines in them as there are in their drawings by other artists.

Dave called today to tell me that the people from the AGO Art Rental Gallery would be coming into the gallery to look at work. He wanted to know if I'd let them take some of my work if they wanted it.

I cut the stencil for the print for Nelson's book today. I worked on a drawing, but it was unsuccessful. I have abandoned it.

23 October, 1970. Friday

Dave called late last night. He told me that the people from AGO had chosen two of my drawings, but they chose two of the unframed ones so I will have to have them framed. He told me they had looked at the five framed drawings, but didn't like them. I said no to more framing; the AGO Rental Gallery will have to do without. Either they choose the drawings that are already framed, or nothing. This exchange took an extremely long time. It was after midnight when I got off the phone.

24 October, 1970. Saturday

I'm beginning to think Nelson lives on the moon. I hardly see him. It was after nine o'clock last night before he got home.

I talked with Dave at Aggregation about the pricing of my drawings. I think we got things straightened out. Dave and Lynne don't take the cost of the frame into account when they price a framed work. They know that the artist receives less for his work when it is framed than if the same work were sold unframed, but they don't know why — as Dave said, "it just always turns out that way." I tried to explain that when the commission comes off the top, the value of the frame must be marked up by the same percentage, or the artist can't recover what was spent on the frame. It was hard to get this idea across to Dave. He told me that he didn't think I should be trying to make money on my frames. I tried to get him to see that I would not make money on the frame (he would), I was trying to not lose money on my drawing. I don't know if he's got it, but he has agreed to go with my prices.

25 October, 1970. Sunday

We have spent the whole day on our CC bursary application forms. We began last night and got nowhere — almost got into an argument over it. The forms that each of us are sending to the people who will write letters of recommendation have to be sent out, and on them, one outlines the project. Nelson thought he could write only, "I want to write" and that would do. I thought he should write more than that — give a short account of his plan for a year of work. Today, we both completed our reference forms and they can be mailed. There is time now for each of us to work on our own applications. Nelson is applying for a writing grant and I'm applying for a visual arts grant.

I talked with Victor yesterday about a colour reproduction for the invitation for my show in February. If the reproduction of the print for the cover of Nelson's book had an extra printing it could be used for the invitation. It sounds like it will work.

Victor offered to write a review of my show for *Artscanada*. Fine, if he's willing to do it. He said he will talk to Anne Brodzky.

29 October, 1970. Thursday

I've been working on drawings these past few days with uneven success. I set up the cover for Marty's catalogue. I will soon be ready to print; I have to take materials over to my print studio on Markham.

We've been working on our CC applications.

The class last night at St. James Town went refreshingly well. This group is small enough to handle. One of the students told me that she had gone to Aggregation to see my work. She mentioned *Still Life* (acrylic on paper), where I used words to describe the forms (bottle, jug, orange, orange, orange). She told me she didn't know why I would do that, but it started to dawn on her as she was walking home. She seemed happy that she "got it." She said that she was beginning to "see" differently because of the classes. And, of course, that made me feel good.

31 October, 1970. Saturday

We have finished our CC applications. They should give some sort of award just for having completed those forms.

The children's class went well this morning. The two 11-13 years' classes were combined. Mitch [Ted Michener] was away, so Gernot Dick took his place. Gernot was really good to work with — he's disciplined and conscientious.

Thursday's class at Northern went well. At last, I've found a way to deal with all twenty-nine of them.

Yesterday, I went to see the David Hockney show at the Pollock Gallery. The show includes some early lithographs, his illustrated *Grimm's Fairy Tales* and a *Cavafy Suite*. While I was in there, the girl and one of the boys I talked to about the Motherwell painting that day at Mirvish came in. They had seen me from outside and wanted to know what I thought of the show. They wanted to know if I liked Darby Bannard's work. Much talk; it was kind of fun. When they left, they said they were going back to the Mirvish Gallery to look at the Bannard show again.

3 November, 1970. Tuesday

I went over to my print studio yesterday. I managed to get things organized. I put the stencil on a screen, set up the registers and mixed inks. I'm worried about the paper Victor brought me; it's not as smooth as I would like and it varies slightly in size. Now that I'm ready to go ahead, I'm having misgivings. Will the print be right for the book?

I dropped in to see Carol before going to my studio. She was so depressed I hated to rush off, so I spent more time there than I'd intended. She has gotten herself into a poor state over her CC forms. She has not been able to get references for her application. She has had the forms longer than we have had ours; she kept saying she was "keeping cool" about it. She was hardly cool yesterday. She spent most of the time crying. I hate to see her like that. She has shown her work to Alan Toff and to Dennis Young, but neither, she said, responded very well, so she is not going to try Barry Lord. So far, she has only asked for support from the people who are supporting me, so I suggested some names of people she knew (who I don't know and don't know me) who would likely give her support — like her friend, Earle Toppings — and encouraged her to get on it and get her application in.

I spent last night collating sections of Marty's catalogue. Nelson worked on the stencils for Victor's book and later, we decided on the colours for four of the covers for the Weed Flower Press books in the works. Nelson will take the covers to the printer this week.

4 November, 1970. Wednesday

Last night's class went well. I'm finally getting control of what's happening with these large classes. Nelson met me outside when I got home and we went over to Markham and got Carol to come out for a coffee. She was much better.

Dave called today. He offered me a spot in the Christmas group show and I turned it down. I thanked him for asking, but told him to offer the space to someone else. He was a little surprised, but it was okay. I didn't tell him that the fee each artist will pay to be in the show ($75) is more than I can handle right now. Even if I hung a work and it sold, I would still owe the gallery money, so I'm willing to let it go.

5 November, 1970. Thursday

I worked at my Markham studio yesterday. I pulled two colours (the yellow, the grey). I began to pull the blue area, but it was not going on smoothly so I stopped. I will remix the blue, using more pigment and mixing more thoroughly.

10 November, 1970. Tuesday

Last Friday, I worked on the print. Despite my care, the blue area dried badly. What looked like a good print while I was pulling it dried with an uneven blue area. There is nothing to do but make it over again. I can't find the specific cause of this failure, so I will correct all my suspicions. I have stretched a new silk; I will cut a new stencil, use smoother paper, change the intermixture for the blue, and hope.

Nelson came home with flu on Friday, so he did nothing over the weekend. He stayed home from the library yesterday, but will go in at noon today. I did little — I set the lettering for the envelope for Marty's catalogue, prepared the new screen, but much time was lost.

20 November, 1970. Friday

These are slow and restless days. Neither of us feels well enough to do much, yet we're not sick enough to justify all the inactivity.

I cut the new stencil today.

22 November, 1970. Sunday

On Friday night, we went over to the studio. I pulled two colours of the new print. We worked until midnight. All went well, so yesterday we pulled the third colour. I say "we" although I did the printing. Nelson stayed the whole time and did all the carrying, making any difficulty more manageable because he checked every print and any imperfection was caught immediately. This print is far superior to the first one.

Steve McCaffery and his wife, Maggie, visited last night. Steve brought his *Carnival*, a sixteen-page typewriter concrete piece using black and red inks. He spread it out on the floor; it is really impressive. He is going to bring us a photocopy of it this week so we can look at it at leisure.

23 November, 1970. Monday

A new worry. The prints have a very delicate surface and the blue area is slow to dry. At this point, I'm so insecure that I expect them to disintegrate just to spite me.

I went over to the studio yesterday to clean a screen. I want to make more prints, some to combine with a poem as a Christmas card. This experience with the print for Nelson's Coach House book has been devastating. I need to experiment to get control of the medium. I want to be painting by Christmas.

I dropped in to Carol's studio. She seems alright. She was about to begin a new canvas.

Last night, we gathered the pages of David Rosenberg's book, *Headlights*, and even got a few of the covers on [cover drawing by Arlette Smolarski]. It's good to see a book go together again.

24 November, 1970. Tuesday

I worked on stencils for a small print yesterday. I've cut four stencils for three separations (red, yellow and blue) and an overlay of a black, reduced to a transparency.

That's the idea, at least. It is a small composition of stacked squares and white spaces.

The print for *The Pre-Linguistic Heights* has dried beautifully. I'm pleased at last.

26 November, 1970. Thursday

I began printing on Tuesday. I printed two of the colours, then stopped half way through the third because the screen was picking up colour from the prints. This ink needs more drying time than I've been giving it. Yesterday, I finished printing the third colour. When I tried the overlay of transparent black, I had to stop again. I quite like the look of it. I will try the overlay again today, but already I know I have too many imperfects — well, it's an experiment after all.

I saw the Steiner sculpture show at the Mirvish Gallery yesterday. There are some beautiful low lying things; they are the best for me. The small pieces that stood high were the least satisfying; the large ones that had height accommodated it by their size. Robert Downing came in with some friends. He spoke to me and introduced me to Peter Kolisnyk who was with him. Kolisnyk's show is at the Pollock Gallery so I went over to see it. It's a beautiful show — verticals, clean canvases of one colour, very demanding work. There is a series of drawings with fine vertical lines. In some drawings, the lines are one-eighth of an inch apart; in others, a quarter-inch apart. The forms are tight — line to space to line.

30 November, 1970. Monday

The children's class on Saturday was a double load for me. Neither Mitch nor Gernot Dick showed up so I did both classes together alone.

Saturday evening I tried printing again. My paper stencil broke after about ten pulls. I will cut another to continue. The difficulties are maddening. I'm going toward an interesting print, if I could only print it! I've called Naz-dar for their catalogue; I want ink that will dry faster.

Nelson printed Anselm Hollo's book on Sunday [*America Del Norte & Other Peace Herb Poems*]. I gathered the pages in the evening. I have done the lettering for the cover. David Rosenberg's book is finished.

Nelson took my print for his book to Coach House, along with a mock-up of the invitation for my show in February. We'll see if the double printing is possible.

I received my slides back from Barry Lord today. He enclosed a letter saying he liked the work. He said my work was "amongst the most interesting colour work being done in Canada." Wow!

1 December, 1970. Tuesday

I was really quite excited about Barry Lord's letter — more than I realized. I went out for a walk along Bloor and Markham Streets, looking for someone I could tell about it. I found no one, so came home laughing at myself.

I cut more paper stencils yesterday. I recut the final stencil for the small print and three new stencils for another print.

7 December, 1970. Monday

Nelson has been printing Weed Flower Press books. The pages for Victor's book are done. They will be sewn; the cover is ready [*Old Friends' Ghosts*]. Anselm Hollo's and George Bowering's pages [*George, Vancouver*] are finished, too. Hollo's cover goes to the printer today; Bowering's isn't ready yet.

I did some printing at Markham. No success. I figured out, however, that the paper I have been using for stencils is too heavy. I have gotten new ink; the oil I was using dried too slowly.

We both spent Sunday at Marty's. I read while Nelson filled the orders received from Marty's catalogue.

8 December, 1970. Tuesday

I haven't been noting any of my reading lately. I've been reading more from the set of Mark Twain — two books of short stories and articles and the two volumes of *A Tramp Abroad*. Read a book on Homer Watson last week that was loaned to me by one of my students. I enjoyed it; it was nostalgic for me because of my time spent at Doon [Doon Summer School of Fine Arts]. I am reading some Sapir and a book called *Colour Theory* that Nelson brought me from the library. It is a study on colour and language (the evolution of the mind) that was done at Berkeley, California.

9 December, 1970. Wednesday

I did the class at Northern last night. This is the last week of classes there before the holiday — we finish early this year. The students in both of my classes are painting now.

This afternoon, I went to the Mirvish Gallery to see the Robert Motherwell show — the *Open Series*. I hadn't known that Motherwell worked with so much colour; I've only seen the blue paintings from this series. He has worked with orange and black line as well as the blue and black line. One painting combined blue and orange — a nice use of the complements. In two paintings, he has laid a transparent red over green, neutralizing or greying both colours (although no "grey" is used) — another use of complementary colour. I don't really understand his use of line beyond the fact that it disturbs the shape of his canvas. It reaches for the wall. (I don't know how to describe what I mean by that.)

I went into the Pollock Gallery where I talked with Jack and another man — a collector.

11 December, 1970. Friday
That talk at Pollock's was interesting. There was some gossip, but mostly the talk was about painting and painters. I was surprised that Pollock would engage me in conversation when he was already involved in a conversation with the collector. This man talked about a work by Eva Hesse that he had bought. He loved it, but found that he could not live with it. It was a Hesse sculpture that combines several tall narrow elements made of fiberglass, but the fiberglass had not been sealed. The work gave off a smell that at first was not unpleasant, but it was pervasive. Air conditioning didn't dispel the smell, so finally with regret, he returned the work. He told Jack that Mary Martin had died. Jack clearly didn't know who he meant (I didn't either), so said hesitantly, "Peter Pan?" Mary Martin was a British artist whose painting is "structurist"; she was married to the British artist, Kenneth Martin (whom we didn't know either). I will look them up.

I cut new stencils yesterday and pulled two colours for a small print. Good results.

14 December, 1970. Monday
I finished the small print on Friday. We have tipped some of them into cards with a poem, but won't send any out yet — I'm still uncertain. I do have more control of the medium as a result of this print and aside from its technical imperfections, the colour and forms work well. I am going to deal with it as a 60" x 60" painting. We stretched a piece of canvas on the easel-boards last night.

I will see Dave Tuck this week to decide what goes on the invitation for my show in February.

16 December, 1970. Wednesday
I sized my canvas today. I'll begin work on it tomorrow.

I went to Marty's yesterday to help Nelson fill a large order. I read the titles from the catalogue while he pulled the books from the shelves; it made the job go faster.

17 December, 1970. Thursday

I began laying tape on the canvas last night. This painting will follow the print, using the same colours (red, yellow and blue) in the same positions. I will make adjustments for the size. I feel tentative about starting, a little afraid of the new canvas. It's such an aggressive piece of material at this point, and me, so small and insignificant. Making the painting is like an exchange of blows with me only appearing to be in the lead. The painting finally wins, must win. And yet, it is none of that. It's a piece of cloth; I put paint on it.

18 December, 1970. Friday

I worked a long day yesterday. I mixed and applied the red and the low-keyed yellow areas. I applied only one colour at a time. I'm still mixing the blue; I will apply it today. The red is quite magnificent; it looks like a magenta alone with the yellow. Already I am projecting further paintings.

22 December, 1970. Tuesday

I finished my painting on Friday [*Colour Lock, Second Series #1*]. On Saturday, we put it on a stretcher. I've had time to look at it and I'm satisfied that it works. On Sunday, I made some compositional sketches and yesterday, I began to work with the felt tip markers (designer colours). The felt tip colours lack subtlety for this work, but I got some useful things down. This work is strongly about colour. I don't know if I'm doing anything "new," but I feel it needs to be done.

It's also involved with size. I'm projecting some pretty big works, like six feet by eight feet and four feet by twelve feet. This is not really very big, but I won't be able to put paintings that size onto stretchers in here. My projections are still unsettled and will need more thought and work. For now, I'm going to go ahead with another 60" x 60" painting; I have ordered the canvas.

I spent this afternoon at my Markham studio cleaning screens. I want to try some new things there. Dave Tuck called last night; he'll come tomorrow to talk about the invitation.

30 December, 1970. Wednesday

Dave and Lynne did come about the invitation although not on the day arranged. The invitation is coming along slowly with much worry on my part. I've been to Coach House to choose paper stock, etc. The text will be typeset.

I have stretched and sized the new piece of canvas.

bpNichol and Ellie Hiebert were here just before Christmas. bp brought us the original photocopy of his hand as a gift. He is surprisingly sentimental about Christmas.

1971

1 January, 1971. Friday

The invitation for my show is working its way toward realization. Dave will order envelopes and I'll start to address them as soon as they arrive. All of this has kept me from any other real work. My canvas is still untouched.

Carol came by last night for a brief visit; she was on her way to a party. Carol's exhibition at Aggregation has been scheduled to follow mine in February ("back to back," as Dave says). She seems so uncertain. She said she may put it off for another month.

4 January, 1971. Monday

Although this is only the second painting in this new series, I am aware of a distinct change in my colour. I am working with greater intensities and as a result, with more demanding interactions. It's too early to draw any conclusions, but the possibilities are exciting.

5 January, 1971. Tuesday

I worked on the new canvas yesterday. It is five feet square; it will have nine areas, three colours, each repeated three times. Green, red and blue. I have applied the first two colours, green and red. They are close in tone. The blue, greyed, will be slightly lower in tone. I plan to apply the blue today.

The three green areas are packed together at the top, the centre and to the right. The red areas are dispersed. I expect the red/blue contrast will itself contrast with the red/green. The concentration of the red/blue is large compared to the small red/large green areas. Because the green areas are packed, the painting will be green dominant. The reds promise to show immediate changes of effect because of their position. This is still speculation; the painting is not complete.

I worked with much uncertainty yesterday, taking a long time to arrive at these colours and their positions. I still feel out on a limb. But I seem to have more control of the shapes and the spaces between the shapes in this painting. The edges of the shapes vary with their colour and position — more active, more still — and some shapes are slightly larger, or slightly smaller. The choice of colour and position was determined intuitively; once the physical work began, an intellectual ordering began. I am curious to understand my own choices, to recognize my own approach.

My work has been described as *too* intellectual. It is not really so, I believe, because so many of my decisions are made intuitively. I am becoming more aware of colour and its interaction both from study and from the experience of painting and I think that has to be acknowledged intellectually. I believe it's impossible to know too much about anything (where knowing = understanding). As Josef Albers says so simply, "One must have sensitive eyes."

I'm reading John Dewey's *Art as Experience* (1934). It reinforces some of my own thinking and opens some new ideas. Dewey takes seriously some ideas that I have felt and believed, but considered frivolous — e.g. the relationship one has with one's work (like in my entry of 17 Dec., 1970).

I have sent a painting to be viewed by the CC jury. Professional Fine Art Services picked it up this morning. I begin teaching classes tonight.

6 January, 1971. Wednesday
Yesterday's painting is finished and seems to be working. I will have until the weekend to watch it. We won't stretch another piece of canvas until then.

I saw Carol briefly yesterday. She will call today. She's in a terrible mood.

7 January, 1971. Thursday
Carol came for lunch yesterday. She was in a better mood and was going to work at her studio all day and in the evening. She is still so doubtful about her show.

Dave Tuck called. He has a friend with a truck, so wants to pick up my paintings today at 5:30. (They'll have problems parking on Bathurst.) I have them ready — got them ready last night.

8 January, 1971. Friday
The paintings weren't picked up yesterday. The guy with the truck didn't even make it downtown, never mind parking on Bathurst at rush hour. Now, the plan is to take the paintings to the gallery on the 30th. The show opens on Monday evening (February 1st) and continues to February 20th.

I read most of yesterday. Dewey's book and a book on Malevich. Class last night was good. I am preparing my mailing list.

11 January, 1971. Monday
What a mess! Carol came by Saturday night after working at her studio. She was in a terribly negative mood. She showed us the design she had made for the invitation for her show and the title for her work was Soft Squares. I thought the title was odd because it doesn't describe her work, but I made no comment about it. She started to become abusive by putting things on me, like blaming me for keeping her working (she said she should have stopped painting years ago, and would have if it weren't for me — so it's my fault!) She is so self-effacing, but brutal when

she gets this way. Nelson has never seen her like that and he was alarmed. I was upset when she left and didn't sleep. I spent the night worrying about her and her show. It was toward morning when I realized that the situation was impossible. Soft Squares describes *my* paintings better than it describes hers! The title could cause confusion and my title, Colour Lock, would add to the confusion. (Carol's paintings use overlapping and interlocking shapes.)

In the morning, I told Nelson that I thought the two shows should not run together. He agreed that it could cause confusion if they did. I knew it would be impossible to talk to Carol about this, so I called Dave Tuck and explained it to him. He agreed that Carol's title would have to be changed, but separating the shows would be more difficult to do. He will get back to me about it. Then Dave got into the question of me committing myself to the gallery — I'm there now; what more does he want? It makes no sense.

I'm feeling down today, whipped by circumstance.

12 January, 1971. Tuesday

Lynne from Aggregation called yesterday. They have separated Carol's show from mine by three weeks by putting the printmakers' group show between them. It wasn't so difficult after all; in fact, Lynne said it works to their advantage because of the framing and the fees for the print show.

She told me that the Aviva people had been in [Aviva Chapter of Hadassah] to choose works for the Aviva Art Show and Auction in April. They took a long time choosing something of mine and finally settled on one of the drawings. Graphic works will be offered by silent auction.

I talked with Victor. He said the invitation will be done this week or early next week. Again, he said he would contact Anne Brodzky about reviewing my show for *Artscanada*.

We stretched a new piece of canvas on the easel-boards last night. We rolled the last painting temporarily.

13 January, 1971. Wednesday

I've been reading the recent *Artscanada*. There's an interesting article on Carl Andre. There's also a piece on Jim Dine by Victor. It's a poor piece; Victor is grandstanding.

I sized the new canvas yesterday. I've settled my sketches; I'm ready to begin painting.

I expect my painting to be returned from Fine Art Services today. There is nothing to be learned about the CC jurying — have to wait until April.

14 January, 1971. Thursday

The new painting is complete [*Colour Lock, Second Series #3*. 60" x 60" acrylic on canvas]. The colours are a blue, a purple and a low-keyed orange. The purple dominates by its position and the concentration of the shapes. The blue and the purple are close in tone and the orange (lowered) reaches toward them. The orange is an unlikely colour to stabilize the composition, but it does that here by its position and its contrasts.

I worked the full day yesterday mixing the colours and applying the purple, then the blue shapes. I applied the three orange shapes today.

I have become more and more involved with colour in these last three paintings. The nature, the character, even the "personality" of each colour becomes more complex (or should I say simple?). The experience (my awareness) of colour increases as I go on. I'm a little afraid of over-simplification, but it is the [complexity of] simplification that is exciting.

Carol called me this morning to tell me her "news"; the gallery has rescheduled her show. She seemed alright with it; she was calm, in a better frame of mind — almost cheerful. She knows nothing of my intervention and it's best if she doesn't. God, I want her to have her show and I'll help her as much as I can, but I don't want to be beaten to a pulp doing it.

15 January, 1971. Friday

I saw the show of Olitski's sculpture at the Mirvish Gallery. They are strange panoramic pieces with constant changes going on as one moves around them. The surfaces are spray painted in Olitski's usual manner.

17 January, 1971. Sunday

I've been thinking about the new paintings, questioning the way I am repeating colours. I consider disturbing the order of the repetition. The order in the last three paintings is very flexible; I have not repeated the positions of the colour nor the colours themselves. Each colour changes in relation to another (or to itself) and to the positions the colours have in relation to each other. Still, it's possible I could use four colours in a composition of nine areas, using the colours not three times, but once, twice (twice) and four times. It's a thought, but I don't want to do it now. I want to work further with what I have been doing; I need to know more about the colours' energy through the discipline of the orderly repeat. The order is satisfying. The sameness of each area (similar to the first series of paintings) makes a strong, formal composition. The stability of that composition gives emphasis to the colour interaction.

It has occurred to me that what I'm doing in this work has had other answers, fine answers, in other works that I know. I wonder about introducing one area of a new colour, or changing the tone of one of the colours to three different tones of that colour. It's a thought. But, the changes that occur in a single colour, by its position, its juxtaposition, interest me more.

The line. The line formed by the spaces between the colour shapes (the canvas ground) is a field of activity, too. The loose edges of the near-square areas of colour form that line and its energy bursts at four vital points on the canvas. Each point is a centre which gathers around it four squares and each gathering is different. The colour activity is intensified by the lines of raw canvas and each colour area gives a singular performance in the activity of the whole.

I ask myself what the next painting will be. I have sketches for so many.

19 January, 1971. Tuesday
Nelson went to Coach House to pick up a copy of the first run [the reproduction of the print] of the invitation. We wanted to see it. Thank god we did. It is on the wrong paper. It will look terrible as an invitation. It is printed on that light-weight paper, glossy on one side, dull on the other. It's a book wrapper; to make it a folded invitation, it would be folded *inside out*, the text printed on the dull side which curls in the opposite direction — the folder wouldn't stay folded. I called Victor. He made some lame excuse about it looking better this way, "rather unorthodox." He told me I was worrying too much about an invitation for the show; it wasn't very important because, he said, "most people just throw them away when they get them." (Thanks!)

Nelson called Stan and told him we would pick up the copies printed for the invitation and take it somewhere else to be finished. Stan said he wanted to finish it himself, so we went over to see what could be done. I asked to see the plate for the text. The wrong lettering had been used, there were changes in the text and the plate was the wrong size! It was too big; it couldn't even have been printed on the paper with the reproduction. Stan was sobered by the mess (he was pissed with Victor because none of these changes needed to be made), but insisted that because Coach House had started the job, he would finish it. It will be done by 5:30 p.m. on Wednesday.

The plate has to be made again, smaller. I chose a grey cover stock for the folder. I accepted most of the changes on the plate to be sure the thing will get done on time. The reproduction is going to be cropped to the size of the original print, and I will tip it inside the folder. It should work, but it's a disappointment compared to the original design.

Aside from all this hassle, I worked on drawings yesterday. I got some good results.

24 January, 1971. Sunday

On Wednesday, Stan hadn't begun to print the invitation when Nelson went to get it at 5:30 p.m. (he forgot!). By eight o'clock it was printed and folded, and the reproduction was cropped. I used double-sided tape (faster and cleaner than glue) to tip in the reproduction. I worked on it until 11:00 p.m. Wednesday night, on Thursday and on Friday. On Friday evening, we delivered it to the gallery to be stuffed into envelopes and mailed. Nothing left to do now except hang the show and see what happens.

On Thursday afternoon, Milly Ristvedt and Henry Saxe came by. They thought the invitation looked good and I was glad to hear it (they don't know how it was supposed to look). Henry is quiet, like Nelson, but he listens. He asked to see more of my work (there was only one piece visible on the boards). I showed them the new drawings. I said that I'd seen the Olitski sculpture show and liked it and got a rise out of Henry about that. He had seen the show and said he thought it was "shit." The structure bothered him — he said the works were "junk" just thrown together and used as a vehicle for colour. Henry is a sculptor; so I listened carefully. I will have to think about this and see the show again.

I saw the Five Painters show at the AGO Rental Gallery on Saturday.

27 January, 1971. Wednesday

I have two things I want to write about here: the drawings I made last week and the Five Painters show at the rental gallery at the AGO.

The drawings relate to the three new paintings. They are graphite drawings — nine shapes, three tones, each tone repeated three times. I cut stencils to make the shapes and drew each shape with a graphite line that flows diagonally across the shape. The stencil holds the edges of the shape. I made twelve drawings (10¼" x 10"), each one a different tonal composition. So far, they hold for me. Each one is an independent piece, but it's good to see them all together. Working with graphite, I eliminate hue, or colour, and focus on other energy factors of the composition. I showed these drawings to Lynne and Dave and to Milly and Henry and got a good response.

The Five Painters show is a good collection [paintings by Milly Ristvedt, David Bolduc, Dan Solomon, Paul Fournier and K.M. Graham]. Of Milly's work, I thought *Sweet Earth* was the best. It had a large area of dark flowing up from the bottom and colour tongues (wide brush strokes) dropping down from the top.

The raw canvas left between this activity was fine. Because this was the best piece, the rest were a bit of a disappointment. They didn't pursue the same things. But Milly told me that she was working on three different series at the same time. Upstairs, there were two more paintings where the colours were falling into the canvas from the top onto the raw canvas. The spareness of these made them more demanding, although less satisfying. Milly has worked right on the edges of the canvas. I get the feeling that the greater activity occurs outside, or just above the painting, where I can't see it — I am seeing only the tail end of it as it falls into the painting. I know this isn't true, but it is a very strong feeling and it makes me dissatisfied with what I can see on the canvas. There was a small painting with three colours moving horizontally across the canvas and two arcs of raw canvas dropped into it from the top and the top of each colour. This one was very nice, but not as clear as *Sweet Earth*.

Bolduc's paintings were like the pastels he's been doing that I've never understood. The looseness, the floating colour, all had a good feel — there were three big paintings, all satisfying. A yellow piece had three floating swatches of yellow-green that repeated themselves by after-image. It was very effective.

Dan Solomon's work had less appeal for me, yet each one was a solid piece of thinking. His control of the surface was fantastic. The game of surface to infinity was carefully played out. The titles related to music. I think he's a thoughtful painter.

Paul Fournier's and K.M. Graham's paintings didn't seem to do much. Fournier's pieces are amorphous, astral looking things. (The newspaper review called them "underwater pieces.") He's a careful painter, more careful than thoughtful. I felt impatient with K.M. Graham's work for the most part, but for one small piece, *Orange Forward*, her best there. Strangely, it was the only piece of hers that had neither sold nor been rented when I saw the show.

I didn't teach at Northern last night. Snow storm, icy streets — colossal traffic tie-ups.

Mike Ondaatje called to tell us he'll be showing his film on Friday night. We are going. My paintings will be picked up on Saturday, we'll hang the show on Sunday, the opening is Monday night.

28 January, 1971. Thursday

Dave called yesterday to tell me that the man at OISE had called to say he wanted to buy the painting reproduced on the invitation. Problem: that's not a painting; it's a print. Dave knew that, but he wanted me to consent to making a painting like it as a commission for this person. I suggested he talk to the person (Dave didn't take the original call) and urge him to see the show. He will get back to me about it. I know Dave doesn't want to miss a sale, but I think he's jumping the gun on this.

Last night, I read aloud to Nelson the Milton Acorn manuscript that Marty let us have. One of the poems, "I Shout Love," is an earlier piece revised. The longer poem (44 pages), "On Shaving off His Beard," is new. They are a great read. Marty may publish the two poems.

29 January, 1971. Friday

I went over to the Mirvish Gallery to see the Olitski show again yesterday. I considered the works from Henry's point of view. I'm still on the outside of this work, but I like the small pieces and the big round piece. I like the effect of the arcs that close, the pressure of the corrugation, the surprises in the structure. Olitski *is* using the sculptures as a vehicle for his colour, but I'm not disturbed by that. Yes, I prefer his big paintings, but I stay open to the sculpture for the time being.

There is a show of prints and multiples at the Pollock Gallery, a companion to the tapestries at the AGO. Victor Vasarely is on the main floor; Josef Albers is upstairs. Albers is my favourite — *Homage to the Square*, some earlier prints and some more recent ones that are architectural. Jack showed me a recent Robyn Denny print (British) to point out some similarities to Albers. The Vasarelys had some surprises; his work (the prints, especially) have become so popular that it's easy to feel jaded about them. I enjoyed this group, but I find his work a bit too academic.

My own work has slowed to a halt. I don't plan to go on until after my show has opened.

We will go to Kim Ondaatje's show at the Merton Gallery tonight. Mike will read and show his film.

30 January, 1971. Saturday

I went into the Pollock Gallery again yesterday just to see the Albers prints. I stayed and talked with Pollock for over an hour. He talked mostly about the Five Painters show; he was very critical of some of the work.

I phoned Dennis Young to remind him of my show. He was cheery and enthused — said he was looking forward to seeing the work hung. This was more than I expected, so I was left not knowing what to say.

Last night, we were late getting to the Merton Gallery, arriving just after Mike Ondaatje had begun to read. There was quite a crowd; most people were sitting on the floor. After the reading, I met Kim Ondaatje and spoke with Mike. Before the film began, I could only exchange nods or waves with Stan Bevington, Nelson Adams, bp, Victor and Sarah who were among the carpet of people.

The film, *Sons of Captain Poetry*, is about bp. It has some great images of bp pressing through a fence and through a window frame; there is an interview, some background of Plunkett, some cartoons. The sound was poor, so I missed a good deal of it. I'd like to see it again.

I talked with Stan. He has made up a bill for me for $100 for the invitation. I know that isn't enough for the job and said so, but that's all he wants. I won't argue.

I talked briefly with Victor and Sarah, then with Steve McCaffery. I got a big kiss from bp. Of course, I told everyone about my show opening on Monday. Of course, everyone promises to come.

This morning's class was slide painting in the gallery studio with the 14-18-year-olds. There were eight students, a good class. We worked until 12:30 p.m.

My paintings were picked up and taken to the gallery at six o'clock tonight. At 8 p.m., Nelson and I went over and put the 60" x 120" painting [*Colour Lock #15*] on a stretcher. We placed all nine works in their positions; Lynne and Dave will hang them tomorrow. We may go over tomorrow, or I may go on Monday. I want to look at them alone for a while. I want to see them, see their colour, see them work.

1 February, 1971. Monday

The show opens tonight. It is bitterly cold; I hope some people will come out. We plan to go to the gallery early so I can see the work alone.

I slept late yesterday; I was exhausted. I called the gallery in the late afternoon and learned that there was a problem with the stretch job we did on the large painting, so we went to take a look at it. We ate first, so when we got to the gallery, the bubble had corrected itself with hanging and we didn't have to touch it. Then for diversion, we went to a movie.

4 February, 1971. Thursday

The show opened Monday night with a pretty good turn-out in spite of the cold. I didn't get there early; in fact, we were a little late.

Jack Pollock and Bernie Taylor were at the gallery when we arrived at eight o'clock. Pollock was full of compliments about the work. Bernie didn't say a word, but I really enjoyed watching him look at the paintings — he seemed to be drinking them in with his eyes and he did that the whole evening. Before they left, Pollock whispered to me that he was buying #7 [*Colour Lock #7*. 60" x 60" acrylic on canvas], but it was a surprise gift for Bernie, so I wasn't to tell anyone. (Later, I asked Lynne and Dave if Pollock had actually bought the painting and they said that he did.) One of the drawings also sold.

bpNichol came and Jim Spence and his wife Kathie. Mr. Spence had told me he wanted to meet bp, so I had Nelson introduce them. Doug Fetherling and Gernot Dick came and so did Barbara Hall and Richard Sewell. Carol and her nephew Peter Martyn came together, and Joy Walker, an artist friend of Carol's, came, so I met her for the first time. There were people there I didn't know and didn't meet; some were Lynne and Dave's friends, others were regular "opening" people who come and go and nobody knows. The brash young kids I talked with about the Motherwell painting at Mirvish walked through as if they owned the gallery. When they saw me, the mouthy boy asked what I was doing there, so I told him. Marty and his friends came and made me regret that I'd invited them.

When I invited Marty (he came to my last show), I asked Nelson if I should invite one of his friends, too. Nelson suggested that I invite David Mason and Richard Landon (I know them both slightly), so I did. Marty told Nelson that he, Mason, Landon and their wives planned to go out for dinner together, then on to the opening at the gallery. Fine. When this party of five arrived at the gallery, I expected they would look at the work or even at me at some time over the course of the evening. Nelson spoke with them, then they got into a huddle to talk with each other, *leaning against a wall*. They were bumping one of the paintings, so I asked Nelson to tell them to stand away from the walls. Mason walked about, looked me up and down several times, never making eye contact, so I couldn't even say hello. None of them spoke to me. When they were about to leave, Richard Landon strode over to me and said, "You can't do this." (Jim Spence and another of my students overheard him and they both moved in to listen.) I said, "I *have* done this; what's the problem." He told me I couldn't paint with just colour, that colour had to be something coloured. I told him that wasn't true; it hadn't been true for a long time and I quoted Fernand Léger: "We, Robert Delaunay and I, have liberated colour. Before us, blue was the sky and green was the grass. Now, colour is colour." He just stared at me, then turned and left.

On Wednesday, I went to the Lamanna Gallery to see Ron Martin's show. I talked with Lamanna briefly. I told him my show was on at Aggregation and that I'd even sold a painting. He shrugged and muttered, "Some friend..." and I could say nothing because of Pollock's secret. Lamanna told me he didn't like Milly's work in the Five Painters show. I don't like hearing this — it's a dealer's job to talk his artists up, not talk them down.

I went to Aggregation, arriving while Kay Kritzwiser was there seeing the show, so I had a chance to talk with her about the work. There will be a review of the show in *The Globe and Mail* this weekend.

8 February, 1971. Monday
Steve McCaffery came by on Friday. The conversation wound up being silly and insulting. Nelson and I have been in disagreement about it since.

Kay Kritzwiser's review of my show was in Saturday's paper. It was a good review. Lynne and Dave said that there were a lot of people in to see the show because of it on Saturday.

10 February, 1971. Wednesday
I've finally finished writing a piece about the paintings (the "artist's statement"). I took it to the gallery yesterday. I met Tony Tudin (he does ceramics and weaving) who was there to see the show.

I had a long talk with Lynne and Dave. I talked out the business about prices again with Dave. I want him to make the prices on the "grey work" the same as the Colour Lock paintings, but Dave thinks that the "old" work should be cheaper than the new work because it's "old." The 60" x 60" paintings from the "grey work" were $250, then Dave raised them to $350; the 60" x 60" Colour Lock paintings are $450. I want them all to be $450. Dave will call me when he's made up his mind. (I could take the "grey work" out of the gallery if I don't want it sold at a lower price, but I'd rather not do it that way.)

I got a phone call from the Aviva Chapter yesterday telling me that I had won the graphics award ($100). What a surprise.

11 February, 1971. Thursday
I talked with Carol yesterday. I told her about the Aviva prize. A few minutes later, she called me back to tell me that she had been rejected by the jury for the RCA show. She was struggling with tears. I felt terrible. I went over to her studio a little later with a couple of coffees. When I got back, I sized the new piece of canvas.

Dave called to tell me he sold another drawing. That will take me over the top, I think. My sales will pay off all my expenses with the gallery.

12 February, 1971. Friday
Yesterday, I began working on new graphite drawings on full sheets of cartridge paper, 22½" x 29". I am stacking and packing shapes. I made a new set of stencils, 2½" square. I made four drawings; I think three of them are successful, so far. In one piece, 6 x 8 shapes are stacked, drawn with a 2B pencil. The shapes are sometimes separated and some overlap slightly. The surface of the shapes varies with the pressure of the hand. I am attempting to draw the surface with as little variation as possible while still drawing with ease. I'm watching a "natural" variation occur in the work from my breathing, or from my hand, or my body. I have decided to

repeat this drawing four or six times, allowing the space and overlap pattern to change slightly. (The alchemist's bag.) I am reminded of Yves Klein, his blue paintings and his red paintings.

The class at Northern went well last night, but I was talkative. Mr. Everett, my retired minister, paid me a great compliment. Very seriously, he said, "Do you realize how much you have taught us in so short a time!" Things must be opening up for him. He gave me so much resistance at the start, certain that a little thing like me couldn't teach him anything.

14 February, 1971. Sunday
I worked further on drawings on Friday. I will go as far as I can with these, then select from what I've done.

At 3 p.m. I met Nelson and we went to hear Andrei Vosnesensky read his poems at U of T. The hall was full, standing room only when we got there, so we heard only two poems, then came out. We looked at Downing's building [Medical Science Building] and went inside to see his wall sculpture. We had a Chinese dinner, then took a cab to John Robert Colombo's place for the evening with Vosnesensky.

We were early. There was a discussion about teaching and social politics going on between Ruth Colombo, Robin Skelton and an older couple whose name I didn't get. The place soon filled with poets and "friends of poets." We met George Swede and his friend (and I didn't get her name throughout the whole evening).

People roamed or camped in every room as if waiting for something to happen. (I did, along with George's friend.) Francis Sparshott and his wife were camped in the kitchen. They are a funny pair, the cryptic comments between them were the best entertainment of the night. Phyllis Gotlieb was talkative and maybe a little drunk; she sparred with Miriam Waddington who sat on the kitchen garbage pail wearing her long velvet dress. They were funny, a little silly. Doug Fetherling was there, and Walter Gordon for some unknown reason. It was a great people-watching party. There were two men in suits with Vosnesensky who stayed on each side of him the entire time. I heard them referred to as "security men," "party police," "KGB" and "flunkies" at various times.

There was a reading to end the evening, but it hadn't been planned in advance. There was huge tension in the room when Colombo asked for poets to read. To organize the reading a "conference" took place among the poets (the older, or *real*, poets and the young poets), while those of us who were "friends of" were asked to wait in the back porch. There must have been twenty of us standing or sitting in the porch, waiting. The one thing we had in common, finally, was that everyone had run out of cigarettes. Suddenly, Robin Skelton dashed through the porch and out the back door. A minute later, he came back in, *opening a fresh pack of cigarettes.* I said, "Oh, you have cigarettes." Skelton, a gentleman, said, "Yes, would you like one," offering his pack. George's friend, beside me, said, "May I have one, too?" And everyone in the porch gathered with "may I..." and "thank you," until Skelton's package was empty. He did manage to take one for himself.

The reading took place downstairs in the rec-room. Irving Layton, Robin Skelton, Miriam Waddington, Phyllis Gotlieb, Francis Sparshott, Joe Rosenblatt and Colombo read, then Vosnesensky read. It was particularly interesting because of the contrasts of styles — the rich, spirited Russian style of Layton and Vosnesensky and the quiet, almost demure, British style of Sparshott. Clearly, it was important to be one of those "chosen" to read one's poems in this situation.

We got a ride home with George Swede and his friend.

18 February, 1971. Thursday
I haven't begun my painting yet. I hope to begin next week after the show is down and things are back to normal. I have worked further on drawings with some good results.

The gallery is having someone take installation photos for me. The reviewer from *Artscanada* will want to use them. Dennis Young hasn't been in to see the show; he won't make it before it closes, but he told Dave that the Aviva graphics prize was "no contest" (he was one of the judges) — my drawing was way ahead. Nice to hear.

Jim Gordaneer and Thelma Van Alstyne have been in to see the show. The man from OISE hasn't been in yet. I expect nothing will happen with that.

24 February, 1971. Wednesday
Days of tired, much reading, much sleeping, some laundry and a pretense at house-wifery are all that I've accomplished.

On Saturday, about 9 p.m., Nelson and I took down the show and covered the paintings with plastic. Lynne and Dave want to store the whole show at the gallery.

On Sunday, Jim and Tessa Lowell visited us here.

I had a class last night. Nelson went to the bookstore after work at the library, so I didn't see him until after 10 p.m. I don't like that.

26 February, 1971. Friday
On Wednesday, I began to work on my painting. I took a long time mixing pigments to arrive at the colours: a red, slightly lowered below its intensity, an orange, lowered even more, but still intense, and a blue-purple, raised slightly to lie with the red and orange. I applied two colours on Wednesday, the third yesterday.

It's a warm painting, strong although the contrasts don't have a lot of opposi-tion. I was doubtful about the aggressive combination of the red and orange against the blue-purple. So far, I'm satisfied with the results. It was exciting all the way through, watching each colour go into position and changing as each other colour's shapes were added [*Colour Lock, Second Series #4*. 60" x 60"].

I talked with Jack Pollock. He wants to include a piece of my work in a Canadian exhibition at the Robertson Center for the Arts and Sciences in Binghamton, New York in April. There will be a show of graphics in a private gallery in the same place (same time) and he wants some of my drawings for it, too.

Aggregation called to tell me that a 48" x 96" Colour Lock painting has gone out on approval.

Later: I went out to the galleries today and spent the whole day looking. At the Dunkelman Gallery, I saw acrylic paintings by William Pettet (American). I went on to the new (a Spanish name) gallery which was showing plexiglass sculp-tures by a Mexican artist; I spoke with the artist about the work. I went into the Mitchell Gallery and saw a selection of works there — six Gary Slipper paintings (paint on plexiglass), a Tom La Pierre, a Tib Beaumont, among others. Talked with Mr. and Mrs. Mitchell for some time. At the Albert White Gallery, there was a group show of paintings and prints. At the Morris Gallery I saw Ivan Eyre's large acrylic paintings — still figures that reminded me of Egyptian wall paintings. Talked with Mr. Morris. At Gallery Moos, there was a print show hung. They were about to hang a show by Brian Taylor, large acrylic optical works. I talked with Taylor and the young man who works there. At Carmen Lamanna's I saw three conceptual pieces by Robin Collyer. Isaacs had a new show of photographs by Gar Smith. A group show at the back of the gallery interested me more. I met Greg Curnoe in there — brief exchange. Then, I went to Aggregation where the show of prints by five printmakers is hung. I thought Sylvia Singer's work was interesting and a young man named Kelly had done some nice monoprints.

I got a taxi back to Bathurst and walked over to the Mirvish Gallery where I saw the Olitski show again. Had a talk, a good talk, with Alkis. I went over to Pollock's where the Wayne Eastcott show was still not hung — it rested on the floor. Then, briefly, I went into Adams Gallery to see Wendy Toogood's show.

I'm very tired and saturated with looking.

1 March, 1971. Monday
David Rosenberg was here on Friday night. He has been back for a week from France. He told us a lonely, frustrating story about his time spent in London and Paris. Arlette has stayed on in Paris to visit her brother for two weeks. David did a

lot of writing, so he's happy about that. He came here again last night; he brought his poems and read them to us. He wants to print about 100 copies of this manuscript, *Paris & London*. He will type the stencils for it here and Nelson will print it for him on the Gestetner.

The Saturday morning class began what is to be a three week painting project. The students (14-18) said that they just wanted to fool with the paint. I sounded off to Gord White about that.

After class, Jim Williamson told me that he'd seen my show. With a little urging, he told me his feelings about it. He seems to have found it acceptable, but was doubtful that I would be able to hold my own (continue) in this "most difficult area of painting." He went on to tell me what he thinks I could or should do next — the options, in his mind, are limited. I listened; what he said was of no value to me and it was a great disappointment to hear it.

Carol is back from Ibiza. We had a talk at her studio Friday night.

I'm reading *Face to Face*, a book on Emily Dickinson by her niece, Martha D. Bianchi.

3 March, 1971. Wednesday
We stretched a new piece of canvas on the easel-boards on Monday night. I sized the surface yesterday.

I called Aggregation yesterday to find out if they had heard anything from *Artscanada*. Dave said he had phoned several times, but he was not put through to Anne Brodzky. He asked me to try. I called and spoke with Anne Brodzky. She told me that she had asked Gary Michael Dault to see my show to review it for the magazine and he told her he could not review it, because (as she said) he felt there was nothing he could add to it. (He probably didn't like it.) She made an appointment to meet me at the gallery to look at some of the work. I'm not sure why. This is the second review for *Artscanada* that hasn't panned out. Last year, she got Doug Fetherling to write a review of my first show at Aggregation, but what he turned in to her, she said, "just couldn't be published."

I talked with Alan Toff on Monday. That three-man show for Scarborough College has turned into a five-man show. The two new people are fourth-year OCA students. Pollock told me that I should ask *who* will be in this show, then he told me not to show with students. I don't know what I should do.

David Rosenberg was here all day yesterday typing his poems on stencils. He worked in Nelson's room and I worked in the front room, so mainly, we stayed out of each other's way. David told me he had been at Coach House talking with "the boys" when my name came up. Greg Curnoe was there and someone asked him if he knew me. Greg said that he did. So David said to me, "Greg Curnoe says that he knows you. I thought you should know that." I took this as a matter of fact and said, "Yes, Greg knows me. I met him at the Doon School and we were at OCA at the same time, although we weren't in the same year." David looked at me a moment; I could see there was something I hadn't understood. He said, "No. Greg Curnoe *admits* to knowing you. (Pause.) I thought you should know *that*." I got it.

5 March, 1971. Friday
I've been working on graphite drawings for the past two days. Earlier, I made eight drawings using the 2½" square stencil — 6 x 8 unit squares [*Graphite Drawings, Series 2, Set 1*]. Now, I'm using a smaller stencil, 2" square — 8 x 10 unit squares [*Graphite Drawings, Series 2, Set 2*]. I have made five drawings and I want to go further.

Dave Tuck is really disappointed about the *Artscanada* review. I think he's more brought down about it than I am.

8 March, 1971. Tuesday
On Friday night we went to a reading on Dupont Street. There were performances of sound poetry by bpNichol, Steve McCaffery and Rafael Barreto-Rivera, separately and as a group. Two opera singers read their own poems, each using their singing voices as part of their poems. Joe Rosenblatt read his "bee" poems. I thought the best piece of the night was Rafael's solo performance of "In the Middle of a Blue Balloon." The poem was entirely that line repeated, as song, in dance, with the word *blue, blew, bloo-o* blown out to the listeners. It was wonderful to watch and to hear. The last piece of the evening involved everyone, including the audience. It played with the letter (sound) "O" and bp, the central performer, tossed handfuls of Cheerios to the audience. They went wild.

We went outside at the intermission and a young man (Will Kennedy) spoke to me. He had seen my show at Aggregation. He is an artist; he works in the studio space on the main floor of the building and he took me inside to see his work. There are nineteen artists sharing the space — it's huge. There were only a few people working, but my presence stopped them all. They are a cheerful, friendly group, but I know I couldn't work in that kind of environment. Kennedy showed me two pieces of his work. He was tense with expectation, so I questioned him about them and commented. He seems to think I'm a "perfectionist." He asked me if I was part of Therafields. When I said no, he said, "I can't imagine anyone being able to paint like that unless they have gone through Therafields." Strange idea.

10 March, 1971. Wednesday

I saw the Jack Bush show at the Mirvish Gallery yesterday. It's a beautiful show. I prefer this new work to the earlier works that involve a loop. Large paintings that use large bars of colour. In all but one painting, the bars are contained. The colour bars are like strokes, ragged at their short ends and crisp along their lengths. In the one piece, the bars reach the edges of the canvas as if they continued beyond it; the bars are so strongly directional that they seem to move in and out of a negative field and the colour areas become a secondary experience to this strong chevron of space. All of the other paintings invite a positive colour play that stays on the surface of the canvas. The colours, the changes in the size of the "strokes" are immediate and control the plane. These are high contrast works with oppositions tied down by the immediacy of the stroke (colour bar). I think they are "high risk" works. The field (or ground) in each painting is painted with a high tint — almost neutral. This is a brilliant decision. The ground (by not being raw canvas) is different in each painting and gives each work a new open environment.

Almost all of the colour bars are diagonal, or at an oblique angle to the picture's edge. The colour bars are parallel to each other although they move in four different directions (angles that relate to the four sides of the painting). The colour bars repeat their width (there are two or three different widths of bars in each painting), but always vary in length.

The colour is fresh and bright with contrasts and the contrasts of size and direction make these works complex.

One painting has three colour bars (dominant) parallel to the picture's edge — the only piece that works this way — and it has two short bars on an angle. This one works like a teeter-totter, the activity controlled by the angular bars. This piece, like the "chevron" piece, seems exploratory and looks tentative, but it works better than the "chevron" piece. It was impossible to "see" the whole show. I will go back.

bpNichol came by yesterday. I told him what Will Kennedy had said to me about painting and Therafields; he said, "That wipes out just about every painter in the world."

16 March, 1971. Tuesday

Carol's show opened last night at Aggregation. It was a successful opening; there were a lot of people there throughout the entire evening. Carol is good at hosting her show. Milly phoned her from Montreal to congratulate her. Two of her small pieces, colour felt pen on paper, sold. Still, she seemed let down when it was over.

The work looked good hung. The large paintings, however, still look too heavy even up off the floor. The space problem in them is most disturbing — only one painting seemed to have it resolved.

No, I don't really like the work. It's heavy and not thoughtful enough. But yes, I think she should show it and let people judge for themselves.

After the show, Florence and Carol drove us home. In the car, I told Carol I thought it was a good opening; she must be pleased by the turn-out. She gave me a hard look and said, "Well, Jack Pollock wasn't there." Jeez! I wish she wouldn't do that.

I've been working on drawings these past few days and I completed the new canvas. Three colours repeated three times in nine areas — yellow-green, purple and blue. I thought I might lose this one, but it works [*Colour Lock, Second Series #5*. 60" x 60"].

The gallery called to tell me that the 48" x 96" Colour Lock painting that went out on approval has sold. The couple have decided to keep it.

17 March, 1971. Wednesday

I made two drawings yesterday. I looked at all the drawings I've made over the past four weeks. There are twenty-five pieces and most of them stand up.

Carol came over at noon yesterday. She seemed to want to cry, but couldn't find anything to cry about. We talked and it passed. She is leaving for Mexico on Thursday.

I want to go out to galleries today. Greg Curnoe's show is at Isaacs and there's a group show at Lamanna.

18 March, 1971. Thursday

I worked on drawings yesterday. I made one in the morning before I went out and a new piece after I returned. The new piece uses a 1" square, 16 x 22 unit squares. I drew with an HB pencil very lightly. I want to try this with a 4H pencil [*Graphite Drawings, Series 2, Set 3*].

I saw Curnoe's show. Greg was there and I spoke with him briefly. It's a good show; I especially liked *Victoria Hospital*. The works are autobiographical, are accompanied by diary pieces and there are sound tapes involved. Each of the large works had a tape that was recorded in the studio — random sounds of working, a radio playing, some speech. The tapes add a dimension of time (the time it takes to make the work) to the works and are a kind of sound poetry.

Lamanna had a group show up. One of Milly's paintings from her show last year was in it, with Bolduc, Ron Martin and Molinari, a Rabinowitch, a Beveridge, Robin MacKenzie and another sculptor, Van someone.

I was a little depressed last night. We both seemed to be feeling low, so we went to a movie for diversion. We saw *The Graduate* and *Charly*. Enjoyed both of them.

19 March, 1971. Friday

I had lunch with Carol and her niece, Paula Jocelyn, at Gaston's yesterday. Carol was leaving for Mexico at 3 p.m.

Afterward, I ran into Tony Tudin and went with him to his studio to see some of his work. He has a nice studio; his wall hangings are very good. We had tea and talked about working, showing and teaching and the insanity of being with a gallery.

I spent the morning on a drawing (1" unit squares). I began a second drawing in the afternoon and finished it this morning. I've been thinking of having a show of drawings, but the framing would cost me a fortune. Each time Aggregation frames for me, the cost of the frame goes up.

I called *Artscanada* today, as arranged, and spoke with Anne Brodzky. We will meet on the 30th at Aggregation. Then, I called the gallery to give them the date and to ask them to hang some of my work in the small space at the back of the gallery on that day. The Bruce St. Claire show will be hanging in the front.

The weather has turned bad — snow and wind.

25 March, 1971. Thursday

Nelson has been writing — some really fine new poems and some earlier ones revised. I have been writing, too. I have a few things worth keeping, I think. Nelson thinks they are good. Then, I tried working on an old idea that turned out to be a waste of time. I was surprised by Nelson's reaction to it. He seemed disturbed that I could write something so bad. Then, he suggested that I had done it deliberately to reassure him about his own writing. Not true; I just write some pretty shitty things sometimes.

26 March, 1971. Friday

I made another drawing yesterday. I am going to try to combine the 1" square and the 2" square in a drawing. I will try it today.

I typed up some of my poems. Only one of them stands up. I flounder.

Nelson got another sheet of plywood for me. We are going to extend my easel-boards by two feet so I can make larger paintings.

27 March, 1971. Saturday

I worked on drawings all day yesterday. I am surprised that I could sustain the work; these pieces are demanding [*Graphite Drawings, Series 2, Set 4*]. I made five drawings that I think work and a sixth that I will reconsider.

This morning's class was pastels with the 14-18-year-olds. It was a small group because of the holiday. There was a lot of discussion among the instructors in the halls during and after class; Rick McCarthy was making much wind.

Aggregation called. A couple from Buffalo have bought one of my drawings.

Carol's show is doing well. There have been two reviews (I didn't see them) and another one of her coloured pen drawings has sold. She should be pleased when she gets back.

I should call Pollock to see if that Binghamton show is still going to happen.

29 March, 1971. Monday
Jack Pollock was here today. He was to be here at 1:30 p.m., but it was after three o'clock before he arrived. He stayed an hour. As a result, I didn't print as I had planned.

The show for Binghamton, NY, is still on — the preview will be April 17th; the show opens to the public April 18th and it will run for three months!

Pollock wants my *Colour Lock #5* (60" x 60") — it's at Aggregation —and *Colour Lock #8* (48" x 96") — it's here — for the show. As well, he wants three of the new drawings for the private gallery show of small works. I will take the drawings over to Pollock's tomorrow; he will have one of them framed. I will have two paintings brought here from Aggregation (the one for Binghamton and the one Pollock bought from my show); we can walk them over to his gallery on Sunday (April 4); all the paintings for the show will be picked up on Monday by Fine Art Services and transported to Binghamton.

It's a bigger show than I thought. Fifteen artists, two works from each. Pollock said he was getting work from Jack Bush, John Meredith, David Bolduc, Paul Fournier, Peter Kolisnyk, Robert Downing, K.M. Graham, Thelma Van Alstyne, Cathy Senitt-Harbison, Dan Solomon and I don't know who else. And me.

Pollock saw my newest painting, still on the boards, and really liked it. He suggested taking it for Binghamton, but I said no. He was quite excited about the new drawings.

Nelson spent yesterday afternoon at Marty's. He saw bp and Ellie; he said that bp didn't look well. William French wrote about the Governor General's Awards in the weekend *Globe and Mail*. He vetoed Ondaatje and bp for the poetry award, suggested Pierre Berton. *Pierre Berton!* I hope bp knows not to be brought down by that.

30 March, 1971. Tuesday
I met Mrs. Brodzky at Aggregation at 11:30 a.m. After self-conscious introductions, I found her an easy, open person. She is blond, very tall, slim-legged, but she is

thick-waisted. She was elegantly dressed in black. She seemed interested in what I said and impressed by the work I could show her. She was especially interested in the drawings. She took a photograph of one of them to show to someone. She wants to see my new work and she said she may bring this person with her to the studio to see the new paintings. It was a very pleasant interview — I enjoyed her; enjoyed myself. She was very definite about seeing me again soon. She said she will call me first of next week.

I came home, picked up my three drawings and took them to Pollock's. I looked at the shows there. Donna Rae Hirt (not very good), an uneven solo show of prints by another woman and Ruth Weisber's photo realism which left me cold. I went over to the Mirvish to see the Bush show again. I became aware of some new subtleties in the works. I met Alan Toff in there. He's off to Greece this weekend until mid-June. He wants me to call him in June. The Scarborough College show is postponed again, but it is still on.

31 March, 1971. Wednesday

The past two days have been so exciting that I'm quite tired out by them. I still have done nothing on the print that I plan. I cut the stencils for it on Sunday.

The person to whom Anne Brodzky wants to show my drawing is John Noel Chandler. He is presently at the Boston Institute of Contemporary Art. Mrs. Brodzky said that he may be coming to Canada permanently. He has a long article in the October issue of *Artscanada*. I reread it now.

1 April, 1971. Thursday

Yesterday, Victor Coleman called Nelson and asked him to go to Coach House to read the proof for the cover of *The Pre-Linguistic Heights*. The cover will be printed today. The book is a disappointment. We don't quite know what to do about the print. Victor decided on his own to put a black and white reproduction of my print right on the title page. That makes it impossible to tip the original print on the facing page as a frontispiece for the special edition. Nelson discussed this with Victor yesterday and Victor agreed to tipping the print on a separate folder that will be laid into the book.

Lynne called from Aggregation yesterday about the delivery of the paintings. They'll be here tomorrow between 2-4 p.m. Pollock still hasn't called them about *anything*, not about the show at Binghamton and nothing about the painting he is buying. They are worried he will change his mind about buying it. Dave asked me to talk to him about it; I said I didn't think that was appropriate. When I asked Dave if he had invoiced it, he told me that the gallery doesn't invoice; their accountant advises them not to; they only write up an invoice when the buyer comes in to pay. Strange.

Later: change of plan. Fine Art Services has just picked up the painting here and is on the way to Aggregation to get the others. Pollock called here saying, "The shit hit the fan." Everything has to be done immediately. I gave him the titles, sizes and prices of the paintings on the phone. Priced the drawings at $150 framed. Everything is away now. Pollock said he will call Aggregation to invite Lynne and Dave to the opening at Binghamton.

3 April, 1971. Saturday
I finally got over to my Markham studio to print yesterday. The print combines a red, a green and an orange; each colour is repeated three times. I lowered the red to bring it closer in tone to the green and I raised the orange slightly. I pulled ten prints. I like it. I'm pleased that I kept control of it. Maybe I'm finally learning this medium. No mean trick.

4 April, 1971. Sunday
I worked with the 8-10-year-olds yesterday morning. I have forgotten what a strain it is to work with that lively bunch.

Nelson met me at the AGO after class and we went into OCA to see the student exhibition. Then we went to Aggregation to pick up the framed drawings; Dave had three of them done. We brought them home by cab.

6 April, 1971. Tuesday
I didn't go to the Markham studio yesterday, but stayed here in case Anne Brodzky should call. I worked on drawings. I made six drawings using the 1" square stencil, each on a 12" x 9" page — 10 x 8 unit squares. I changed pencil for each drawing, using HB, 2B, 3B, 4B, 5B and 6B pencils. I drew with an even hand pressure throughout; it is the pencil weight that changes the surface of each drawing. I'm pleased with the results.

We went to Simpson's Avon Galleries last night to see the Aviva Art Show. I thought it was a poor show; the good pieces even looked poor in the surroundings. Dennis Cliff's piece seemed to be the best there. I've heard the complaint that artists don't give their best pieces to this show; maybe it's true. I looked at all the graphics in the room where my (prize winning) piece was hung. There were some good people showing — David Blackwood, Jo Manning. My drawing seemed pretty far out by comparison to the rest, but I was still happy with it (and the prize) even in this company. I was feeling pretty good. But on the same wall as mine, hung just below it, was a drawing by Christiane Pflug — a "black flag" piece, with the cab of a pick-up truck in the foreground. It is entirely different from mine; there is little to compare, but the tension in this work was so strong, so perfect, that I had no doubt that it was the piece that should have been given the prize. The jury made a mistake. I was deflated.

We went for coffee, then to a bookstore. I bought *The Sacred Mushroom and the Cross* by John Allegro. I am reading it today.

8 April, 1971. Thursday

Yesterday, I cut stencils for a print in the morning and went over to Markham and printed in the afternoon — blue, blue-green and a low-keyed yellow-orange. I don't think I made it with this one. The blue and blue-green are too close in hue and in tone. The yellow-orange works beautifully in spite of it, possibly because of it. I'm disappointed, but it printed well; at least, I'm gaining control of the medium.

On Tuesday night, I did the last class with that group; tonight's class will be the last one at Northern.

10 April, 1971. Saturday

Yesterday, I prepared the stencils for another print. I thought I would print, but instead, I stayed here and read *The Little Disturbances of Man* by Grace Paley — also, finished the Allegro. Nelson has been writing. We haven't extended the easel-boards yet; we'll leave it for another week.

11April, 1971. Sunday

It's Easter Sunday.

Yesterday, I went over to Markham and printed. I pulled an edition of 15 of this new one — blue, red-purple and a low yellow-orange. The red-purple shapes are gathered; the blue and yellow shapes are dispersed. I think it is quite successful; the colour is more controlled than in the last, although I'm finding that last one very satisfying to look at.

Nelson has been working on poems. I haven't seen anything yet. This is new work and he's not ready to show it to me. I wait.

12 April, 1971. Monday

Yesterday, I cut the stencils for a new print. Because I have sketches projecting more prints, I cut the stencils for two more. I went over to Markham and pulled one print — a blue lowered with red (gathered), a blue-green and a yellow-orange (dispersed). The yellow is very high, but it rests quietly with the blue and blue-green. I'm pleased with this one. Next, I'll work with reds and yellows, both very high. I want to take colour risks with the prints to see what happens.

The prints (on Nutex paper) are 10¼" x 10". The printed area is about 6½" square. The size allows me to try dramatic colour relationships. I can explore in a sense that I can't (yet) on a large canvas. I am finding out a lot about colour and I'm enjoying the process. Printing is exciting now in the way painting is exciting. Silkscreen is the most direct of the print media, and that makes it the best medium for colour. Its directness is important to me now.

Nelson and I have been talking again about doing a book of prints and poems. I am more willing to do it now and with *The Pre-Linguistic Heights* out of the way, Nelson can begin working seriously toward it. We would do a limited edition — maybe 50 copies [*Points of Attention*].

Nelson hasn't shown me his poems yet. Yesterday afternoon he was quite discouraged by the very work he was so excited about in the morning. He said he was writing "doggerel"; I think he is trying too hard. He needs some space. We should hear from the Canada Council soon.

I finished reading McFadden's *Great Canadian Sonnet*, Vol. 2. I want to reread Vol. 1 and 2 together. Joe Nickell called Nelson last night. He is coming over on Thursday night. I want to get down to Open Studio this week and I want to see the Stella shows at AGO and at Mirvish. I have a nice feeling of freedom now that the classes at Northern are over. Saturday morning classes finish at the end of this month.

Later: The letters from Canada Council came at noon. I opened mine — I got the grant. I opened Nelson's — he got his grant, too. I tried to phone Nelson at the library, but I couldn't reach him — the line was busy, so I went out to do my bit of shopping and reached him when I got back. He could hardly believe it either. *$4,000 each.*

I couldn't go print. I just sat around here doing little things like tidying up my mailing list. At 3 p.m. Nelson came home; he had taken the afternoon off because he couldn't work (no one objected). It still seems unreal. We will receive travel funds — *I will see Europe, at last* — in the fall. Nelson will resign from the library. The grants are for 12 months, and the library won't hold his job that long. Tenure begins on June 1st; he will resign effective that date. We have so many plans to make.

I want to get down all the work that is in my head before we go to Europe. Nelson will want to get solidly into writing before going, too.

13 April, 1971. Tuesday.
I'm still a little stunned by yesterday's news. We spent the afternoon in the back porch, just looking out at the sky, talking from time to time. Nelson seemed to go from "happy" to "scared" and back again, or so he said. Me, I just sat there feeling like Mother Earth — Mother Earth never gets excited about anything.

We decided to go out for dinner at Sai Woo. David Rosenberg called, wanting us to get together either for dinner or afterward to celebrate — David got a CC short-term grant. It seemed wrong for us, so Nelson made excuses. We went late to dinner; it was nice just to have each other's company. After dinner, we walked to City Hall and saw the Moore sculpture in the Square.

Later: Nelson is resting in the front room, so I will write here.

This afternoon, I went over to Markham and pulled a new print — an intense red, a low blue (lowered with yellow, then raised slightly with white) and a tint of a tone of yellow. The yellow, although raised with quite a bit of white, remains intense. The colour activity is amazing in this one. The red shapes are gathered and change in tone. While the eye is on the reds, the yellow shapes seem very high-keyed. When the eye moves to the yellow, it lowers and each shape changes tone. The blue changes too, but it is not as immediate. The blue is the most dispersed of the three colours and it is the lowest in tone.

Between pulling the colours, I went downstairs to Mrs. Pollock's [Jack Pollock's mother] coffee shop on the main floor for a coffee. Jack Pollock was there and I sat with him. He told me that Kay Kritzwiser had been at his house last night and she was very impressed by my painting. He has it hanging in his living room on a wall with three small Jim Dine "heart" pieces. There is a large Paul Fournier painting in the room, and prints by Jack Bush, Olitski, and Barnett Newman. He said my painting stands up well; it has "real presence." (That's awesome company.) He said I could come and see it some time.

I told him that Nelson and I had received CC grants and said that we would take a trip to Europe (our first) in the fall. He told me that he will be travelling in Europe this summer. He will suggest some people and places I should see.

14 April, 1971. Wednesday
I worked at the Markham studio today, printing. A rich red-yellow (gathered), a yellow-orange and a green, each more dispersed. This, and the last print, break into high intense colour. Now, I want to deal with blue-purple.

I went downstairs for coffee and Pollock, who was there with Claude Yvel and his wife, invited me to sit with them. He introduced me to them by my painting at his house which they had seen. We talked mostly about Yvel's work, for I asked him some questions. We talked a bit about the Binghamton show.

Yvel is a small, dry-looking man. He looks a bit peeled, despite his beard. Perhaps "polished" is a better word for it — not the neat, polished look one usually thinks of, but polished in the sense that he has been gone over with a linen cloth. He spoke no English, although he seems to understand some. His wife translated into French for him.

I read *Scantlings* by Gael Turnbull last night. I enjoy his poems. Some seemed laboured or deliberate, but fine all the same. I suspect he knows he's mortal.

15 April, 1971. Thursday
I had a good time today; it was a little wild and a lot of fun.

There was one disappointment — the 48" x 96" painting that Aggregation sold has been returned to the gallery. After having it for a month and a half, the couple have changed their minds. It means that I am back to only breaking even on expenses with the gallery.

I went over to Yonge Street and saw the Gordon Rayner show at Isaacs. The show was strangely mixed; the works were from 1969 to 1971. While I looked, I felt there must be a great painting somewhere in there; I just couldn't find it — each one fell away.

I went next door to Lamanna to see the David Rabinowitch show. Rabinowitch was in the gallery and he talked with me. Carmen, too. I looked at the work — David was at my elbow all the while — and I commented on the pieces as I looked. David was enthused about my response to his work, "Carmen! Do you know this girl. She understands my work!" Carmen said, "Yes, I know Baba." (I was tickled by that.)

David wanted lunch, so we went next door. David ate and I had a coffee and we talked about the Bauhaus, Klee, Albers, Carl Andre, etc. — pros and cons. David has a fantastic ego; in fact, he's a madman. It's easy to catch a bit of his madness.

Then, we went into the Isaacs Gallery to look at Rayner's work (David hadn't seen it yet).

He looked around and said, "These are truly execrable paintings." I must have looked puzzled, because he said, "Shit! They're all shit!" (He goes a bit too far.) Back in Lamanna's he expounded on Rayner, saying that he was "an honest painter, painting truly crappy paintings." There was more talk — from Rayner (no), to Solomon (no, no) to Bolduc (yes). Carmen seemed to be getting a big kick out of all this. I think it's the first time I've ever seen him smile.

I went to Curry's to buy some supplies, then took a cab to Open Studio. Richard Sewell and Barbara Hall have a good set-up there. I hope they can keep it going. I don't think I can make use of the place, but they will order solvent and screen wash for me. I talked with Barbara until six o'clock. She showed me her work. Her prints are gentle exploratory things — tiny, dear things. She is involved in technique, seems only peripherally involved in making something happen.

When I got home, I talked reams to Nelson about the Rabinowitch work and about David. It seems that the madness I caught from him just unraveled.

I got two of my drawings ready to send to be juried for the International Print and Graphics show in Montreal.

Joe Nickell came at 8 p.m. I was still at my drawings, so Nelson talked with him in the kitchen. When I finished, I came in and had a coffee with them. Joe has just returned from a tour of Europe. He was in England, France, Spain and Morocco. He kept a journal of drawings and notes that he showed us. It was a travelogue. I was reminded of Jack Cain.

16 April, 1971. Friday

I went into the Mirvish Gallery today to see Frank Stella's show. There are three paintings, huge pieces — I guess they are 10 feet high and 30 to 50 feet long. They are beautiful. The colour! Brilliant work. They are so big, so imposing. I got saturated by the experience; it was impossible to do anything but gaze. I stayed until the gallery closed.

17 April, 1971. Saturday

The Binghamton show, Festival of Canada, is opening tonight — probably right now. I wonder what is happening.

After class this morning, I went into the AGO to see the Frank Stella retrospective. (I ordered a catalogue.) The show is hung chronologically. The early work is strong and direct; it is not as overwhelming as the later work and perhaps is the better for it. There's a good transition from work to work from 1958 to 1960. The shaped paintings from 1962 to 1964 sometimes use a fluorescent paint; some don't seem to solve their own problems. Then, into the squares — very satisfying — where the colour anticipates the 1970 work. In the gallery room with the 1970 works, there are two 1969 paintings with pale colours; they look weak beside the others.

The prints and drawings are a delight. They are easy to look at; one can investigate at leisure. That's different from the largest, most recent paintings that have so much energy, such size, that one loses one's sense of stability.

I met Gernot Dick at the gallery. We talked about the show. He was impressed, but he doesn't like Stella. Gernot gave me a ride up to the Mirvish and we both went in to see the new work there. Gernot talked down the show a bit, but it didn't matter. I saw the prints and drawings in there this time. I can write no more now.

19 April, 1971. Monday

Nelson spent Saturday morning putting legs on a piece of plywood 8 x 2 feet. He will use it for a writing desk. The large board that he has been using, he made into a drawing table for me for the front room.

Tonight, we lowered the easel-boards to the floor [three attached sheets of 4 x 8 plywood] and Nelson added two feet to them. He (I helped a little) lifted them back into place, so now the easel-boards are a wall 14 feet long and I can work on paintings 6 feet square and 4 feet by 12 feet long.

So far, the paintings [*Colour Lock, Second Series*] are 5 feet square. I have one of them on a stretcher; I will order four more stretchers. I want to see them all now. The areas of colour in them are about 20" square. In a painting that is 6 feet square, the areas of colour will be about 24" square. The same in a 4 x 12 foot painting. I will know if it's workable with the next painting. A new size and new shapes will be difficult; I've done this trip before and I know the dangers.

I printed today. Red, green, blue-purple. I discovered a beautiful green, a mixture of blue, red, yellow and white. It's earthy. The reds are gathered in this print. I lowered the red with blue with no white added. The blue is pressed to purple with red, then opened slightly with white. I like what I've done.

We are working toward a book of poems and prints. Nelson suggests *Points of Attention* for the title. He is working on the layout now. I have begun drawings toward prints. I am thinking about making five prints.

Nelson says I fill these books to keep from talking to him too much. That's what it's all about. He is right; at least, he's partly right. It works for both of us.

21 April, 1971. Wednesday

The list of Canada Council awards was printed in yesterday's paper. There were fewer awards granted this year than last.

I pulled another print at my Markham studio yesterday. A low red, a red-purple and a low blue. This print and the last one are heavier than the earlier ones; they are pitched low. I'm fairly pleased with these two, independently of each other.

I went into Pollock's to see Claude Yvel's show. I'm not as impressed with this body of work as I was with the last show. This work spanned a number of years and it seemed a little scattered, although it is fine work. Only half of the works shown can truly be called *trompe-l'oeil*.

23 April, 1971. Friday

I cut stencils yesterday — three sets for three more prints, then I went over to Markham and printed one of them. An orange, a green and a purple; it was only while I was printing that I realized that they were the three secondary colours. I had arrived at their relationship by a different route of thinking than the theoretical.

When I went downstairs to Mrs. P's for coffee, I met a girl, Shelley Graves Shaw, and talked with her for quite a long time. I was late getting home.

I want to make twelve prints and I begin to believe that I will do it. I have made eight now (nine actually, but I will take out the second one). The editions are uneven, but I will be able to get a few sets of twelve out of them when I've done them all.

25 April, 1971. Sunday

bpNichol was here on Friday when I got back from Markham Street. He seemed a little down; maybe he's overwhelmed by the Governor General's Award. He talked about his fear of losing anonymity — something he seems to prize. He admitted he wants "recognition"; in fact, he said, "I crave it," but his "anonymity" means more to him. There's something false about this, I think.

I went over to Curry's early on Friday to buy supplies and stopped at Lamanna's to see the Molinari/Rabinowitch show. Molinari's paintings are very fine — triangles. I like his work in spite of what everyone says. The Rabinowitch sculpture was a bit weakened by it; they are not as forceful as they are seen alone.

I came back to Markham to print. A red-orange, a yellow-green and a rich brown. The "brown" is a mixture of red, yellow, blue, black and white. I'm pleased with this one.

The Saturday morning class did drawing in the sculpture court at AGO. I got the Stella catalogue and I read most of it yesterday.

Nelson and I discussed the book of poems and prints quite thoroughly last night. We are going ahead with it.

The Aviva auction took place last night.

Later: I went over to my Markham studio today and printed. A yellow-orange, a purple and a light brown. This "brown" (or low red-yellow) again combines red, yellow, blue, black and white to yield a different colour.

I have talked with Lynne. She and Dave went to the auction last night. My drawing was not called while they were there. The last bid they saw on it before they left was $60. She said things were going well below their value. A piece by Robert Sinclair sold for $75. (The artist will receive 50% of that amount). The price on that work in the gallery is $150. The auction is for charity. No wonder artists complain; they are making the bigger donation to the cause when a work sells this low.

26 April, 1971. Monday

I looked over all the prints last night, eliminating one. I put them in the same order as the twelve drawings I made earlier (I didn't print them in this order), so #10 and #11 are missing. I laid them on the floor in three rows of four prints to look at them together. I was able to decide what I wanted for the last two prints, and I cut the stencils for them. Today, I printed #10.

I got a letter from Milly Ristvedt today, saying that she didn't get a grant (no mention about mine). She has sold a painting to the Museum in Montreal. (Good. That's where we want to see stuff hung.) She said there will be a review in *Artscanada* of her show at the Waddington Gallery (I'll watch for it) and that she will be having a show at Lamanna this year (yes, Lamanna will do that even after what he said).

28 April, 1971. Wednesday

Yesterday, I printed #11. In Mrs. P's, I met the girl who spoke to me at Aggregation when my show was on and learned that she is Lois Steen. She is a lively person. She compared art to a religion (I don't really get that), but we had an interesting talk. I may see her again because she has Albers' book on colour and she wants to show it to me.

Last night, I went over all the prints and signed and numbered them. I have six complete sets [*Colour Lock Prints #1-12*] and because the editions are uneven, I have single prints in editions up to 30. I have two sets marked "artist's proof"; I gave one to Nelson.

Today, I worked on sketches for the prints for *Points of Attention*. I will make six prints for it in editions of 50. I made tonal drawings first, then made master stencils, adjusting the drawings. I went ahead and cut all the stencils (I cut two paper stencils for each colour in each print). Now, I only need the paper to print on and I'm ready to begin printing.

Carol is back from Mexico. She called yesterday; I called her last night; she'll call again today.

29 April, 1971. Thursday

Last night we stretched a piece of canvas on the easel-boards for the next painting (72" x 72"). Nelson raised my bench by two inches so I can reach the top of this one. I sized the canvas today.

I went out for a while this afternoon; I went in to Pollock's where I talked with Anne Winter who is working there now. She talked about ballet; she is a dancer.

Carol called yesterday. She was upset. She believes the affair with Pinto is over and says that she can never go back to Mexico. I think this will probably pass.

2 May, 1971. Sunday

I have not begun to work on the new canvas yet. My stretchers were delivered on Friday and Nelson and I put two of the 5 x 5 foot paintings on stretchers last night. We will stretch the other two tonight.

Saturday was the last children's class at the AGO. Nelson met me at noon and we went in to see the Stella show. We ate in Chinatown, then went to Coles on Yonge Street. I bought Werner Haftmann's two-volume *Painting in the Twentieth Century* and Barbara Rose's *Readings in American Art since 1900*. The Rose book is a compilation of writings by artists on their work — something I don't see often enough. I got a book on Mondrian and one on Moholy-Nagy that has a good deal of his own writing in it. I also bought *The Second Sex* by Simone de Beauvoir.

I browsed all these books today and began reading *The Second Sex*. I have finished the Stella catalogue and I'm reading *Magic, Science and Religion* by Malinowski; I've just finished Rex Reed's *Do You Sleep in the Nude* — some artful portraits drawn there.

On my way over to Carol's studio this afternoon, I stopped in at Dennis Cliff's opening at Pollock's. Pollock told me that he had seen Nelson's *The Pre-Linguistic Heights* — Kay Kritzwiser has shown him a copy. She told him that she had thought I was a very lonely person who needed someone to love; when she saw that the book was dedicated to me, then read the poems, she told him she was so happy for me. (Pollock told her I was married to Nelson — she hadn't known that.) When I got back here, I told Nelson about this and he was almost moved to tears.

Nelson will be interviewed on Tuesday night by a man from CBC. He's not sure what it is about. I plan to go out on Tuesday night, to be out of the way.

4 May, 1971. Tuesday

We put the other two paintings on stretchers on Sunday night. I was able to look at all five paintings together. I laid out all of the prints while the paintings were in view. (I have learned a lot from those prints.) Yesterday I continued to look at the paintings, then last night, we covered them with plastic and stacked them away from the boards.

I worked on the new canvas today. I've been working toward this one for a week. The larger size gave me some difficulties at first. I am working with a green, a purple and an orange. I mixed the colours, tested them and applied the green and the purple areas today. I will apply the orange tomorrow. I think the colour is right, but I will reconsider it before I apply it tomorrow. Today, I worked from 10 a.m. through to 5 p.m. — I forgot to eat.

There seems to be some sort of order to the change in a colour when there is a change in its size. I test each of my colours as I mix them by putting a 2"-3" swatch of the colour on a test sheet [a small piece of canvas, tacked to the boards beside the painting I am working on]. I test each colour beside each other colour, changing the mixtures until I have what I want. I have to see the colour dry (there is a change in appearance between a wet colour and a dry colour with acrylic paint) before I apply it to the painting. There are also always changes in the appearance of the colours when they change size; the value changes when a colour goes from a 2" square to a 20" or 24" square (or the 30" square I worked with in the first series). I wonder if there is an orderly ratio to these changes.

The changes seem to be, for instance: 1) a 2" square of yellow will appear more brilliant on the test sheet than a 24" square of the same yellow and 2) a 2" square of blue or purple will appear darker, or lower in value, than a 24" square of the same colour. If the 24" square were to be extended to a 6 foot square, there would have to be some thought given to the distance between the viewer and the painting. I don't think there's anything I need to work out about this, but I think the observation is important.

I've been thinking a lot about size because of the Stella show. Mirvish is showing Helen Frankenthaler now.

Pollock has a show by Dennis Cliff — I saw it only briefly on Sunday. All the works use two colours, often complementary colours. They are easy on the eye, and they have a shallow illusion of space. One aspect of these works is disturbing — they are backed with fiberglass (the canvas is glued to it), making them about ¼" deep to the wall. They are so lean that I don't think that even the shallow illusion of space can work. Another thing: there was a strong smell in the gallery on Sunday. I wonder if the fiberglass is sealed. I'm reminded of the man who owned the Eva Hesse sculpture and found he couldn't keep it.

The man from CBC, Allan Anderson, called Nelson to postpone the interview until Thursday night. Nelson has talked with Victor Coleman (he was interviewed, too) and learned that the interviews are taped and will be used for a series of seven half-hour programs on seven poets on CBC Radio's *Anthology*. Nelson is not at all excited about this. I am.

6 May, 1971. Thursday

I completed my painting yesterday [*Colour Lock, Second Series #6.* 72" x 72"]. I will leave it on the easel-boards for a few days so I can look at it.

Aggregation called yesterday to tell me that the woman from the AGO Rental Gallery was there choosing paintings. Dave said she wanted my 4 x 8 foot Colour Lock paintings, but not the ones at the gallery, the ones I have here. I only have one of them here; the other is in the Binghamton show. She described the cartage, handling, insurance and terms to me on the phone. (If the work sells, the AGO takes 20%, Aggregation receives 25% and the artist, 55%.) The consignment period is one year. I looked at the painting last night. I think I will have them take it [*Colour Lock #9*].

I went over to see the Frankenthaler show at Mirvish. The paintings are large with large colour fields and smaller areas of raw canvas involved in all but one piece. Frankenthaler has used a slow meandering line, almost a straight line, in these works. The lines have the look of having been drawn slowly and deliberately (this is a bit surprising, because a straight line is usually a "fast" line — the eye moves fast along it) and they cross the colour field and the raw canvas field, describing the surface and tying area to area. The lines are mostly black, a few are red. I think this is a brilliant use of line. Without the lines drawn in this manner, there probably would have been "holes" in the paintings, or an illusion of space as in a landscape. With the lines, everything holds the surface.

The surface colour is a stain; it's lean and active with strokes and water marks. I don't find the work as exciting or as immediate as a tougher surface would be. I know that's my subjective response to stain, but these are fine paintings to my eye because of what has been achieved by the line.

I went back to see the Cliff show at Pollock's. I still don't think the leanness of the pieces works. Cliff is trying to make the illusion of space go *into the wall* by using the thin fiberglass backing instead of a stretcher for the canvases. Theoretically it's sound, but it's difficult. Face on, one can get the illusion, but seen on approach from the side one sees the paper thinness of the works and is disturbed by it. Worse, the pieces curl out away from the wall in some places, causing a shadow. They must do one thing or the other, not a little of both. Cliff doesn't have control of it; the material, the thing he has tried to minimize, has gotten away from him.

I mentioned the smell in the gallery to Pollock and told him what I thought it might be. He said that the fiberglass is raw; he seemed concerned about it. I don't know about this material.

Pollock knew who bought my drawing at the Aviva auction. He said it has found "a very good home." (It went for $80 — not bad.) He had no news about the Binghamton show. It seems that I'm the only painter in the show represented by two works. Robert Downing is represented by two sculptures, but the rest have one piece each.

8 May, 1971. Saturday

On Thursday, I went with Nelson to Bell Offset to choose the paper for the book of poems and prints. Since then, Nelson has gotten the type set for the pages at Coach House. He did a mock-up this morning. He's ready to set the actual pages and will deliver them to Bell to be printed next week. He will pick up my paper at the same time and I can begin the silkscreen prints.

I saw Carol in her studio on Thursday night while Nelson was being interviewed by Allan Anderson. Nelson seemed unhappy with the interview, but from what he has told me, it's probably not as bad as he thinks.

10 May, 1971. Monday

On Saturday, Nelson tipped the print for *The Pre-Linguistic Heights* onto card. I went over them, signed and numbered 100 and about 15 artist's proof copies. The prints generally look good, but I'm not pleased by them on close inspection. We put tissue over them and set them into envelopes. Nelson will deliver them to Coach House this week and he'll sign the 100 copies of his book.

We stretched a new piece of canvas on the easel-boards yesterday for a 4 x 12 foot painting. I sized it and last night I put the edge-tape in place. I can begin today. I have been working over the sketches for this painting for ages. I determined the four colours (each repeated three times) this week. Everything seems to be right about it, but when I look at that tremendous expanse of canvas, I'm petrified.

Later: I'm super-tense, super-excited. The painting is underway. I thought for a while that the positions of the reds and yellows should be reversed. I went over the drawing again, got out colour chips and tried it both ways. I decided to stay with the gathered reds. It is the riskier, but it will be the better painting if it works. I am applying the red now.

11 May, 1971. Tuesday

I sit here in front of my painting. I worked from 9:30 a.m. to 5:30 p.m. yesterday applying the red and yellow shapes. Today, I worked just as long applying the green shapes and the brown shapes. I'm super-tired.

The painting is working, but it is very difficult. I am uneasy — *something* is not working and I can't figure out what it is. First, the painting is too large to really see in this room. Is it that? I'm not certain. The red collects, but it seems difficult to get started into the painting. I will let it sit and watch it for a few days. Unfortunately, I will have to roll this one; it's too big to put on a stretcher in here. I would like to leave it visible and go on immediately; perhaps I would recognize the problem that way. Still, I plan to make prints and I need more paint and canvas anyway, so I will leave it on the boards and watch it. By moments, I look up and it holds and I'm overwhelmed by how well it works. Other times, I look and it seems too dispersed and it falls away. My eyes are saturated.

12 May, 1971. Wednesday

Today, the painting bothered me so much that I changed it. Yesterday, it had looked so good until I laid on the "brown" areas; I was suspicious that the whole painting was not working because of that colour. As well, one of the brown areas had a poor shape and that kept biting at me.

I laid tape along the boundaries of the brown shapes and cut through it with a knife, peeling away the inner excess. (I've never tried this before.) On one shape, I cut a new boundary, enlarging it slightly. I mixed a new brown that was softer, a brown that leaned more toward blue, raised it slightly with white and applied it. It went on well. I can see that the one shape has been changed, but the painting works so I'm not sure it matters.

The first brown was a red-brown. It competed with the intense red shapes and over-intensified the green shapes. This new brown (more blue) is compatible with the green and it separates from the red, letting it work independently. *Now* the reds gather and one can get into the painting [*Colour Lock, Second Series #7*].

13 May, 1971. Thursday

Because of yesterday's successful colour change, I decided to make a change to the painting the AGO Rental Gallery wants, *Colour Lock #9*. I have held this painting back because I have been uncomfortable about it. The red shape is too brilliant (it is a red-orange). I mixed a new red, lowered it with black and raised it slightly with white. I am amazed at the effect of this change. Because the new red is greyed, it intensifies the green and the orange shapes in the painting. I'm very pleased with this work now and will not feel reluctant to put it out.

My paintings are very direct; there is no allowance for change. I make them that way deliberately — I give myself only one shot at it. I have to be right. (That's why I spend a long time sketching and thinking about a painting before going to the canvas, and I take a long time mixing and testing the colours when I have begun.) Now I know that a change, a limited kind of change, is possible. I can't change the hue of a shape (I can't change a red area to a blue area), but I can change a colour to another value of that colour if it is keeping the whole painting from working. The difficulty is in knowing which colour is the culprit and what to do about it.

Mike Doyle from Victoria visited us this evening. He is in town for a conference at U of T. He looked at my prints and chose six that he wanted. He will send me $50 for them. There was talk about the University of Victoria, about the conference, about Coach House Press and about Vancouver artists and writers. It was a good visit, but it was short. He and Nelson should have had more time to talk together — too much time was taken up over my prints. He gave us a signed copy of his book, *Earth Meditations*.

14 May, 1971. Friday
Carol came by today at noon. I showed her the twelve prints and she saw the new painting.

This afternoon, I called Aggregation and was told that my big painting, *Colour Lock #15* (60" x 120") is at the Medical Arts Building on St. George Street. Pollock arranged it. The painting was picked up last Thursday; the building was opened on Saturday. I learned that Lynne and Dave plan to renovate the gallery, so they will be closed for the month of July. They are going to extend the gallery space right to the back of the building.

Later, I went out for coffee at Mrs. P.'s. Jack Pollock came in and told me about the exhibition of paintings he put into the Medical Arts Building and about a jury show of prints. I went into his gallery to pick up the forms for the print show and there was more talk about framing, fees, etc. At one point, Pollock said, "You know, an artist gets more money when a piece is sold unframed than he gets if the piece is framed. I don't know why that is, but it always comes out that way." I couldn't believe my ears.

16 May, 1971. Sunday
Today, I began to print for *Points of Attention*. I began with the fourth print for the book, printing one colour. To be safe, I pulled almost 25 extra copies. All of the prints will have three colours, so will go through the press three times. I have to be ready to lose some. I want 50 for the edition, another 10 as proof copies and whatever over-print survives can be separate from the book.

Pollock seems to be playing some kind of game with me. First he says that I would be crazy to frame my work with anyone but him; then he says that it can't be done because it would cause hard feelings with Aggregation.

I would like to write about colour, about my ideas about colour perception. I should get it down in writing now, because memory is a great deceiver. It is easy to believe that all of one's insights have always been clear, when in fact, they accumulate and relate to each other bit by bit, over a long period of time. If I record what I think I know about colour perception now, I will have something with which I can compare future ideas and insights. The problem will be finding the words.

17 May, 1971. Monday
I printed today at my Markham studio. I finished the first print, #4, and pulled two colours on #5.

Nelson and I each got a letter today from the Canada Council saying that the first installment of our grants is on the way.

It's interesting that not many people have congratulated me on getting a grant. Nelson's friends congratulate him; in fact, they congratulate him on both grants. The evening David Rosenberg was here, he said to Nelson, "Eight thousand dollars! You may never have to work again!" Nelson has been told this sort of thing so often, that even he got confused about it. He asked me that night how much of the money I thought I would need. I asked him what he meant. He wanted to know how much of my grant he should give me so I can paint. I reminded him that when the money comes, it will be sent to our separate accounts: the writing grant will be deposited in his; the visual arts grant, in mine. He was painfully embarrassed. So we made a plan about the money.

Carol told me that when she told her friend, Gerald, that we had each gotten grants, he asked her, "How did he swing that?" She asked him what he meant and he said, "How did he get one for her, too?" Carol really tore into him for that.

18 May, 1971. Tuesday
I worked at Markham again today. I finished print #5, began and finished #2. I brought the three prints home to show to Nelson. He thought they were great, just right for the book. I was so relieved; I thought he might have a strong preconception after all of our talk about the book and the actual prints would not meet it.

I saw Lois Steen again today. She wants to have a "study group" over her Albers book. She thought Dennis Cliff might be interested and she's going to ask him about it. I don't know about this — I'd just like to see the book. She said she won't be ready to get started until mid-June.

I was rejected from the Montreal graphics show. It's the first rejection I've had that I've felt relieved about — I didn't really want in.

21 May, 1971. Friday
On Wednesday, I printed #3. It was hot (over 80°) so I stopped work at 3 p.m. Yesterday, I printed #6 and today, #1.

Yesterday was frustrating. Carol dropped in while I was pulling the print. She was quite excited; she had just had lunch with a friend whose marriage has broken up and she started telling me about it. I had the screen loaded with ink so I kept pulling until I finished, barely hearing her. We went downstairs for coffee (I wanted to get her out of the studio) and the conversation deteriorated to defensiveness and we were left with nothing to say. I had an encounter with Lois Steen that did not improve my day. I'm getting tired of people telling me that *I* make *them* feel guilty because *I'm* working. What do they want? If I stopped working, would it make them feel better? It's not that I talk about *what* I'm doing (they never ask that) — I put that here.

Carol is going to Stratford for the weekend. I won't see her for a while; there will be time to get over my irritation.

23 May, 1971. Sunday
We have tipped one of each of the six prints into the mock-up of the book. I am considering reversing the position of #3 and #6 to put the stronger contrasts at the end. Yesterday, I went over all the prints, signed and numbered 1-50 and 10 artist's proofs. I found trouble with #6 — pinholes I had missed before. I printed that one on Thursday, the day Carol came in and bothered me and I lost my concentration.

24 May, 1971. Monday
Last Friday, I talked again with Shelley Shaw. She invited me (and Nelson) to her studio to see her work. I said that I would go over after I finished printing and, since it was 5:30 when I was done, I called here to see if Nelson would come. He did, so we went to Shelley's for tea. Shelley is the girl (she wants to be called a "woman," not a "girl") with whom I have had a few interesting talks about feminism, or as she prefers to say, "womanism."

We saw three of her drawings and one painting. She calls her work "biomorphic." They are like some of the drawings I was making about six years ago, but they are more intense and more refined. This "landscape of the mind" is something I mistrust. Her images deal with birth, death — they are writhing organic compositions, and seem to be about aspects of childhood.

25 May, 1971. Tuesday
I went into Pollock's today to see Paul Fournier's show. It's a good show, but Fournier's work always seems to disappoint me. I don't know what it is. It's competent, but there's something soft and sweet about it.

Pollock showed me some prints by an artist named John Pearson (American, from Cleveland, Ohio). His concerns are similar to mine. Pollock told me that

Pearson will be at the gallery on the 6th of June and if I came to that opening, I could meet him.

I made an appointment this afternoon to have our passport pictures taken. It was done this evening.

27 May, 1971. Thursday

I have decided to make one of the book prints over again — #6. I may also try to print #4 again. I'll see.

Yesterday, I had an interesting talk with Shelley about her work and about mine. There was more to contrast than to compare. I learned that Shelley greatly admires Salvador Dali. She says she understands everything he says. She read an interview and she's pretty excited by it. I'm afraid I agree with some of the other Surrealists who have said that Dali has "talent up to the elbow," but I didn't say that to Shelley.

I talked with Anne Winter in Pollock's about gallery operations in general. She made a good point about framing. She said her father, William Winter (Anne is the little ballet dancer who appears in his paintings), says an artist should not frame with the gallery where he is showing. He should get his frames wherever he can get the best price and take framed works (with a framed price) to the gallery. This is worth thinking about.

I looked again at the Pearson prints. There are three prints, each done with the same stencil changing colour, changing relationships, creating new complexities.

28 May, 1971. Friday

I worked at the Markham studio yesterday. I made print #6 over again. It will be #3 in the book. I also began a new #4 print with colour changes as well as shape changes and finished it today. The transition from #3-#4-#5 in the book will be better.

I ordered canvas yesterday; it was delivered last night.

Nelson worked on poems last night. This is his last day at the library.

30 May, 1971. Sunday

Yesterday, Nelson and I went over to Pollock's to see the Fournier show, but especially, I wanted him to see the Pearson prints. Pollock told us he had talked with Anne Brodzky and she had talked about me and my work. She compared my work to Albers and she said something about "*it*" — the unnamable thing that artists have. She said, "Whatever *it* is, she's got it." Meaning me.

Nelson was up early this morning writing. He is in a good space now. We will stretch a new piece of canvas tomorrow.

I have arranged to go over to Aggregation on Thursday evening to talk with Lynne and Dave about my position with the gallery.

31 May, 1971. Monday
Nelson stayed up writing last night until 4 a.m., so he slept late into the day. He was working in the back porch (we have fixed it up to serve as another writing room for him). He has begun his CC tenure, and we will work separately in the same place now. We've decided against all-night working sessions; they cut too much out of the day and the light is important to me. (He would wreck himself if he kept this up.)

I stripped the staples out of the 4 x 12 foot painting today. We rolled it and stretched another piece on the easel-boards. I have sized the surface. I want to do a piece that gathers one of the four colours. I have sketches prepared for it, but the final decisions haven't been made yet. I have drawings for works that involve gathering two, even three of the four colours. I hope to find paintings out of these, too. Everything remains tentative up to the final moment — that "moment" lasts through the days that it takes to execute the painting.

I got a reply to my letter to CAR from Kim Ondaatje. I was not on the list of members, but that has been corrected now. Kim and Mike are moving to Toronto in the fall, so we'll probably see them then.

We plan to see some galleries together tomorrow.

1 June, 1971. Tuesday
We went out to the galleries today. We saw David Diao (American) at the Dunkelman Gallery. The paintings are large works, single gesture pieces. The application of the paint seems to have been with a very wide instrument, almost as wide as the canvas — perhaps a squeegee. There were eleven or twelve large paintings and about six small pieces on paper. There is a build-up of paint at the edges of each painting, creating a natural "frame" for the smoothly dragged centre. The effect reminded me of Olitski in one case and Rothko in another (that's an observation, not a criticism) and these were the most satisfying. In them, the layers of colour became monochromatic, having been mixed by the scrape of the squeegee down the surface. In one painting green was laid over red; another used orange over blue over orange. The mixed complementary colours became grey, or a non-colour, despite all the colour that was there. Two other pieces divided in the centre using two areas of colour. These were not as satisfying for me; they reminded me of Larry Poons' recent work. One of them was red and blue with a yellow line at the centre. Another piece had an open line at the centre, not drawn, but left uncovered. It reminded me of Newman. The small pieces varied, but each

was executed with a single pull of the squeegee vertically down the page. One of these had a very strong thrust (no similar force on the canvases although the technique was the same). The technique dictated the form in these works; the results were dependent on the method. The show was completely sold out. All the pieces were made in 1971. Fast work.

We went in to the Mitchell Gallery mainly so Nelson could see Gary Slipper's work. Slipper is being talked about a lot right now. I saw some work there by Richard Gross, someone Shelley has mentioned whose work is like her own.

We went to the Morris Gallery and saw a show of American and Canadian early small works — Varley, Casson, a Jock Macdonald (1934), Thomson, Dufy, Whistler, FitzGerald — good to see. In the stairway, we saw Town, Claude Breeze, Nakamura, de Niverville, a Bloore, Hedrick and some others. A lot of good work.

At Gallery Moos, we saw a show of work by Jean-Paul Riopelle, spanning 1958-1967 — most of them small pieces. I found them strangely dull. I was most interested in a work dated 1963; there were works from 1967 that I liked, too. We saw two pieces from the Pol Bury show. We spent quite a bit of time over them; I'm sorry I missed that show.

We were getting saturated, so we stopped to eat — hamburgers and ice cream. Then we saw David Bolduc at Lamanna and Dan Solomon at Isaacs.

2 June, 1971. Wednesday
I didn't finish yesterday, partly because I didn't know how to describe the Bolduc and Solomon shows. I saw both shows, and talked with Bolduc briefly.

The small works in Bolduc's show were most satisfying; they were solid, exciting, yet quiet. The large paintings seemed tentative by comparison. Bolduc said the small works were earlier; the large works had all been painted since February. They had colour-grey fields, sometimes yellows, that varied in tone with strokes disturbing the surfaces. Vertical lines occurred at the bottom of a canvas (David called this "putting in some foreground"), or, at the centre, three sides of a square or a right angle were drawn. The paintings seemed weak and evasive; I had expected something stronger after seeing his work in the Five Painters show at the AGO. I thought I was missing something. When I met Bolduc over coffee, he was just as evasive as the work. I asked him if he thought of himself as a colour painter and he said, "There are no colour painters, except maybe Cézanne." (If that was supposed to put me in my place, it didn't — I liked that "maybe.")

Dan Solomon's show at Isaacs reminded me of the clutter of the Rayner show. His paintings are overloaded with shape play, overlapping shapes, and a splashing or pouring of blobs of grey or brown. I thought one piece, *Devil Music*, was the only good painting in the show.

We came back to Markham and saw the Frankenthaler show again, and the Fournier show at Pollock's, where I bought copies of the two Victor Vasarely books, *Vasarely* and *Vasarely II*.

I saw Carol last night. She was in a state. Sometimes she doesn't make sense and it's impossible for me to talk with her.

3 June, 1971. Thursday
I am working on my painting.

5 June, 1971. Saturday
Although it is well past midnight (2 a.m.), I date this Saturday. It has all been a tremendous strain.

On Thursday night, I went over to Aggregation to talk with Lynne and Dave. When I arrived, Dave was at the desk. He looked up and said, "You owe us $500." (He'd just worked up the statement.) The amount covered the fee for my show and the shared expenses for it. (Galleries usually charge an artist a flat fee to do a show, or they charge the artist 50% of the expenses — split costs — for that show. Lynne and Dave charge the artist both a fee and split costs.)

The costs were higher than I had been told they would be — again (this happened with the last show, too). The total was almost $700, but it was reduced by two drawings that sold and had been paid for. I asked what the settlement will be when monies for all the sales were received. Dave said it will be about $30. I would not break even after all. Then, he told me that he hadn't charged me yet for the two frames done the week after the show. Okay.

Before I could say anything about why I had come, they said that they had formed a gallery policy. It took four hours for me to hear it out. I wrote it down. I questioned some points; I wanted to think it over.

The policy is this: Aggregation will take a one-third commission on sales in the gallery; on sales out of gallery (through another gallery, or agent), Aggregation's commission will be 15% to 25% if the other gallery takes 25% to 35% (the total commissions will not exceed 50%); and Aggregation will claim 10% of all other sales — like *studio sales*. This could stack up badly for me. There is no contract and the gallery has few contacts. The contacts that have been most valuable to me, I have made for myself and for the gallery.

They outlined new exhibition arrangements. They will charge fees and split costs (no change there), but if there are no sales, or insufficient sales to cover the artist's debt, they will take the artist's work at 50% as payment. This might sound good, but when I consider it in terms of my show last year (from which there were no sales), where the costs were about $400 and the prices, set by the gallery, were very low, the gallery could have taken half the work in the show.

With the exception of the doubling up on costs (which I agreed to and have paid from the start), the policy is standard. But Lynne and Dave change their terms without notice. This new policy could change within 24 hours. I don't want to appear to have accepted it.

I cannot accept the gallery's claim on [sales of] work in my studio. My work is either consigned to the gallery, or it is not. I make prints, book prints, my drawings appear in publications — I am not paid for that work, but the gallery is not entitled to anything that is not consigned to them. As it is, Lynne and Dave have a huge amount of my work at the gallery and they call me for paintings that are here (like the piece for AGO Rental Gallery) instead of putting out on my behalf what is at the gallery.

On Friday, I called the gallery to give them my objection to their policy. I had decided to withdraw all but the Colour Lock paintings from the gallery. I told them that I would not pay them a commission on work in my studio.

Nelson had gone (he'll be away for a week) and I was left to think over everything that had been talked about. Today, I called again to say I had decided to withdraw completely from the gallery.

I spoke first to Lynne. She suddenly left the phone and apparently started crying. Dave came to the phone; he was angry because I had made Lynne cry (oh, god). I had to start all over again with him. So we talked.

I will withdraw by mutual agreement, and now I feel unbelievably relieved.

Dave did admit today that there may have been "a few mistakes."

13 June, 1971. Sunday
I have just read the last entry — it's sad. I am firm about my decision to leave Aggregation — as quietly as possible and without hostility.

I had begun my painting on Thursday. On Friday, Saturday and Sunday, despite the distressing talks with the gallery, I continued to work with a clear head on this 4 x 12 foot painting. I finished on Sunday, late in the afternoon (too late to go over to Pollock's to meet Pearson). I am looking at the painting now and I'm amazed at how well it works [Colour Lock, Second Series #8].

I have been sleeping a lot. With the decision made about the gallery and the painting completed, I found I was exhausted. Nelson got back yesterday.

14 June, 1971. Monday
We went over to Markham Street for coffee tonight at about ten o'clock. Carol

was at her studio and had coffee with us before going home. It's nice to sit at the outdoor tables when the street is quiet.

We are going to a reading at the Mitchell Gallery tomorrow night. There will be a series of readings; David Rosenberg's will be the first.

19 June, 1971. Saturday

On Thursday, I talked with Lynne and arranged to arrive Monday morning with a truck to pick up my work from the gallery. Also on Thursday, I told Pollock that I would be leaving Aggregation by mutual agreement, so that the work from Binghamton and the painting at the Medical Arts Building will be returned to me, not to the gallery. I haven't mentioned it to anyone else.

Thursday night, Dave called and asked me to bring a cheque for $375.89 on Monday — the balance now of my expenses. My comment, that he had made sales to that amount, didn't impress him. Dave wants me to pay the bill now and the gallery will send me two-thirds of the payments on sales as they are received, or, he said they could recall the work, cancel the sales and give me back the paintings. I said that I didn't think it was wise to involve the clients in this matter. I asked him to give me an itemized bill for the expenses and 30 days to pay it. He asked me if I would still be in the country in 30 days. I assured him that I would be. (He is anxious.)

On Friday, I saw my doctor (my usual appointment). I guess I didn't look very good and it came out that I was in the process of leaving the gallery. He suggested legal counsel; I said I didn't need it, but he knows a lawyer who deals with art matters and he wants to put me in touch with him "just for advice." Maybe.

Today I have been making lists of everything that is at the gallery and of the things that have gone out from there and from here.

20 June, 1971. Sunday

It's raining today and rain is forecast for tomorrow. We may not be able to pick up my work at Aggregation.

21 June, 1971. Monday

This day went better than I believed it would. Nelson got the truck from Hertz and we were able to pick up all the work at the gallery. There were a few problems collecting everything; I would have missed some things if I had not made the lists.

Bills and receipts were clarified. I did not pay them anything, nor did they credit me with anything. However, we have agreed that I will make payment and have my works returned, or get credit if the pieces are paid for by August 6th.

So much talk — and I have written it here so briefly.

22 June, 1971. Tuesday
I have just gone over the bills from Aggregation. Total expenses plus the fee: $394.39. Framing, etc: $266. This year at Aggregation has cost $660.39. I owe them $394.73. If Pollock pays for the painting by August 6th, I will owe them $94.73. I have no idea if Pollock will pay before he leaves for Europe. If the client who wanted the other drawing picks it up and pays for it, my debt would go down by $55.60.

24 June, 1971. Thursday
The work from Binghamton has returned (except for the two unframed drawings). I will let Aggregation know about it.

I talked with Pollock this morning. He is arranging a group show in Winnipeg for the fall and he said he wants my work in it. He will call me about it later in the summer.

We stretched a piece of canvas on the easel-boards yesterday and I sized it. The painting will be 6 x 8 feet. I have been working for quite some time on sketches toward this one and I'm just about ready to start.

I'm reading Kenneth Clark's *Civilization*.

25 June, 1971. Friday
I began my painting today. I have applied one colour to the canvas — a low-keyed red. The shapes couple at the centre and one is at the top right. This red will be dominant. I have mixtures of the three other colours, but I'm still working on them — a blue-purple, a yellow-green and an orange. The relationships are not right yet.

The reading at the Mitchell Gallery last Tuesday was by Victor Coleman. It was a good reading, the best I've ever heard from Victor. David Rosenberg was there. He told me that he and Arlette had split up; she has gone to New York. I was sorry to hear it.

27 June, 1971. Sunday
I worked long hours on the painting yesterday applying the blue-purple and the yellow-green shapes. Today, I applied the orange shapes and the painting is finished [*Colour Lock, Second Series #9*. 72" x 96"].

I saw Carol on Friday night. She was in a terrible mood. Many tears and much verbal abuse directed at me. I will try not to see her for a while.

2 July, 1971. Friday
I am really pleased with my painting. I am thinking of making a print that uses the same colours, the same composition. Or, I will stretch a new piece of canvas. I'm

out of medium and it will take a week to get a new supply — there is time to print. I'm working on sketches toward two new paintings. One is a 4 x 12; its sketch is the most advanced right now; it will probably be next.

Carol called on Tuesday night to tell me she had sold a painting. Earle Toppings went back to the gallery and bought one of her large canvases. This could not have happened at a better time for her; she has been so depressed and she is strapped financially. Still, she got her licks in at me even while telling me her good news. I will still stay away. I'm tired of it.

I was a little surprised by the sale. Toppings is a friend of hers, but he didn't seem to like the work at her opening. He seemed uncomfortable with it; I talked with him that night, explaining what Carol was doing in the paintings. When I told Nelson, he said that I shouldn't speculate on why a person seems uncomfortable; maybe he was uncomfortable because he has haemorrhoids.

On Tuesday, we mailed our applications for passports. We had shots: smallpox vaccination (required), typhoid, tetanus, polio booster (recommended). The typhoid shot made us miserable until today. As well, the weather has been hot until today — over 90°, about 94° in here.

Tonight, we went over to Markham to cover the paintings from Binghamton with plastic. (I am storing them, and a few others, in my print studio.)

Points of Attention is at the binder's now. We are anxious to see it.

Our trip to Europe is beginning to take shape. A book fair in London, another in Frankfurt help determine the route. Yvel in Paris, Vasarely's museum in the south of France — we have done some talking and much looking in the Atlas. We will determine our route soon so we can petition for our fares from the Canada Council.

Nelson bought me a CC present, *Mayan Letters* by Charles Olson.

14 July, 1971. Wednesday
I have neglected this book.

David Rosenberg spent two days here typing stencils for another book of his poems, *A Star in My Hair*. Nelson will print 100 copies for him on the Gestetner. We got along well enough; actually, I kind of enjoy him in spite of his clumsiness.

Jim Gordaneer visited for an evening, meeting Nelson for the first time. I think they liked each other.

We have finished off the two Weed Flower Press books: *Dragon Fly* by Bill Bissett and *Before the Golden Dawn* by David UU (David W. Harris).

Points of Attention is done. After getting advice on how to price it from Marty ($50), Jim Lowell ($17.50) and Jack Pollock ($75), Nelson decided on $47.50. Thirteen copies have gone out already and we have sales on four more. Nelson is still tipping in the prints.

Pollock paid for my painting before he left for Europe, clearing my debt with Aggregation by $300. I still owe them $94.73.

I have made two new prints. In each, four colours are repeated three times. The first one follows the 6 x 8 foot painting; the second has a blue-green, a purple, a green (toward yellow) and a red. I am thinking of taking this second one into a 6 x 8 foot painting, too. The colours are challenging. The prints are on 12" x 14" paper, with a 8" x 10" printed area.

We went to the Mitchell Gallery last night to hear bpNichol read. I spoke to him about doing a collaborative print. He is interested. I've been thinking about this ever since he saw my 4 x 12 foot paintings. They remind him of his drawings with cartoon frames and he said he'd like to draw right on them. I think there's a way of doing something like that with a print, but *not on my paintings*.

19 July, 1971. Monday

I have completed my painting [*Colour Lock, Second Series #10*. 72" x 96"]. The colours and their positions follow the second print. The tonal range differs from the print to accommodate the scale. I'm going to leave it on the easel-boards for a while to look at it.

I have talked with the AGO Rental Gallery. They will deal directly with me for consignments. I have written a letter to Aggregation giving the details of the transfer.

Points of Attention is doing well. Twenty copies have sold.

21 July, 1971. Wednesday

We went to Mitchell Gallery last night to hear David McFadden and Roy Kiyooka read. I spoke with McFadden before the reading and he seemed depressed. He gave a good reading, but it was subdued. Kiyooka's reading was powerful. He read poems and some letters. One of the letters was written to Kim Ondaatje about CAR — I guess Kiyooka's name got left off the membership list for a year like mine did. Another was written to Coach House — Kiyooka, we learned, was not entirely happy with his book. His letters are rich, pointed, insistent.

Anne Brodzky, Dorothy Cameron and Ronald Bloore came to the reading (to hear Kiyooka, I think — they've never come before). I spoke to Mrs. Brodzky. I am to call her next week for a meeting.

26 July, 1971. Tuesday

I received a letter from Aggregation saying that they have received payment for *Colour Lock #7* (Pollock's painting). They are extending the date of the settlement of my bill to August 18th.

30 July, 1971. Friday

The 5 x 10 foot painting that was at the Medical Arts Building was returned today. Nelson and Dan walked it over here from Pollock's. It came in through the back, so we don't have to strip it from the stretcher. It is leaning in the hallway now; it's too big to keep in this room.

Mike Doyle wrote Nelson and asked if I would do a cover for his magazine *Tuatara*. He also asked for some graphics.

I expect bp tonight. We are going to talk about the collaborative print. I have made a contour drawing with twelve shapes (two rows of six) like my 4 x 12 foot paintings. If he wants to treat that as the frames for his drawing, I will give him my large pad of tracing paper to draw on.

12 August, 1971. Thursday

I've done a lot of work since last writing here. My last painting is still on the easel-boards. I have begun sketches for another 4 x 12 foot painting.

I have been working on drawings. I have five large pieces that treat the square shape with only one drawn line — the diagonal. I've made a series of twelve small drawings (5" x 5").

The drawings came out of the cover drawing I made for Mike Doyle's *Tuatara*. The cover went down swiftly, then I made some "Interval" drawings — I made ten and sent six of them to Mike as graphics. The new drawings followed this work quite naturally.

bp liked the idea for the print (or prints). He took away the contour drawing and the pad of tracing paper and a few days later returned with a series of six draw-ings and some rejected attempts. His drawings use words and his Milt the Morph figure. I have used one of his rejected pieces to print some trials. I have pulled two prints to work out how I can best cut his hand on a stencil (that is, his drawing; I want it to look as if he drew on the print himself). I have paper ordered (15" x 30" sheets) and a large screen is ready. I have cut the first profilm stencil, so I'm ready to go ahead.

When bp showed me the six drawings, he said he was dissatisfied with the last one. I asked him if he wanted to work further on it. He said he did. I expected him to take the pad of tracing paper away with him and return with it again, but instead, he got up, went over by the easel-boards and got down on his knees with the pad of paper in front of him on the floor. He got out his felt tip pen and began drawing. It was interesting to watch him. He was down on his hands and knees drawing, ham-fisted, concentrating. It was like watching a child draw. When he stopped to look at what he had done, he stood on his knees. He didn't like his first attempt, stood on his knees and said, "Nope, that's not it." He began again, down on all fours. This one got a "Nope" too, so I went over to see what he had done. I asked him what he wanted, and on his knees, he explained what he was after, so I told him he could leave it with me and I would correct it. He was happy to let me adjust the drawing for him. bp is a big guy, but I felt like I was teaching the children again.

I talked with Pollock on Tuesday about the paintings for the Winnipeg show. He will take a one-third commission in the event of a sale. The Winnipeg show will be in a private gallery.

We each received travel funds from CC today — $730 for air fare and a Eurorail pass.

15 August, 1971. Sunday
I began the first long (collaborative) print this week and ran into problems. I've overcome them little by little. I printed two colours yesterday. I will print again today.

Dave called on Friday to tell me that I owe them $4 more. I couldn't make out what it was for (an earlier miscalculation, I think), but I told him to put it on the bill. We settle on Wednesday.

22 August, 1971. Sunday
Yes. I settled with Dave on Wednesday.

The AGO Rental Gallery picked up two of my paintings — the 4 x 8 and a 5 x 5. The consignment contract is with me.

I got a letter from Mike Doyle. He will use my cover for *Tuatara 6* and the "Intervals" in *Tuatara 8/9*, an all-Canadian issue — Nelson's poems will be in it, too.

I finished the first three prints for the collaboration with bp. The stencil for the fourth one is on the screen. The prints have been a lot of work. There have been several hang-ups like pin-holes and slips because of the large sheet of paper. But I'm pleased with them and anxious to see the six complete.

26 August, 1971. Thursday
David Rosenberg came by and told Nelson about a review of Weed Flower Press books by Kildare Dobbs in *The Toronto Star* that is brutal. It is the first notice the newspapers have taken of Weed Flower Press and Nelson has been sending them review copies for years. David said, "After you've worked for nothing for all these years, you should be bitter." It sounds bad. Of course, Nelson is upset.

12 September, 1971. Sunday
We saw the Kildare Dobbs article. It was bad; Dobbs ridiculed the Press, but the book, George Bowering's *George, Vancouver*, was treated well. Nelson wrote a letter

to the editor to correct misinformation, but it wasn't published. Instead, two weeks later, parts of the letter appeared in Dobbs' column, cut to give him a second round at sarcasm. I was furious, but Nelson said that at least the letter wasn't ignored and some of his points got made even if that's not what Dobbs intended. Peter Martin (the publisher) has written a letter in support of Nelson and the Press. It hasn't appeared yet, but it will probably be published; they'll know who he is.

I finished printing the six prints (editions of 25) for the Nichol collaboration. bp has seen them (we both signed them) and he seems to like them. He was surprised to see his black line drawings appearing as white line in the prints. (I know I explained that to him when we started this thing, but I guess he hadn't visualized it.) I think he is happy with the outcome all the same. We aren't going to release the set until January. We have to figure out how to package them; it will be difficult because of the size (15" x 30").

I showed the six prints to Jack Pollock and he told me I should show them to Dennis Young.

I made another print on the last day of August. It is very small. It's on a 5¼" x 4" page with a 3¼" x 3¼" printed area. It has three colours — a yellow, a purple and a blue, but the colours are repeated in a different manner here. It has two yellow shapes, three purple shapes and four blue shapes. It will go into a little book of Nelson's poems, *Round Stone*, that he is printing in an edition of 35 to give to friends.

We each sent a first report to the Canada Council and were notified of approval. The second installment of the grant ($1,200) is being sent. We bought our airline tickets and Eurorail passes last week. The trip gets closer; we will leave on the 28th.

We have a full week ahead. On Tuesday, we are having dinner at Pollock's house with Mrs. Kritzwiser. I am to take some of my prints. On Wednesday, we will have a Chinese dinner with Marty; he will fly to London, England on Thursday. Next Sunday, we are going to the official opening of Captain George's Gallery of Comic Book Art.

We have both been working on Marty's next poetry catalogue at the bookstore. I have done no work (no painting, no drawing, no prints) since the first of September. I make sketches and notes for projected works.

Nelson is trying to set up an appointment with Anne Brodzky to show her *Points of Attention* and the six Nichol collaboration prints.

17 September, 1971. Friday
We had dinner at Pollock's on Tuesday with Kay Kritzwiser and Donna Rolfe. We took the prints and a copy of *Points of Attention* and everyone looked at them.

Donna Rolfe wants to buy a copy of the book; her sister, Niki, is in Paris, and she will put us in touch with her. I told Mrs. Kritzwiser about Captain George's gallery opening and encouraged her to see it for a review, but she refused. She doesn't think comic book art is a legitimate art form. It was a comfortable, pleasant evening. I saw my painting.

We worked on Marty's catalogue at the bookstore on Tuesday and Wednesday, then had dinner with Marty at Sai Woo on Wednesday night. Marty left for England yesterday.

Before going to the bookstore on Thursday, we went to see Dennis Young at the AGO offices. I took the Colour Lock prints (#1-12), the Round Stone print, *Points of Attention* and the Nichol collaboration prints. He was enthusiastic about everything except the Nichol collaboration. He didn't like bp's drawing hand. I told him bp was a concrete poet, but he was too put off by the clumsiness of the drawing to see anything happening in the prints (except one, which used words only). He told me that he believed people in the art community would think badly of me if they saw these prints — it could ruin my reputation. Obviously, he was giving me his best advice (but I didn't believe it). It was *his* reaction that disturbed me. I called Pollock about it and he told me that Young was not into what he called "mixed media" and probably has never heard of bpNichol. Sure, but the "mixed media" thing doesn't make sense. Young told me to visit Art & Project when we are in Amsterdam and I know he likes Jan Dibbets — that's far out stuff.

This morning, we saw Anne Brodzky at her office and showed her the same things. She liked the prints — all of them, especially the Nichol collaboration. We left her a copy of *Points of Attention* for review and gave her Mike Doyle's address in Victoria. He is willing to review it.

We saw Doug Fetherling today at the bookstore. We also saw bp. I told him about Anne Brodzky's response to the collaboration; then, to my horror, Nelson told him about Dennis Young and what he had said (I wouldn't have told him). Of course, bp was hurt by it, but he said he couldn't worry about "people like that." That disappointed me. What happened with Dennis Young wasn't about him; it was about me and I don't think bp gave that a thought.

18 September, 1971. Saturday
We went over to the Pollock Gallery to deliver a copy of *Points of Attention* for Donna Rolfe. We saw the Cruz-Diez show that was opening there. I intended to go into Mirvish, too, but we ran into Jim and Kathie Spence outside and had a coffee with them at Gaston's. There was much talk about what we have been doing.

I have arranged to have Peter Martyn, Carol's nephew, take slides of some of the new paintings on Monday night. I want to take my slides to Europe — for whatever it's worth. I should not go empty-handed.

26 September, 1971. Sunday
Two more days and we are away.

Peter took slides and they have been processed. I have slides of six of the new paintings. I have left a key to my print studio with Pollock; the paintings for Winnipeg are stored there. I have been cleaning and clearing, tidying up my supplies. I'm ready to pack.

I went with Carol to the first Toronto CAR meeting last Thursday night. Twelve people showed up; we were told there are twenty-eight members. Afterward, Carol and I had coffee with Vera Frenkel and Judy Gouin. I think the talk over coffee was more valuable than the meeting.

27 September, 1971. Monday
Last night, I cleaned up my Markham studio and left the paintings for Winnipeg where Pollock will easily see them. Today, we wrapped and stacked all of my paintings here. bpNichol came by to pick up his author's copies of *The Other Side of the Room*. He visited for a while, said *bon voyage* and was away.

Nelson has gone to finish at the bookstore. There's nothing left to do except pack.

Europe

28 September, 1971. Tuesday
We are in the air.

Our take-off was delayed until 9:30 p.m. We will fly for 6 hours 35 minutes. The take-off was a grand and scary experience, going up and out over Lake Ontario, seeing all of Toronto traced below in ribbons of light. There has been some turbulence, briefly alarming.

We have had dinner. It is almost 12:30 a.m. now. In a few more hours we will be in London, England. It will be a new morning there.

London

29 September, 1971. Wednesday
We arrived!

The landing was double the excitement of taking off. The countryside from above was a beautiful geometry. We are staying at the Edinburgh Hotel (bed and breakfast) on Bernard Street. It is a charming place, but the toilet paper, like at Victoria Station, is incredible.

We left a message for Marty at his hotel. He called at 3 p.m. and we went to meet him at the Antiquarian Book Fair at the Europa Hotel on Grosvenor Square. In the booths we looked at holograph manuscripts, autographs, early illuminated manuscripts from the 12th century to the 14th century and an 18th century Ethiopian manuscript. At one booth, I was shown a box of tin soldiers that had been used to train foot-soldiers. It was a wooden box with two drawers. Each drawer was filled with tiny metal soldiers in troop formation; the troops were separated into sections in each drawer. The tin soldiers were about a half-inch high. By inserting a key into the keyhole on the front of each drawer and turning it, the dealer could make the troops turn left, turn right, about face, etc. This was not a toy; rather, it had been used to demonstrate formations and commands to soldiers who were illiterate. I was fascinated and the dealer seemed to be having fun showing it to me.

Richard Landon was with Marty. The four of us went to Marty's hotel, the Britannia, across the Square from the Europa, for coffee in Marty's room. It was a very small room, but Marty thought it was grand. We talked for about an hour, then Nelson and I walked along Oxford.

We plan for tomorrow.

30 September, 1971. Thursday
We took a bus tour this morning from Victoria Station. It has helped us get a sense of the city.

This afternoon, we went to the Tate Gallery. We began in the first gallery and kept going for as long as we could. Hogarth was a surprise to see. Things I have considered dull were lively and fresh. Copley, Gainsborough, Reynolds. The Turner collection was a revelation. There were four rooms of Turner, early through late work. I kept thinking how exciting it must have been for Turner as he made each painting, seeing his own work advance. The later pieces remain relevant to the early work but move ahead; this seems evident in the structural works, from his early to middle years. The late works are loose and impressionistic. I was surprised by the colour. Some use a high-keyed yellow — beautiful — I would never have guessed.

We saw William Blake and the Pre-Raphaelites. Blake is better than I thought from what little I've seen in reproduction. There were two unfinished watercolours that show his art better than others that are heavy with allegory and heavy-handed as well. The Pre-Raphaelite works are so fine, but seem so empty. Ford Maddox Brown and Rossetti were most prominent.

We found Stanley Spencer's paintings in a stairwell and hallway. There were two huge paintings and about eight smaller pieces. Each was masterful and so full of human energy that it became disturbing to look at them.

We saw the Impressionist room. Van Gogh's chair is here. There was a small Seurat painting, a sketch for *La Grande Jatte* that I saw in Chicago. There were two Gauguins. I saw a painting by Edvard Munch — the first painting I've ever seen by Munch — and a landscape by Emil Nolde.

In the rooms ahead, I could see Willem de Kooning and Jackson Pollock, but we were finished for the day. We will have to go back.

1 October, 1971. Friday

Today we went to the British Museum. We looked at the collection of illuminated manuscripts, the room of holographs and autographs. The illuminations were Italian, Dutch, French and English. They are so seductive; we had to examine them all. There were many letters and documents — the Magna Carta, poems and manuscripts by Elizabeth and Robert Browning, the Brontë sisters, a letter by Defoe, Sterne, Captain Cook, Pepys. Nelson was intrigued by a signature done by Queen Victoria when she was four years old. We were done in by one o'clock.

Around 3 p.m. we went to Trafalgar Square. It was full of tourists taking pictures (we didn't bring a camera) and feeding the pigeons. There were a lot of kids with knapsacks. We had our letters of introduction from the Canada Council with us, so we went on to Canada House. With some reluctance we signed and asked about addresses. We sat down for a bit not knowing what, if anything, to do with our letters. The place was depressing with so many "homeless" kids hanging onto knapsacks just sourly looking around, as if they were waiting for something to happen. A few of them were reading letters; the rest just watched them read. Some older people were reading Canadian newspapers in a reading room, but it was no livelier in there. Finally, I took my CC letter to the desk, showed it to the young woman there and asked who I should approach with it. She shot off with the letter to another woman who rushed over to me to say that she would get the Cultural Counsellor. I was amazed. She returned shortly to say that I should call next week for an appointment and she brought an invitation to an exhibition of work by Raymond Chow that will open next Tuesday.

We crossed the Square to the National Gallery. What a wealth! We saw some early Italian and Flemish paintings (Jan van Eyck!) and some magnificent Rembrandts. Our time was short; we will go back.

2 October, 1971. Saturday

This morning, we went to the Compendium Book Store where Nelson met and talked with Nick Kimberley, a long-haired, self-conscious young man. Compendium has been buying Weed Flower Press books and Nelson wanted to meet Kimberley and to see the store. Nelson gave him an advance copy of bpNichol's *The Other Side of the Room*, a copy of his own *Round Stone* and showed him the copy of *Points of Attention* that he brought with him. We browsed the stock and Nelson bought a few books and had some set away for him until December.

We went into a workman's cafe and had ice cream and coffee. The dishes were dirty! But no one seemed to care *who* we were and there was a certain comfort in that.

This afternoon, Nelson phoned Larry Wallrich of L. A. Wallrich Books and we went there. Mr. Wallrich operates out of his home, so the visit was interesting from that point of view. Nelson showed him *Points of Attention*, gave him a Weed Flower Press catalogue and bought some books by Gael Turnbull. We had a short, but interesting, talk, and Mr. Wallrich suggested we look him up again in December.

3 October, 1971. Sunday

This morning, we walked around this area. I bought some apples and pears in a fruit store and asked the owner about the South African Outspan oranges (I know they are not popular at home). He said that only certain crops were good, but the best oranges came from Spain. I asked if they got California or Florida oranges in England. He said no, that even they were not as good as the Spanish oranges. He reminded me that the American oranges were grown from seeds originally imported from Spain (Cortez), so the Spanish orange, grown in its natural environment, was still the best. I was struck by my own cultural indoctrination — the new country produces the best; the "old country" is too old to be as good.

We went back to the British Museum this afternoon. We looked at the main floor Egyptian rooms. We saw pieces from Assyria (500 BC and earlier) and Egypt from 30 BC to 360 BC (Ptolemaic period) and earlier to 1200 BC-1450 BC Among the latter were colossus heads (Rameses?) and sculptured figures of Amenhotep. I began recognizing some of the pieces. There were a variety of steles, Egyptian and Assyrian. There were obelisks, pointed and stepped.

We sat in Russell Square today watching pigeons and children. It is so pleasant and everything is a curiosity of some sort. Even the sidewalks. I think they are granite; they sparkle.

We have decided to leave for Amsterdam on Thursday.

4 October, 1971. Monday

Today we did everything wrong. We got lost, went to the wrong place at the right time, then to the right place at the wrong time. We had been directed to a BEA office on Regent Street off Piccadilly Circus to have our tickets to Amsterdam endorsed. We never found the place. Instead we arrived at a cathedral by the BBC building; it was a good place to stop after so much walking.

The church was built by an architect named Nash. It had been bombed during wartime, then reopened. Inside it was small and blue — the blue of Wedgwood (or so it seemed to me, even in its patterning). The altar was dark wood with a painting above it; the windows were plain frosted glass. It was cool and tasteful, unlike anything I've ever seen.

Walking by Victoria Station, we saw a BEA office, went in and had our tickets endorsed after all.

I called Canada House this morning and spoke to the Cultural Counsellor, Ian Clark. We will meet him at the opening of the exhibition tomorrow evening.

5 October, 1971. Tuesday

We went to Better Books on Charing Cross Road this morning. We were early so we went into Foyles to browse. At Better Books (the poetry and film store), Nelson asked for Lee Harwood and learned that this was his day off. Nelson left a note and a copy of *Round Stone* for him.

We decided to go to the Marlborough Gallery on Old Bond Street. When we got there, we found we had to walk to an entrance on another street. The gallery was showing Ben Nicholson, works made over the past three years. They were relief paintings, done with masonite —white, blue, green and an earthy red, isolated colouration that was gentle and ancient. The circle, that perfect shape, occurred in its perfect context; the square appeared here and there, forced by other shapes to be about itself. Contained shapes, shape on shape, shape inside of shape, the edges made soft with scrubbed colour — warm browns with white scrubbed on. Titles like *Greek Landscape*, *English Landscape*, *Winter* (blue) and *Eagles Nest* (blue with circle) leaned toward the ancient, for land and rocks and seas are ancient. Sometimes a line was drawn with pencil, or scored into the surface, or lines were sanded roughly, disturbing the surface yet drawn at the same time. There was a small collection of prints (about 12).

They were lean and linear, but it was the paintings that were the more exciting for me.

I showed my slides to the young man there. He was friendly and seemed curious about us. He looked at the slides carefully and said that he believed I could have a successful show in London with the work. He suggested I try around, naming three galleries. One was the Woodstock Gallery on a street of the same name. We walked there. The gallery had a three-man show on. The feature room had the poorest work I've seen in a long time. I would consider it poor *student* work. It was the artist's first exhibition. I did not show my slides to anyone. I've tried to figure out if I had been "put on" (or, "put off") by the man at Marlborough. I suspect that the Woodstock, which has been operating since 1958, has a reputation for starting people and that would make it seem appropriate. Anyway, I was a bit brought down.

Tonight, we went to the opening of Raymond Chow's show at Canada House. There was an incredible amount of booze being served; there were peanuts and crackers everywhere and trays of tiny sandwiches were being passed around. We met and talked with Ian Clark (Scotch on the rocks!). He is a painfully handsome man. He talked with Nelson about writing, for he had written and published poetry. He told us he had published a magazine that ran four issues; it was the first place that Leonard Cohen appeared. [Nelson told me later that this was not Cohen's first appearance, but his second.]

The show was called Windows of London. It was three months of work by Chow, who is from Vancouver. There were about forty playful, well-executed drawings and four paintings. It was fun to look at (and to read), for there were words (puns) threaded throughout the images, but I was not particularly excited by it. The man in the cloakroom really liked it; he was delighted by the puns and pointed them out to us in one of the drawings nearby, so one enjoyed the show twice as much if one had checked one's coat. We met and talked with Jerry Santbergen at the opening.

We got a cab back to Russell Square and ate at the Milk Bar near the hotel. Nelson is sleeping now in his clothes, so I must wake him up to go to bed.

6 October, 1971. Wednesday

Such a full day and a beautiful sunny one. We took a tour to Windsor Castle and Hampton Court. The tour conductor, Mr. White, was a well of information and the bus rides to and from were chock-full of details as were the visits at the sites.

At Windsor Castle (the Queen was not in residence) we entered the St. George Chapel. Marble and semi-precious stones decorated the walls. The Chapel was built by Queen Victoria; it housed a tomb for Albert (although he is not buried there). There were carved portraits of each of Victoria's children around the walls. There was a small altar of inlaid wood. The windows were high and there were so many that I could not concentrate on them in so short a time. One window showed the architect. Outside we saw the cloisters and were shown an old entrance and a small fresco portrait of St. George, then another fresco portrait which has been glazed — no one knows who it is.

We were able to go through "state apartments" that were open to the public. There was marble everywhere, solid silver tables and mirrors, the Knight of the Gauntlet, shields, swords, armour, French tapestries, paintings by Holbein, Rubens, Van Dyck, Dürer, Canaletto and portraits everywhere. We had a half an hour to pass through these rooms. Nelson and I were the last ones out.

Windsor Castle was built as a fortress; we were shown its original structure and where the moat had been. The Castle is a wedding cake of history. Next, we had tea, then drove to Hampton Court.

Hampton Court was built as a residence by Cardinal Wolsey, then presented to the King. We did not go inside, but walked around it and through its gardens. We were shown the parts of the structure that were built by Christopher Wren, a section added by Queen Elizabeth, the part built by Wren for William and Mary. We saw individual gardens, a herb garden, a rose garden and Queen Mary's Arbour — "Mary, Mary, quite contrary, how does your garden grow..." We were shown a canal that once served as an entrance by boat. There was a small maze on the grounds; some people walked through it, but Nelson and I didn't. We went to a little pub, then got on the bus for the ride back to London. We first passed through parklands where there were deer by the dozens.

When we reached London, it was as if Mr. White could not stop. He pointed out the homes of Swinburne, Rossetti, Ian Fleming (007), William Hogarth, James Whistler and so many more. Passing a row of pubs in Battersea he recited a spiel of cockney rhyme to everyone's delight; my memory can not do him justice.

Tomorrow, we go to Amsterdam.

Amsterdam

7 October, 1971. Thursday
Our 1:25 p.m. flight didn't leave Heathrow until after three o'clock. The plane was a Trident, quite small, and our seats at the emergency exit were backwards, so we flew backwards to Amsterdam, watching England disappear. Through the clouds, we saw the English Channel, spotting a few boats. Then we were over land again, a rectilinear landscape. The city from above was so ordered. Even the airport reflected the cool rectangle. On the bus to Central Station, we passed buildings, long rectangles with vertical windows repeated; then the buildings became tall

and narrow, packed together to form vertical rectangles with gables pointing to the sky.

We are at Hotel Aalders on Jan Lukenstraat, walking distance from the Rijksmuseum and the Stedelijk Museum. We went out to eat at the Rembrandt Restaurant — good food, good coffee, so different from London. And here, the toilet paper is soft.

8 October, 1971. Friday

We walked to the Stedelijk Museum today. We were there for over five hours and have just come back. I'm tired now, almost too tired to write. Nelson has gone out to walk around the area while it is still light.

We saw four rooms of work by Kazimir Malevich, a huge mural collage by Matisse, a late work. Rooms with paintings by Monet, Picasso and Chagall. We saw the van Gogh collection, drawings and paintings. Nelson was very interested in these. For me, it was meeting at last so many works that I had seen in reproduction. The van Goghs filled five or six galleries (1883-1890). The last painting he did is there.

We went into the print rooms and saw a show of etchings by Anton Heyboer (b. 1924). They were incredible things that seemed to break every rule in the book. They were strongly horizontal/vertical even in the early figurative pieces. The later pieces (1952-1958) lose the figure and maintain a loosely drawn formality. I was reminded of Ben Nicholson's work; the colour and structure, a particular linear quality could be compared. This artist lives in Haarlem.

9 October, 1971. Saturday

We went to Central Station today and took a canal tour in a glass-topped boat. The guide spoke in Dutch, English, German and French. We moved from the core of the city (Singel) to the Princes Canal (Prinsengracht), seeing bridges, early and late (15th to 19th century). Architectural sites and details were pointed out — patrician homes, early gables, the Prince's quarters, the narrow bridge, a draw-bridge still operated by hand. In the harbour we saw boats in dry-dock, a floating dry-dock. An 18th century *warehouse* was pointed out; it was as elegant as a public building. Not a lot of detail was given because of the necessity of saying everything in four languages.

We went to Rembrandt's house (the house with green shutters). I had expected to see the house as Rembrandt had lived in it, reflecting his life-style. Instead, it has a stripped cool interior. It houses a large collection of his prints (200). There was a press on the ground floor where printing was demonstrated. (From my reading, I think Rembrandt printed on the top floor, in the gable room of the house.) In all the literature that was posted, there was only one reference to "a financial ruin." It was noted that the inventory of the Jodenbreestraat house was known. (Yes, there would be a thorough inventory.) It did not say *how* it was known that Rembrandt had owned so priceless a collection of art and art objects, just that it was. The house was opened as a public museum in 1911. Rembrandt lived there from 1639 to 1658. What took them so long!

The prints were worth seeing. Many were early states. The best works — tiny studies — were on the second and third floors. On the third floor was the "Hundred Guilder Print"; it made me sad. The house depressed me.

We bought some vitamin pills tonight. We have gotten colds.

10 October, 1971. Sunday

This morning, we woke sick with colds. We got up for breakfast, then went back to bed; I slept until 3 p.m.

We went out, then, and treated ourselves to a royal meal — an Indonesian rice table. There was rice, chicken, eggs in sauce, several curries, meat balls, fish, fried banana, bread chips, two salads, peanuts, grated coconut, apple and cucumber in maple syrup, a curried vegetable dish, other vegetables, some very tender meat on skewers — everything was delicious. There were eighteen little dishes in all and we ate most of it.

We ate early, so there were no other diners; the owner, after serving us, stayed at the back of the restaurant watching a sports program on the television. The sound of the television gave us privacy; it covered our sniffles and the blasts of our nose-blowing.

We have stocked up on Kleenex, newspapers and magazines, and are back in our room, doctoring.

11 October, 1971. Monday

I woke feeling much better today; Nelson is not quite as good. The sun came out around eleven o'clock, so we went out and bought apples, cookies, mints and chocolate.

This afternoon, I went to the Rijksmuseum while Nelson stayed here to sleep. I took an elevator to the second floor to look for Rembrandt's *Night Watch* (*The Militia Company of Capt. Frans Banning Cocq*). I went through Flemish and Italian rooms (14th to 18th century); I saw an El Greco crucifixion, Rubens, Tintorettos (that didn't really impress me), a Goya portrait (that really stopped me), some Italian gold-leaf paintings from the 1300s — wonderful — and so many pieces by artists I was only vaguely aware of, or didn't know at all.

The *Night Watch* and *The Anatomy Lesson* may be Amsterdam's shame. Magnificent as the *Night Watch* is, it is poorly housed, overshadowed by three large paintings by contemporaries. The painting has been cropped and looks cramped in its frame. However, it is better preserved than *The Anatomy Lesson* (destroyed by fire in the 17th century). Only the cadaver, one student portrait and the hands of another remain; seven figures are lost. *The Jewish Bride*, the little portrait of his mother, several small landscapes and interiors are hung among works by Rembrandt's students and contemporaries. I'd have preferred to see these works hung in isolation, not among contemporaries for whatever reason, but on their own to be compared only to each other.

I found the work of Jan Steen, but instead of going through the labyrinth of rooms I saw ahead, I went back to the *Night Watch* and found rooms with Pieter de Hooch, Emanuel de Witte and Jan Vermeer. There were three Vermeers — the woman reading a letter, the maid pouring milk, and the small street. These have an incredible "white," the white of cool light. I went through these rooms twice, then slowly retraced my steps to the elevator.

Walking back to the hotel, I couldn't help thinking that Rembrandt is more present for me in the streets and along the canals than in the museum.

12 October, 1971. Tuesday

Nelson and I went to the Rijksmuseum today. First, we saw the Albrecht Dürer exhibit, a huge collection of prints by Dürer with some pieces by contemporaries (I really don't like this method of display). The prints were mostly engravings and woodcuts; there were a few drypoints and some etchings on iron. It was a beautiful exhibition. We went back a second time to finish looking; we couldn't sustain this great mass of work, since we were moving through it thoroughly. The engraving of *Adam and Eve* (1504) was there.

We went to the rooms I had gone to yesterday, taking the same route together. I tried to point out things of greatest interest, but still we had to look at everything. This time, after the *Night Watch*, we went on to see Jan Steen, van de Velde and others for whom I have no names.

We ate early so we could spend this evening at the Stedelijk Museum. There, we revisited the exhibition of concrete poetry and saw several contemporary exhibitions of sculpture, paintings, some ceramics, drawings and wall hangings made of folded and tied paper, foil and cellophane. There is a tendency toward the grotesque in some of this work, a surprising record of violence in what seems to us a peaceful city. The names of all the artists have left me.

We went upstairs to continue looking at the permanent collection. We saw Jean Dubuffet, Matta, Antonio Tàpies, Harold Town, Paul Jenkins and Antonio

Saura. The upper rooms were cold; we moved quickly through them. We were tired, so came away.

13 October, 1971. Wednesday

It rained today. I went again to the Stedelijk Museum. It is close and I wanted more time there. I saw again the Malevich collection — works from 1909 to 1927. The later works are Suprematist. I went on to find van Doesburg and Mondrian. I toured the van Gogh rooms again. I looked more thoroughly at pieces by Kandinsky, Chagall, Robert Delaunay, Vlaminck and Picasso. It was leisurely looking and all the better for it.

Later in the afternoon, we set out to find Adriaan van Ravesteijn (Art & Project) at 18 Breestraat. It is a walk away. We found the gallery closed, but I rang anyway and the man we were looking for answered. He is a very tall man with a cool, stern demeanor. I told him who we were and that we had been directed to his gallery by Dennis Young. (I was standing on the doorstep, a step below this giant; I felt like a bug.) He told us we could come in on Friday after 3 p.m. to see him. We will.

We have decided to leave Amsterdam on Sunday. We will go to Mainz, Germany, where there is a Gutenberg Museum. Mainz is near Frankfurt.

14 October, 1971. Thursday

We went to Central Station this morning to make our reservations for Mainz. Then we walked up the Damrak to Dam Square. Along the way, we found a street of shops and department stores. We stopped and I bought a wool tam and scarf; further along, Nelson bought a tuque and warm gloves. Then I bought gloves, and Nelson got a turtle-neck sweater. *Now* we will be warm. So we were bundled up like kids in snowsuits passing people wearing light jackets or sweaters — I don't understand it. We walked to Dam Square, around the Koninklijk Paleis, then back toward Central Station on a zigzag route through narrow winding streets. Twice along the way we met barrel organs (calliopes). They were marvelously loud and happy. When the drums roll and the clappers clap there is a thundering of music and we just had to laugh.

15 October, 1971. Friday

We went again to the Rijksmuseum this morning. This time, we went in by a different entrance and found we were in the Chinese, Japanese and Indian rooms. There were Japanese screens and prints, Chinese Buddhas, sculpture, ivories, jade, some Chinese pottery from 2000 BC. We pulled ourselves away to go upstairs to look at the early Dutch paintings. We did not last long today, so we came away, back to the hotel to rest.

At about 3:30 this afternoon, we went to Art & Project to see Adriaan van Ravesteijn. In the gallery was a work of Sol LeWitt. It was on the two long walls of the gallery: on the left wall, 10,000 pencil lines 12 cm long were drawn; on the right wall were 10,000 pencil lines 24 cm long. The soft grey of the graphite made me slow to realize what I was seeing, for there was a vertical window blind and a white radiator to the left on the back wall and my eye was caught by their strong contrasts of light and dark. When my eyes fell on the walls again, I realized *this is it* and nearly shouted, *Hey!*

The difference between the two walls was fascinating. Greater density was achieved not by number, but by the length of the lines. The lines collected in an orderly manner that was not predetermined. One was very aware of the count. Nelson asked how it was done and Mr. van Ravesteijn explained that four men had worked on the walls, two on each wall. After each had drawn 50 lines, the number was recorded. There really were 10,000 lines on each wall. After working for a time, they would stop and assess what area wanted more lines, here or there, until the 10,000 were drawn.

Mr. van Ravesteijn showed us three framed works by Jan Dibbets. One was a sequence of photographs taken from a single point that recorded the 360° circle. Another showed four postcards, representing the event of writing and mailing from the precise spots shown on the cards — along bridges over the canals in Amsterdam. He showed us the bulletins he sends out from the gallery and took my name for his mailing list. We gave him a copy of *Round Stone*. He seemed a bit surprised, but pleased by it, and his coolness warmed when he accepted it. He told us about Espace [gallery] and how to get there.

16 October, 1971. Saturday
This morning, we walked to Espace on the Keizersgracht and saw a show by Co Westerik — drawings using watercolour and ink, and prints. It was a really successful show; almost everything was sold. Downstairs, there was a mixed show of painted sculptures, some doll-like wall pieces by Niki de Saint Phalle, and there were some small fold-out sequential love drawings that were playful — the best things in the show.

We went down the street to another gallery called Kuntzhandel A. E. Boer. There, Geer van Velde was being shown. It was good-looking work. Nelson really liked it; not so me, and I don't know yet why not. It was somehow too easy to look at. A couple of pieces reminded me of my own *Town Image* paintings. In the room downstairs there was a small Jongkind among other works unknown to me.

We go to Mainz tomorrow.

Mainz

17 October, 1971. Sunday

We are in Mainz, Germany, this evening in the Richter's Eisenbahnhotel on Alicenstrasse.

We left Amsterdam at 2:05 p.m. We were warm and comfortable on the train. The route: Utrecht, Arnhem, Emmerich (where we crossed the border into Germany), Duisburg, Düsseldorf, Köln (these three were only 10 minutes apart; Cologne looked large and stately), Bonn (a big city), Koblenz. It was getting dark at this point, so we did not see much more. From Bonn to Koblenz, we could see castles on the hill (mountain?) in the distance. We were very close to the Rhine, on its bank part of the way.

When we left the station to find the hotel, we asked direction from an old gentleman. He walked us right to the door of the hotel, telling us tales of his own travels. He had been to India and Bangkok; there followed a fantastic array of place names and the number of months he had spent in each. He spent three months in Quebec in Canada and had been to New York and San Francisco. He stopped to ask if I was German, if I spoke German. I said no, Canadian; I spoke only English. After asking me this a couple of times he wanted to know how I could understand German (I had been translating everything he was saying to Nelson). I had to tell him I didn't know how I was doing it, but everything he said was clear to me and I was able to pass it on to Nelson.

After settling in we went out and found an Italian restaurant nearby. We had Wiener schnitzel. We shared a table with four others, two older couples. The two gentlemen were very funny in an endearing way. They gave us a fine performance, dispelling the myth that German people are cold. The people here seem to be the warmest we have encountered yet.

At the station, we learned that trains for Frankfurt leave and return almost every half-hour. We will go to Frankfurt tomorrow.

18 October, 1971. Monday

We went to Frankfurt today. It's about a half-hour by train. We took a cab to the International Book Fair. It was huge! We only visited one of the buildings, the Main Exposition; there were two other smaller buildings. We found the Canadian booth. It was much larger than the collective booths of other countries. We found Nelson's Weed Flower Press books (a bit of a thrill). Ivon Owen of Oxford University Press was manning the booth and Nelson spoke with him while I looked at the display. I saw some books illustrated by Elizabeth Cleaver and one illustrated by Doreen Foster.

Many of the booths, like Canada's, represented publishing for an entire country: Israel, Australia, Ceylon — while others represented individual publishing houses. I went into the art section. It was staggering: art books, prints, reproductions, posters, calendars. I did not know there could be so many art books produced; it is a major event when *one* is produced in Canada. Milan was represented repeatedly; Skira had a booth; several booths represented galleries. I tried to browse, but found it impossible to concentrate on any one item, surrounded by so much. We looked in vain for the *Artscanada* booth and the Marlborough-London booth. They may have been in one of the other buildings.

At the train station, we saw a sign posted for the Goethehaus and Goethe Museum. We may go back to Frankfurt to see them. In Mainz again, we went to Tourist Information to find out about the Gutenberg Museum. We'll go there tomorrow.

The toilet paper here is soft, or soft enough. It comes in the world's biggest toilet paper rolls. The roll of paper here at the hotel must measure five inches from its core and it sits out from the wall like a drum.

19 October, 1971. Tuesday
This morning we went to the Dom, or St. Martin's Cathedral, and the Gutenberg Museum. They are very close to each other.

The Cathedral is Romanesque; it was begun in 975 AD. We went into the chapel, its original structure; the altar had a wooden crucifix over it from that date. The nave is later and off it are a number of side-altars. These had altars from different eras, some very ornate, others heavy with stone. A great deal of this Cathedral has been reconstructed since the war, faithful to its past. There is a cloister and an adjoining museum. We spent time in the museum looking at ornate chalices, services, a 12th century crucifix (quite small, very beautiful), carved stone figures, some from 1250.

The windows were delicately glassed with squares of pale blue, violet, grey and clear glass with no apparent order; they worked nicely into this stone setting. The Stations of the Cross were murals (gold leaf) high on the wall. At one point the sun broke through cloud; it was a dramatic moment inside the Dom.

Outside, there is an open food market with stalls of fruit and vegetables, meats. Each stall was under an umbrella. It was busy with shoppers.

We crossed to the Gutenberg Museum where we stayed until one o'clock when they close. The Museum opens again at 3 p.m. until 5 p.m., so we went back then. We looked at the display on papermaking, learned about watermarks on paper and saw a Gutenberg Bible (this is the third Gutenberg Bible that we have seen; we saw two at the British Museum). We saw printing presses through their development and growth. We plan to go back tomorrow.

While the Gutenberg Museum was closed, we walked to the Rhine and watched the boats. I left Nelson sitting on a bench to take a walk by myself. I went south along the river, then west to St. Ignatius' Church, passing an old tower along the way that was part of the wall of the city in the 15th century. Later in the day, we found another tower and saw two boys unlock a metal door in it. When the boys left, they left the door unlocked, so we went in to see what was inside. Nothing at ground level, but there was a stairway that we didn't climb.

It is a pleasure to walk in this town. The streets are a mixture of buildings from the 12th century onward. These early structures are the most interesting. They have a pure Gothic appearance, a refined spare line to their form.

We found another church (Early Gothic, 1200-1300). It had an "ornate rococo pulpit." I thought it was so ornate, it could have been called baroque. It was St. Quintin's Church.

20 October, 1971. Wednesday
We went back to the Gutenberg Museum today. We looked at the section on bookbinding and the collection of Chinese woodcuts. There was a collection of William Morris' Kelmscott Press, 1891-1896 (100 items); books on handmade paper with hand-set pages and woodcut illustrations. In another area there was a collection of illustrators' prints. Toulouse-Lautrec and Aubrey Beardsley were among them.

We walked northward and came upon the ruins of St. Christopher's Church. (This church is where Johannes Gutenberg was baptized.) Buttresses had been built recently; they carried a carved mural. Part of the building seemed to be from about 1200. The ruined nave was a shell; walkways were built within it and a bed of red berry bushes grew at its centre. The altar area was now a closed chapel. We could not enter it at the hour we were there. We walked on past a Carmelite Church and Convent (built around 1350). Walking toward the Rhine, we arrived at the Ducal Palace (baroque, 1730) which now serves as a government building. We passed in front of this building, then, walking toward its back, we found a column, the Pillar of Jove or Jupiter (Roman, erected in 67 AD). We were confused by the information on this pillar, unable to read its inscriptions.

We walked on to find St. Peter's Church (baroque, 1750). It had undergone reconstruction, but three (damaged) frescoes remain. The main altar and four side-altars had heavily decorated marble pillars that may be remains of the original structure. They were broken across their tops as if they had been moved from another position. We went around the side of this church and looked through a locked gate at a walled-in graveyard. There were no tombstones; instead, there were large inscribed plaques cut into the inside walls. Otherwise, it appeared to be a garden.

We went on to the Roman Germanic Museum. It is housed in the former Electoral Castle (Renaissance) — and I don't know what that means. We went into a new section of the museum and spent all of our time on two floors there. We saw finds from Northern and Central Germany, England and Denmark dating from the 7th century BC through the 4th century AD. There were bones and skulls identified as prehistoric (Neanderthal). We looked at pottery, jewellery and pins, spears, helmets, an array of artifacts in an incredible number of materials: glass, precious stones, gold, iron, copper. I could not absorb it all, nor do I know enough about what I was seeing to make sense of it. We will go back.

We are no longer seeing tourists. As well, there are no tours that we can take so we seek out what is of interest from a few brochures and our own intuition. It lends a kind of privacy, or intimacy, to our looking.

The Holzturm (the old tower I saw yesterday) is known as the Wooden Tower, because from it wood was sold. The Eisenturm is the Iron Tower, because from it iron was sold. These towers, along with the Alexanderturm (near the hotel), were part of the city's original wall and served as fortified entrances. The Iron Tower (where we saw the boys enter) is now used for band practice.

21 October, 1971. Thursday

We were foot-weary after yesterday, so today we took a slow train to Koblenz to look at the landscape, the towns and the castles along the Rhine. On the trip north, we watched the east side of the Rhine; returning south we kept our eyes on the west. The train runs along the west side of the Rhine.

Going north, we saw rows and rows of vineyards running up the mountain. Returning south, we could see the people working in the vineyards, the footpaths and stone steps that led up the sides of the hills. Each town seemed to have traces of old fortifications, towers, and in some cases well preserved walls. Gothic spires again and again; towns with narrow streets curving away as we passed. There were castles on the mountain, sometimes near, some far off; some were ruins, others must be partly or fully maintained.

On the trip back (again we chose a slow train that stopped at every town) we were very close to the old walls and towers at Oberwesel. We passed small graveyards that had black stones, or red and white, sometimes crosses with little gables over them. They were colourful, charming sights.

The landscape was beautiful. The mountains were lush with fall colours and hanging green growth in some places. There is a kind of red, low-keyed and rich, and near Mainz the earth is bright orange. Approaching Mainz, the mountains disappear and fruit trees, orchards and gardens appear on the level ground.

22 October, 1971. Friday

Today we took the train to Frankfurt to see the Goethehaus and Goethe Museum and to walk around the area. Goethe's house had four floors and in all those rooms, not one was shown to be a bedroom. There were old utensils in the kitchen and the water pumps were of an unusual design. Each floor had four metal box heaters, some with tiled tops. The heaters were set into the walls of the central hallway and could be entered from behind. They were once wood burning units; now, each heater had a radiator concealed inside. There were iron grills on the first floor front windows. There was a small courtyard at the back. The glass in the windows and the window clasps looked authentic. The furnishings were 18th century. There were a number of musical instruments (pianoforte and clavichord), paintings and a collection of dictionaries in the library. There was a display of books and signatures — Goethe's and other members of the family. We could make out reference to his father, at least one brother and a sister. Goethe was born in this house. There was no information in English; we had to do our best with the German.

In the Museum, we hoped to find answers to our questions, but it housed autographs and manuscript pages by Goethe's contemporaries and literary persons right to modern times. I was struck by how many of them I had never heard of — of the early people, Goethe himself, Immanuel Kant, the brothers Grimm and Nietzsche were the only ones I knew; of the later ones, Thomas Mann (he had a brother), Bertolt Brecht, and Hermann Hesse. It demonstrated to me how unaware I am of German literature and philosophy. There were paintings: landscape, myth and a great number of portraits and many miniature portraits.

From the museum, we walked toward the Main River where we came upon a dome-shaped building, Paul's Church. All the entrances were locked, so we walked on to the Roma (I don't know what this is). It has a stepped gable front. Further along, we passed another church (it was locked, too) and an old tower. We stopped at the river and sat by the iron bridge that is a walkway over the Main.

We made our way to the Dom Cathedral (Gothic). It was begun in 870 AD, was reconstructed in the 13th century, suffered war damage in 1943-44 and was reconstructed again in 1953. There was a pamphlet in English, but it confused us, so we just walked around looking at everything. Back in the hotel in Mainz, we reread the pamphlet, remembering the parts we had seen and now that we know a nave from a transept from an apse, a great deal has been clarified. This church has five naves — we saw them all.

23 October, 1971. Saturday

This morning, we went to the Museum of Antiquities and Picture Gallery. We saw prints and models of old Mainz. Among them is the original of the 1633 print that we have been seeing (we bought a copy) even as a mural in a restaurant. It is by Matthaeus Merian, who did a thirty-one volume book of prints showing all the towns and cities in Europe. It was useful to see the visual description of all the places in Mainz that we have been visiting. We saw some 18th century statuary, early pottery and artifacts dating back to the 4th century. The museum closed at one o'clock, so we walked back toward the Rhine, passing St. Peter's and the Roman Germanic Museum.

We arrived at what was called a Promenade; it was like a carnival. There were rides, carousels of many kinds, electric cars that people could ride and bump together and a "Just from USA" go-cart track and cars that was extremely popular. We walked, looking at the rides, the shooting galleries and game machines. Everyone was having a great time. We sat on a bench just to watch the activity and noticed that a parked motorcycle was attracting a lot of attention. Strolling couples, young and old, groups of boys would gather round the motorcycle, look it over carefully, commenting to each other. There seemed to be nothing unusual about it to us, but when we passed it, we saw "Harley-Davidson" and understood.

At three o'clock, we went to the Roman Germanic Museum to look on the first floor there. It wasn't long before we both realized that we could no longer concentrate on what we were seeing, so we went back outside and sat by the fountain, watching the water until the sun was gone from our chairs.

24 October, 1971. Sunday

We are sitting at our window looking out at the thickest fog we have ever seen. We've just come back from dinner and from the station where we checked on some trains. Coming out of the station, we couldn't see the hotels across the street, just the neon signs hanging in the sky. Now, we are watching the lights from cars and buses pass and disappear out over the bridge.

We spent most of today in our room, resting, reading and sleeping. We ate at the Italian restaurant nearby. The waiters have grown used to us and treat us royally.

We plan to go to Paris on Wednesday night. We will have Monday, Tuesday and all day Wednesday to go along the Rhine, back to some museums and maybe to Heidelberg.

25 October, 1971. Monday

This morning, the fog was lifting. During breakfast, the sun broke through. We decided to go ahead with our plan to travel again by train to Koblenz via Bingen on the west side of the river and to return on the east side via Rüdesheim, to Wiesbaden. From Wiesbaden, it is only 10 minutes over the bridge to Mainz.

We took along a brochure showing most of the castles along the route. The castles were built in 1200-1300; some had additions in 1600 and were maintained or rebuilt as late as 1800.

The trip along the east bank gave us a view of the west bank that we could not see on our first trip. The towns on the east side seemed generally to be smaller and even more charming because of it. Nelson wanted to get off somewhere, but the only next train would arrive very late at Mainz. We planned to stop at Wiesbaden and walk around. As it turned out, Wiesbaden was a poor choice. The station there was miles from anything interesting; it was surrounded by a modern commercial area.

The mist on the hills made this trip a completely new experience. Where there had been bright reds, yellows and greens last Thursday, there were sombre reds and blue-greens now. The sun could not quite make it through the mist and when it did, it scorched the colour rather than brightened it. The hills were more clearly defined; the lower contrast of light and dark made some things easier to see. At some points, the mist was so heavy we would see a castle silhouetted against the grey of a more distant hill. Beautiful.

We made reservations for Paris this morning. We will leave Mainz at 11:07 p.m. and arrive in Paris at 7:10 on Thursday morning.

26 October, 1971. Tuesday

Today, we went again to the Museum of Antiquities and Picture Gallery. We spent both the morning and afternoon there during open hours. It was the picture galleries I wanted to see. The paintings dated from 1250 to 1900; there were a few pieces from 1900 to 1969 — a 1904 Picasso was among them. The works were German, Dutch and Belgian. There were some pieces by Jan Bruegel, a Ruysdael, a Rubens, a Tiepolo. This was not a "major collection," so I felt no urgency to see any one piece in particular.

There was a collection of porcelain: plates, services and figurines. Some unidentified wallpaper (could it be Boucher's?), furniture, large cabinets and clocks.

In the downstairs rooms were stone carvings from 12th century churches in the area (no longer standing). Among them were some delightful figures of saints. The heads were large with long faces, the arms and torsos were short and there was no thigh at all to the seated figure. I speculated that these figures were originally on high pedestals, high enough above a viewer to make their proportions appear correct.

I saw a poster advertising a Jim Dine show at Baden-Baden.

One of the guards told us (in German with a few English words) that a fresco had been taken from a wall and put on canvas to hang in the museum. He went on to tell us that this year he had spent three months in the United States in Arizona, in California, and he visited Mexico. He said that his son lives in Arizona, but he does not speak Arizona. On hearing we were from Canada, he went and got his newspaper to show us today's front page picture of a glum Kosygin in Canada, wearing an Indian war bonnet.

The guards at the Museum are friendly. Of course, we were in and out three times and had some conversation (mostly hand-motions) with several of them.

27 October, 1971. Wednesday
We went to Heidelberg today not quite knowing what we would find there. We knew of the old university and an old bridge. It was a sight approaching the town by train; the hills are lush with fall colours.

We took a cab to the old university. We were taken into the old town, where there was a labyrinth of tiny streets, to a building with "Universitat" over the doorway. There was a notice to visit the "Student Prison" from a back entrance, so we went round to that. Inside the entrance, there were three flights of stairs decorated with pictures and writings on the walls and ceiling right up to the prison room. There, too, the walls and ceiling were covered with names and dates (and commentary) and they were carved into the door and window frames, on tables and chairs. Some dates: 1897 and 1907 — a few fresh signatures of visitors like ourselves. On some doors there were photographs of students, each wearing his coloured hat, signed and dated commemorating the notorious visit. The prison seemed to offer no hardship beyond confinement (there were bars on the windows and a spiked gate was in the stairwell). The duration of stays seemed to be about five days. Drunkenness was probably the most frequent crime. Nelson said it looked a bit Boy Scoutish. It seems that the students were as cynical about the rewards of education as the present generation is, if one can tell from the writing on the walls.

We walked, then, through a maze of cobblestone streets with narrow sidewalks, sometimes no sidewalk at all, to the Neckar River where we sat for a while. On passing a church (locked), we looked at the little stalls that were attached to the walls of the building: book stalls, a shoemaker's, a souvenir shop. On the other side of the building, there was a group of German kids (hippies) sitting on the church steps eating and drinking, making quite a mess. We found another church that was open, but the entire interior was being repainted. The walls were painted white. The interior was thoroughly stripped; it was laced with scaffolding. Dropsheets covered the pews; one man, at the top of a pillar, was painting a leaf green. There was something precious about this sight.

We are at the hotel in Mainz now, waiting in the breakfast room. We were able to store our luggage here all day. In another hour, we leave for Paris.

Paris

28 October, 1971. Thursday

We are in Paris at the Hotel d'Isly on rue Jacob near Saint-Germain-des-Prés. We have a little blue and white room and a private bathroom with toilet, washbasin and bidet.

We spent all night on the train. After Homburg and after crossing the border into France, we were alone in the compartment, so I lay down across three seats and got a few hours' sleep. Nelson, too tall to be comfortable on the seats, was not so lucky. The train arrived at East Station by 7:25 a.m. and we came to this area to find a hotel. Two were full, but this one would have rooms at eleven o'clock. We left our luggage and went out to find breakfast.

We ate in a corner cafe and it was here that Nelson went to find a washroom. He came back to the table incredulous and told me that there was only a hole in the floor in there. We walked on up rue Bonaparte to Place de Saint-Germain and along the boulevard. We stopped for coffee at a cafe that looked more elegant than the first and Nelson checked out the "Men's." He came back (happy) to say there was a urinal and a hole in the floor. This time he gave me a complete description: size, shape, tiles, footrests — he was wondering about the "Ladies'." It was my turn to investigate. It was with overwhelming relief that I opened the cubicle in the "Ladies'" to find a little blue toilet — the regular seated kind.

We returned to the hotel and were given a choice of three rooms: one with a shower, this one with private toilet, or one without toilet or shower. Our choice was obvious.

We slept until four o'clock, then went out to eat and to walk around the area.

I have never seen so many art galleries in one area. Rue de Seine has dozens of them. We found the École des Beaux Arts where rue de Seine and rue Bonaparte meet. Walking back, a young man stopped us to ask directions to the École and we were able to tell him because we had just passed it. Then he said, "You're from Toronto; you used to live at 222 Beverley Street." (When I was at college, yes.) It was Dave Tarnow. We told him where we are staying; he said he would drop by. Nelson knew that Tarnow had published a book of poems (*A Collection of Solitudes*) and mentioned it to him. Nelson had read it; Tarnow's book was favourably reviewed by Doug Fetherling in *Canadian Forum* [1969], in the same article that gave a glowing review to Nelson's book, *Sparrows*, and to Weed Flower Press.

29 October, 1971. Friday

This afternoon, we went to the National Museum of Modern Art on avenue du Président-Wilson. The place was packed with people — such a change from Mainz where we had the museums to ourselves. There was a Picasso exhibition, a collection of his work from museums in Leningrad and Moscow, as well as the collection belonging to the National Museum. The works from Moscow were from 1902 to 1908-9. I enjoyed this show, but I was really more impressed by some works by Sonia and Robert Delaunay, by Vlaminck (five pieces), Juan Gris and another painter I'd never heard of (Manessier). There was a room of work by Georges Rouault and I saw some large Dufys that were a surprise to me. Because of the crowds it was difficult to look, so I spent less time on each work than I would have otherwise.

We have learned that entrance to all of the museums has been free for ten days and today and tomorrow are the last of these free days. This would account for the crowds.

30 October, 1971. Saturday

We got an earlier start today. We left the hotel at 11:30 a.m. and walked down rue Bonaparte to the Seine. The Louvre, in view from the left bank, is huge! We crossed at Pont du Carrousel. The size of the Louvre is forbidding in itself, so today we stayed on the outside. We walked into the garden area between the two wings of the building, then past the Arc de Triomphe du Carrousel toward the Tuileries, on into the extensive promenade with statuary and fountains to the Galerie du Jeu de Paume.

The autumn colour here is low red-brown. The sun only broke through now and then today. There was a low mist over Place de la Concorde. Nelson says that Paris is *too* grand; I say it is grand; we will have to see it bit by bit — there is no other way.

At the Galerie du Jeu de Paume, we saw rooms of Degas, works by Édouard Manet — *Déjeuner sur l'Herbe, The Fifer*, and his *Olympia*. On the first floor, there were many paintings by Pissarro, Sisley and Monet that seemed to fall together for me. On the second floor, however, each came into his own. There were five of Claude Monet's cathedral paintings. The Pissarros and Sisleys were stronger, but I'm not sure even now if I could separate them. There were rooms of Renoir, whose work still doesn't impress me as much as so many others. Some of his portraits were quite fine, but the tendency to pink and white flesh I find not just "sweet," but distasteful. There was a small collection of van Gogh, some of his last paintings. There was a room of Paul Gauguin, early and late paintings, his Tahitian wood carvings: canes, a mask, some small statues, and the Provence snow scene he painted in his last days in Tahiti. There was a small room of Lautrec — excellent to my eye. The works were mostly pastels — they had such energy and by far escaped caricature.

I saw about five works by Odilon Redon, delicate pieces: still life, flowers. I know little about this strange man; his work is mysterious to me. I don't mean his "surreal" work, but the paintings of bowls of flowers. There were three large paintings by Henri Rousseau. I reached them at a time when I was saturated, so I didn't give them much time.

Downstairs at the entrance, two very large Lautrec pieces were hung, each a scene from the Moulin Rouge; both showed the red-haired dancer (La Goulue). They were like wash drawings on raw canvas; one of them had been cut and pieced together.

I enjoyed the collection. I can't name everything we saw (so I will remember). We did see the group portrait by Fantin-Latour. The museum is small enough to go through leisurely.

I have not mentioned Cézanne! The landscapes, the still life paintings so solid and thorough — they were wonderful. The "white" of the white cloth that surrounds the apples has so much colour. I followed brush strokes here with particular interest. Cézanne's landscapes influenced cubism, but I think the still life paintings anticipate it, too. There were four still life paintings, *The Card Players*, a self-portrait, and the painting of a group of figures (bathers) that is awkward and puzzling.

We came back on the Métro so we could walk along the boulevard Saint-Germain to the Denise René Rive Gauche gallery, which shows prints and multiples. Vasarely and Soto were being shown, but the back of the gallery was stacked and being painted so we didn't stay long.

We ate tonight at the place just on the corner by the hotel. Dave Tarnow came in looking for us and sat with us over supper. He told us he is interviewing Canadians in Europe, travellers and expatriates, getting their impressions and ideas about Canada from here. He can sell the tapes to CBC and BBC. We'll see him tomorrow at noon for an interview.

31 October, 1971. Sunday

We went out this morning for a walk in this area and found some bookstores we would like to browse when they are open. We were back at the hotel by noon and met Dave Tarnow coming in. We went to our room and the three of us sat on the bed to talk. Dave taped a 15 minute interview; it was not a bad experience.

At two o'clock we were on our way to the Louvre. Because admission is free on Sundays, it would not be a good day to see very much, but I wanted to get inside to see where the painting collection is housed. We expected crowds, but we had underestimated. I have never seen a gallery packed like a train station; people were streaming through, thick crowds of people. It was like rush hour in a subway.

It was the last day of a "Tribute to Picasso" exhibition. (Picasso is 90 years old this week; he is the first living artist to have his work shown in the Louvre during his lifetime.) We found our way there, getting a glimpse of the *Winged Victory*, passing a large collection of Poussin paintings and a group of Rembrandts too quickly to absorb, and came to a halt at an area filled with a solid mass of people. We hovered at the edge of this crowd, realizing (slowly) that the stream of people we had come through (or with) were coming to this spot to see eight paintings by Picasso that had been borrowed from the Museum of Modern Art of Paris! *Eight!* We got a look at six of the paintings; the other two were hung low and were hidden by the wall of viewers.

Something about this scene at first struck me as funny, then terrible. I turned to Nelson and said, "When the Louvre lets a guy in, it's only by a crack in the door." I don't know what kind of restrictions the Louvre has, nor how it is decided what will hang and what won't hang. But this? A tribute? Eight paintings by one of the most prolific artists in history. And one can walk to the Museum of Modern Art of Paris tomorrow and see these same eight paintings hung in their permanent place! I guess I don't understand the elitist mentality — or maybe I do.

We got a plan of the gallery, so we know what we want to seek out at the Louvre now. I hope the crowds are thinner next week.

This city is hard to see. We have done quite a bit in the past four days, but we both feel remote from things. On the streets, one can only see a short distance ahead, so one always has a slightly confined feeling. The streets are grand, even at their grubbiest, and forbidding because of it. I have been curious to walk on the Champs Élysées, but we were on it last Friday and I didn't know it. For so grand and monumental a city, it is somehow very closed.

1 November, 1971. Monday

Today is a Catholic feast day, so some of the museums, most banks and department stores are closed. This doesn't really affect us, but we were sure that the museums would be packed again today, so we stayed away. Tomorrow is the regular closing day for the museums.

The sun shone today; it was warm enough for pleasant walking. We went along the boulevard Saint-Germain to boulevard Saint-Michel. The shops were closed, but the area was busy and active — the cafes were open and the street stalls were doing a lively business. There were a lot of young people (students?); the Sorbonne is nearby. We crossed to Île de la Cité at Pont Saint-Michel and walked toward the Petit Pont and Notre-Dame Cathedral. We entered the garden along the side of the Cathedral looking at the flying buttresses. We disputed the age of the building (12th century). Nelson thought it was later, but the building has just been cleaned and the freshness of the exterior is misleading. We sat on a bench, watching pigeons, sparrows and people — one man was feeding birds on the wing. Nelson seemed tired of looking today, so it took some persuasion to get him inside the Cathedral. I was tired, too, but I didn't want to miss out when we were so close.

The Cathedral is beautiful; the central nave is a spectacle. We walked the aisles, looking at the side altars. Toward the back there were some magnificent windows and we sat to look at them for a while. There were two great circular side windows; one was dominantly red, the one opposite, blue. The interior was cool and restful; the windows were the colourful complement of the stone pillars and altars. While we were there, someone began to play the organ. There were many starts and stops — the music was fragmented, but not unpleasant. The organ sounds filled the space, yet remained small in it, like the windows.

If I lived in Paris, I would come here and study the windows.

We walked back along the Seine looking at a few of the bookstalls. They sell prints and manuscript pages as well as books. We had coffee at a cafe on the left bank that faced Notre-Dame so we could look at the doorway. There are eight figures at each side portal, twelve at the centre and twenty-four stand above the doorways well below the two towers. We have no information on the details of the Cathedral, but it should be easy to find.

2 November, 1971. Tuesday

This morning, we went to the Church of Saint-Germain-des-Prés. The central nave is decorated with frescoes. The left nave is hung with paintings; the right has stained glass windows. Here, too, there were circular windows at each end. Altars continued round the back of the main (what?) — I don't have the right words to describe this. Each of the four windows above the main altar showed a figure; the others had a patterned motif.

The Church is similar to Notre-Dame, but it is not as magnificent nor as large. It looks more solid from the front; it is not symmetrical, but the single tower (spire) suggests a great height, although it is probably not as tall as the two rather squat towers at the front of Notre-Dame. Both are most interesting from the side or back because of the flying buttresses which give the buildings a surprisingly delicate (fragile) appearance.

Notre-Dame was cool stone and coloured glass; Saint-Germain has windows only at the back and it is fully painted. The pillars were patterned: green, red, yellow, mauve. All the colour was low keyed and restful.

We went to La Hume, a bookstore across from the church. While Nelson looked at the English literature, I went upstairs to the Print Gallery. There were some prints by Alechinsky (I saw his work in Amsterdam) and Tàpies. It was interesting work, but there were few artists with whom I was familiar. Vasarely was prominent and Enrico Baj, whose work I'm not clear about at all.

3 November, 1971. Wednesday
We went out this morning to a cluster of private galleries on avenue Matignon. I wanted to see some contemporary work. We must have gone to six galleries. At Wally F. Findlay Gallery we saw a show of landscape paintings by a Gaston Sebire (it was awful). Upstairs there were two Vlamincks and two Calder drawings. Galerie Tamenaga was showing a Japanese painter, Sano. I thought a few of the collages were the best things in this large body of works. Both of these galleries were plush — carpeted, large space — and the work was so bad.

Knoedler, at rue du Faubourg Saint-Honoré, was showing Picasso prints, drawings and paintings. It was a random collection that spanned his career, a good show. There were some other galleries, but we didn't bother to go in.

Then we went to the Galerie Denise René on rue La Boétie. It is on a second floor (first floor, here). The gallery space is not very large, but it is a pristine white and has good lighting from unobtrusive ceiling fixtures. The show was by Antonio Calderara and it was beautiful.

Before looking at the show, I asked for Niki Rolfe, Donna's sister, and she was called. I had to introduce us, for Donna had neglected to write. Niki seemed unperturbed by this and immediately invited us to her studio on Saturday evening. Her studio is next door to Claude Yvel's. I am to phone her tomorrow about arrangements. I told her about our disappointing morning in the galleries and she brought me a gallery guide. She pointed out the galleries of greatest interest — a handful among hundreds, it seems. She gave me three catalogues: one on Vasarely, one on Le Parc and the Calderara catalogue for the current show.

The Calderara works are small exploratory things that focus on colour, form and order. The pieces date from 1957 to the present. I have never heard of this artist; I was very interested. His colour is delicate; the forms are a manipulation of the square and rectangle on a softly coloured ground — the strong understatement.

We have arranged to take a bus tour tomorrow to get a little closer to this city.

4 November, 1971. Thursday
We did the tour this morning. The bus was a double-decker; we sat in the lower deck, for Nelson said, "If the bus turns over, we won't have so far to fall." (I don't know how he is going to get back on a plane.) There were earphones at each seat;

the commentary was taped and somehow programmed to come on at each site. One could choose to hear the commentary in English, French, Spanish, Italian, German or Chinese. The narration was often very dramatic and throughout there was music for each site — everything from "The King's Dinner" (baroque trumpet), organ music for Notre-Dame, to "An American in Paris." The pretension in this presentation was both funny and moving. Although I think such melodrama is corny, I am always touched by it.

I was most interested in Montmartre. The bus took us up the hill with its steeply stepped streets to Sacre Coeur and everyone got off for ten minutes (it was the only stop on the tour). We were able to look down a misty hillside at narrow winding streets; it is the Paris I have found in books and films about artists' lives. We passed the Moulin Rouge and Pigelle. After seeing so much of palaces, monuments and cathedrals, Montmartre seemed unpretentious, warm and real. It seemed working-class; there life is not so grand and always a little difficult.

The tour took three hours. We were dropped off at the Tuileries and we decided to see the Francis Bacon retrospective at the Grand Palais.

Three floors of Bacon! I have seen Bacon in reproductions, but have seen only about three actual paintings. Here were works from the 1940s to the present. The show was not hung chronologically, so I can't be sure of the earliest dates. The literature about the show was in French, so I didn't take time for it. Everything I have read about these paintings has concentrated on the existential, or on the grotesque imagery of his work, but I found myself involved in other aspects that became apparent on seeing so many of them. There is a consciousness of the plane, even when the "space" in the painting is shallow, rounded, or confined (claustrophobic). The use of a floating blob of white paint (and in one case, a pictured mouse) both affirms the two-dimensional plane and psychologically forbids the viewer entry into the painting. The paintings invite and repel, give all and give nothing at the same time. Is this about the loneliness (pain) of the human condition? The portraits seem to be portraits of portraits (I don't know how to say that).

In earlier works, colour seems not to have been a concern to Bacon. He worked with a lot of grey; his colours are low-keyed and scrubbed on. In the recent work, his colour is higher-keyed and often the ground (background) is painted with one solid colour. This is an odd change for Bacon to make. It doesn't make him a "colour painter" because the colour doesn't "play." Instead, the flat plane of solid colour is almost defiant, both *surface* and a barrier — like the blobs of white paint are barriers.

I have not been able to understand Bacon's work and I can't say I understand it now, but seeing this show has given me enough to have *something* about it begin to come together. We have spent a lot of time talking about this show.

We ate in the restaurant at the Grand Palais — we had lunch when we arrived, and then supper at 7 p.m. We could see, from the restaurant, a large painting by Fernand Léger. There is a Léger retrospective on, but we did not try to see it. We did quickly go through the exhibition of Borduas and the Automatists (Montreal), seeing works by Borduas, Leduc, Riopelle, Ferron, Barbeau, Mousseau and others whose names I have lost.

There is an incredible amount of art being shown in this city.

5 November, 1971. Friday
I made that neglected phone call to Niki Rolfe today, reaching her at Galerie Denise René around one o'clock. It is arranged that we will visit Claude Yvel and Chérie this afternoon at 5:30 and we will see Niki on Saturday evening.

We went out to some of the galleries in this area, those that Niki had recommended. At Galerie Dragon (19, rue du Dragon) we saw a show by Rosofsky — pastels and about three oil paintings that I thought were weak. The pastels on grey, black or coloured paper looked stronger than those on white paper (and should not have). The work was surreal — people in cages and the frequent use of a baby-doll image. We went to boulevard Saint-Germain. La Pochade had a show by A. Nicholas. The work was probably surreal, too — the small watercolours struck me as much more successful than the three or four large oil paintings in the show. There were a lot of graphics in bins. I was not particularly interested. We went on to Denise René Rive Gauche. The Vasarely and Soto show that we saw earlier was still hung, but there was also work by Le Parc, Morisson and Cruz-Diez. There were metal sculptures by Sobrino, highly polished, planar structures. The gallery beside Denise René, Galerie Alexandre Iolas, had a mysterious show of new works by Max Ernst (all dated 1971). Each work had a print collaged into it — a wood-cut or an engraving, or both; the colour was watercolour. They were good things to look at, but I didn't get much from their surrealism and visual puns. A collaborative work brought music, verse and a lithograph together (the litho was Ernst's); it was lost on me.

At four o'clock, we started for Montparnasse, taking the Métro to Denfert-Rochereau and walking to 63 rue Daguerre to Atelier 17. There, I asked for Jan Pachucka and spoke with her briefly. We arranged to meet tomorrow at 6:30. She has been working at Atelier 17 for a month now; she will show us the place and what she has been doing.

We went then to rue Froidevaux to see Claude Yvel and Chérie. Their place is a studio space with an upper loft. The studio is smaller than my painting space in Toronto and the upper loft (their living space) is less than half the size of the studio. We sat in the studio near the door on two small chairs and a bench, well away from the working space where Claude had a painting in progress. The living conditions seem primitive — no refrigerator and, it would seem, little heat. The place is probably drafty; there was a curtain hung across the door. Our poor life in Toronto seems luxurious by comparison.

Yvel was working on a large painting of a motorcycle. The motorcycle (with a helmet resting on the seat) was in the studio and his painting was on the easel in front of it. Chérie explained that this ambitious work was taking up more space than Claude's subjects usually did. He has been working on the painting for the past three months. The bike was a French model (not a Harley-Davidson), small with fine lines, and Yvel's painting of it (his classical realism) was very impressive. The studio has no electric lights (maybe the loft doesn't either). Yvel works only by daylight (the window faces north), so at this time of year he stops work at five o'clock, which accounts for the time set for our visit.

Conversation was good; Yvel seemed enthusiastic throughout — different than I remember him in Toronto. We showed them the copy of *Points of Attention* and they both looked at it thoroughly (Claude speaks English haltingly, but he reads it well) and we gave them a copy of *Round Stone*.

I asked about the tribute to Picasso that we saw at the Louvre. Claude explained, with help from Chérie, that an artist must be dead for 50 years before his work can be considered for the Louvre. The Museum of Modern Art of Paris acts as an antechamber to the Louvre. An advisory committee makes the selection based on reputation and credited value of a work. To have *one* painting shown as a tribute would be a great honour in this circumstance. The eight paintings by Picasso represent the highest honour, for Paris is still considered by most to be the centre of the art world.

We are invited to dinner with Claude and Chérie next Tuesday.

7 November, 1971. Sunday

We got back to the hotel so late after the dinner at Niki Rolfe's studio last night that I did not write here.

Yesterday at about 6 p.m., we went to meet Jan Pachucka at Atelier 17. Because few people were working at that hour, she was able to show us the print rooms and the print she has been working on over the past month. We went to a cafe for coffee. Jan is from Montreal and she speaks French, but she has found that certain expressions that she uses are not understood in Paris. She is delighted to learn of these little discrepancies. She eats regularly at the cafe we were in; the people there are friendly; they know her and tease her about her words. We had a brief talk about the Parisian "hole in the floor" and learned that at the Atelier there is only one washroom for both men and women and it has only a hole in the floor.

Jan said that you get used to it. We had about an hour to talk, so Jan is coming to the hotel today around four o'clock.

We arrived at Niki's studio at 8 p.m. Niki's space is next door to Claude Yvel's; it has working space and a loft, but it is much larger and brighter than Claude's. There is a full kitchen at one end of the studio where the table was set. We sat down to a dinner of many courses that lasted until after midnight with Niki, George and Yannick. It was a thoroughly enjoyable evening. We talked about painting, about the artist's plight in Paris and in general, the gallery situation, about the fact that no Canadian artist or Canadian gallery has a reputation on the international scene. Niki talked about her work, or lack of it due to financial difficulties, and told us that she and George are making jewellery from which they hope to make some money. They looked at our books and at my prints and slides. We talked about printmaking and George had some advice that may be helpful.

Niki is crisp and direct, a bit aggressive in manner (to her credit). She speaks French perfectly, although she told me when I asked that she spoke it with an accent. George, who shares the studio and lives with Niki, is Greek; he is a genuine nice guy who seems amused by the world. His background is in restoration — stone sculpture. Yannick speaks no English; he said nothing for the first two hours of the evening. He is a shy, withdrawn young man, the brother of the painter Claisse who shows with Galerie Denise René and who Jack Pollock has shown in Toronto. He only became talkative after two friends dropped in to speak to him about a plan to go fishing. One of the men spoke a kind of French that Niki said she couldn't understand, l'Argot. It was a discussion about this language that brought Yannick to the fore.

We were back at the hotel by 1 a.m. We will see Niki, George and Yannick again on Monday evening.

8 November, 1971. Monday
Last night was another late night. Jan Pachucka came by at 4 p.m. and we talked until after eleven o'clock. I met Jan at the CAR meeting in Toronto in September; that's where we both learned that we were going to be in Paris at the same time, so promised to get together. We talked over cognac, coffee and beer; no one was interested in supper, so we let it go by. We talked about Toronto, Montreal, the Canadian art scene in general, about painting, printmaking and photography. Jan admires Vera Frenkel's work and was very impressed by her at that Toronto CAR meeting.

We have decided to go to Avignon on Thursday. We wanted to make our train reservations today, then visit some galleries, but we got soaked by rain a block from the hotel and just came back to dry out. We've done nothing but read and sleep and eat. We will meet Niki this evening.

9 November, 1971, Tuesday

It is raining again today, but we did get our reservations made at Gare de Lyon.

Last night, Niki came by at eight o'clock; George and Yannick arrived shortly after and we all set out to find a cafe. Niki had several places in mind, so we walked around the area checking them out. (Niki wanted us to experience a real French meal in a workman's cafe.) She chose one that was slightly less crowded than the others we had seen. The three course meal was inexpensive and the food was excellent. The place had long tables with benches and the occasional chair. The tables had been brought together end to end and there were several rows of these tables parallel to each other — we sat where there was enough space for five, three of us on one side, two on the other, elbow to elbow like everyone else in the cafe. Niki took charge of ordering (in French) and it seemed to be a complex operation. The waiter was an old man who looked almost feeble; he seemed to be chatting with Niki about every item she ordered. I knew that we would not be able to eat there again without Niki as a guide.

After the meal we went to another cafe for coffee and cognac. There were few others there, perhaps because of the rain. Niki and George are going to Canada for three weeks in December. We will see them again before they leave Paris and again in Toronto in January. Yannick is leaving on Thursday to go fishing in the north of France.

10 November, 1971. Wednesday

Last night, we had dinner with Claude Yvel and Chérie. Claude, who is a member of the Independent Artists' Association, was still at a meeting when we arrived at the studio. We sat in the same spot as before, this time at a small table. Chérie showed us a book on Pietro Annigoni while we waited for Claude. I told her that Annigoni had been at the college while I was a student and had worked on a portrait over those few weeks. The students could observe while he painted and ask him questions when he stopped for a break. When Claude arrived, Chérie told him this with great excitement, and I had to retell it to Claude, this time giving details about Annigoni's egg tempera medium, his use of white wine instead of vinegar and Annigoni's glass of the same wine for his thirst. Claude and Chérie greatly admire Annigoni and they hung on every word.

We began a long, leisurely meal with many courses: soup, herring hors d'oeuvre, stuffed peppers as entrée, cheese followed by fruit, coffee and cherries in alcohol. Chérie went up and down the steps of the loft twice for each course, carrying two plates each time. She wears granny gowns, ankle-length dresses; I watched her uncomfortably every time, expecting her to step on the hem of her dress, but she never did. It was admirable. We were still at table at midnight.

The conversation centred for a while on galleries and associations. I described for Claude what I knew about the Ontario Society of Artists and the Royal Canadian Academy of Arts. We managed to discuss Claude's painting, his particular realism; Claude was willing to answer my questions, which Nelson later assured me I had phrased well. We learned that Claude is 41 years old, that he began painting when he was 13 and has had no formal art training; he is self-taught. He talked about his feelings about his style of work, and about other realist painters in Paris. It was an interesting evening; there was the beginning of a good rapport. Still, I was aware that I had no standing as a painter in Claude's mind.

Today, I went out to see some galleries in this area, while Nelson stayed here in our room to write. I went to rue des Beaux-Arts where I looked in at several galleries, but only went into a few. At Galerie Armand Zerbib, I saw work by a Labarthe, or Labisse; these were images of children — one eye, a navel and spaghetti legs described each figure. At Galerie 9, I saw prints (mostly monoprints) by a Mordvinoff; they were pop art, well done, but of little interest to me. At Galerie Claude Bernard there was an exhibition of drawings by Balthus. It was the opening; the artist was there chatting with elegantly dressed women and men all holding glasses of wine. No one seemed to notice me, so I looked at the work: pencil drawings (some watercolours) of figures and portraits. A pose was sometimes repeated in three or four drawings; many of the drawings showed only the legs of the model. I wondered if the drawings were studies for paintings, made before or after the paintings.

I went to rue de Seine, passing by a number of galleries along the way. At Galerie de Seine, there was a show by Serge Poliakoff that greatly interested me (I have never heard of this artist). The works were from the 1920s through to 1966, the latest. The early works looked "futurist" to me; the later figurative works reminded me of Klee and Kandinsky; the colour was reminiscent of Kandinsky. There were three paintings from the 1960s where the colour was muted and the shapes were organic, like Arp's. I will look for information about this artist.

I was on my way back to the hotel, so I passed by many galleries to get to Stadler Gallery. At Stadler, there were two large paintings by Antonio Saura, big aggressive things. There were some mechanically operated rubber or plastic sculptures, hanging like puppets by a Barbieri. They were figures cut out of a rubber-like material; in operation, strings drew up the material to distort the figure until it was a "bunch" (an abstract shape). There were two other artists represented. One was a Bossi, Bussi or Rossi who worked large with wide Kline-like strokes and much splatter, making a grid-like pattern on the canvas. The other, whose name was Naves, worked as if in relief on the picture plane, dealing with objects like a picture frame (within the painting), a chest of drawers (with one drawer appearing slightly opened) and a door (appearing slightly ajar). These works had a spare, dry look. I came back to the hotel along rue Jacob, passing by more galleries.

Nelson seems happy with the results of his afternoon of writing.

Avignon

11 November, 1971. Thursday

Our trip here was aboard the Mistral, a first class train that travels at extraordinary speed. The car we were on was not a smoking car and as a result, everyone on it spent half the trip in the hall outside the compartments where smoking was allowed. There, a young man began talking with us, and it turned out he was from Vancouver. (He knew Toronto well, he said, because he had gone to U of T.) He has been working in Paris for the past year with a cement company (he seemed a bit embarrassed about that). We had coffee together in the dining car and talked about art and about construction with cement. It was interesting; he spoke about the problem of the appearance of concrete buildings (Habitat in Montreal was an example), the colour, or lack of it, of cement, its lack of "warmth" compared to stone and its unsightly wet streaks after rain. It is, he said, a superior building material, but it is unloved for those reasons. He gave us his card and said to call him when we are back in Paris and from it (the card) we learned that he is "assistant to Vice-President" of the cement company (and he was a bit embarrassed about that, too).

We arrived in Avignon at 7 p.m. It was dark enough for us to feel uncertain about where we were and where we should go, but we could see the ramparts so we crossed the street and entered the old town (through Porte de la République, as it turned out). We did not have to go far to find this hotel, Hotel Splendid; we have a room with a shower, sink and bidet — the WC is down the hall.

From the train, we watched the landscape change from flat land just outside of Paris to hills and valleys. We passed town sites and farms. The route: Dijon, Lyon, Valence, then Avignon. After Lyon we followed the Rhône river. Avignon is on the Rhône; it was home of the Popes in the 14th century.

12 November, 1971. Friday

We are flagging. We went out to see the town this morning, but ran out of energy by noon. We spent most of the afternoon sleeping; we had a sandwich for supper to avoid the elaborate French dinner that neither of us can manage to eat regularly.

Our walk was hampered by a strong wind and it was cold. We walked to the Papal Palace. We did not walk around it, nor go into the gardens, because we were cold. We passed the Hôtel de Ville and a theatre on our way, then walked back to the hotel by a different route through narrow streets where the sidewalks were only a foot wide. One walks on the road and steps up on the sidewalk to let the occasional car pass. The walls of the buildings seem ancient and have a warm look to them.

13 November, 1971. Saturday

This morning we went to the Musée Calvet. It is a most unusual museum; it was colder inside than outdoors. As far as I know, we were the only visitors in it. The picture collection was on the upper floor. There were paintings by Sisley, some drawings and a painting by Daumier, a Renoir and a Toulouse-Lautrec. There were two fine pieces by Vlaminck. There were earlier works (from the 16th to 18th century), a Bruegel the most interesting among them. There was a collection of the "School of Avignon"; Vernet was prominent.

The unusual aspect of this museum was its poor condition. Not only were the walls water marked, but water had run down the walls and over the paintings staining them, too. In one room, a small window just below the ceiling (ventilation?) was open and leaves were blowing in onto the floor. Drawings were buckled from the dampness and on one, the matt board was mouldy. The frames on the paintings were chipped and sections of moulding were missing. Many of the paintings were badly cracked; chips of paint were falling off and the paintings on wood were riddled with woodworm. I've never seen anything like it.

The rooms were so cold and damp that our feet felt frozen, so we went to the courtyard and sat in the sun to warm ourselves. There were peacocks in the courtyard moving about lazily; they were moulting and they all looked bedraggled with tail-feathers either lost or trailing them while still holding on. It was a sad and depressing sight.

We went back in to look at the lower floor where there was a collection of wrought iron: locks, keys, lamps, chests. These, at least, could withstand the cold. There were three furnished rooms, but here too, were signs of the lack of care. Parts of the wooden wall paneling looked as if it had been kicked in or hit by a truck. Only the three rooms of "new acquisitions" seemed warm; they were well kept and the displays were well housed.

We have bought a book about Avignon in English. In it, I read that Stendhal visited the Musée Calvet in 1837 and wrote glowingly about it in *Mémoires d'un Touriste*. Were Stendhal to see it today, it would break his heart.

We have been to the tourist office to find out about going to Gordes, Vaucluse, where there is a Vasarely Museum. It is a trip by bus, but we cannot go and return on the same day. We plan what to do.

14 November, 1971. Sunday

Today we walked to rue des Teinturiers to see old paddle wheels on a river which had been used to drive cotton spinning and drying machines up to a century ago. Our book said this street is one of the oldest in Avignon. We found the wheels, old and decrepit and the river (a canal) with about four inches of rank water in it. The river runs along the street in front of buildings, each of which had a bridge to its entrance. One was a church entrance, so we went in. The entrance is an archway where there is a large crucifix (blood painted on the figure of Christ) with statues of Mary and John on each side of it. Then, one enters an antechamber of sorts in which there is a holy-water fountain before passing through doors into a six-sided (or was it eight-sided?) room with a vaulted ceiling in which the fourteen Stations of the Cross and three paintings hang on the walls. Mass had begun, so we sat down. The small congregation faced a central nave; the main altar had a large gold sunburst over it — I was not close enough to see it, but it appeared to overwhelm the altar. I am confused now about the shape of the room because, to the left, there was another nave as large as the central nave which housed a small chapel. We have learned from our book that we were in the Chapel of the Grey Penitent.

We walked out Porte Limbert and along the outside walls of the rampart to Porte Saint-Michel. Then we got a taxi and asked the driver to drive us around the outside of the rampart — twice. It was a fine little tour, all around, beside the Rhône part of the way. The wall is intact; we saw its portals, its towers and the old Saint-Bénézet bridge over the river with its chapel. We had the driver enter through the Porte de la République and drive to the Papal Palace where we got out.

We walked into the gardens of the Rocher des Doms. The gardens rise up and up until one is standing on the top of the rock where one has a magnificent view. We sat in the sun to keep warm, but the wind (mistral) was cold at the top of the rock.

15 November, 1971. Monday

This afternoon we toured the Papal Palace with a small group of people who assembled in the courtyard at 3 p.m. The guide spoke only in French, but we understood just enough to follow the tour. At the end of the tour we bought a book in English and with its help, we have been going over the details of what we saw (and didn't see — some sections were closed and others were not included). Written by "The Keeper of the Papal Palace," it describes how and when the

Palace was built, how it was used, and it gives some history of the seven popes of Avignon. The huge halls and rooms were empty today but for our little group; the guide's voice and our steps echoed everywhere we went. I think about those spaces when they were populated; they must have been full of life, not just with popes, bishops, priests and dignitaries, but with servants, cooks and tradesmen. The court-yard, I suspect, would be a beehive of activity and outside, right against the walls of the Palace, there would be places where people worked at their trades and lived.

Before we left the hill, we went into the Church of Notre-Dame des Doms which is beside the Papal Palace. The church was built 200 years before the Palace was built. There are frescoes on the walls and ceiling of the entrance and statues of Mary Magdalen and Martha. The stained glass windows, two on the left side, one on the right, were a rich sight as the sun was lowering. A chapel at the front left has an altar of white marble, and to the left of the main altar there is a canopied marble chair (the pontifical throne). The paintings hung on the walls were difficult to see, for the church was lit only with candles and the fading light from the win-dows. On the outside, this Church has a huge gold statue of the Virgin on top of the bell tower, too big (and gaudy) for the church. It is a pity; it even interferes with the lines of the Palace. It was the first thing I saw when we walked to this site and I've grown to thoroughly dislike it.

16 November, 1971. Tuesday

This morning we visited the Church of Saint-Pierre. So much detail to account and my terminology is so poor. In the side altars, the walls are frescoed and many have altars of carved stone. At the main altar there are gold pillars with figures on top. The choir chairs have small paintings set into their backs and large paintings hang above them. There is a carved pulpit with small statues set into niches all around it. To the right is a stone sculpture showing Mary (and friends) lamenting over the body of Christ. It is almost life-size; it has an austere look that I liked. We spent a long time looking at everything. The front doors are carved wood; each has two panels with sculpted relief figures on them.

On our walk back to the hotel, we came to the Church of Saint-Didier. We were inside less than 10 minutes when the keeper came to close — it was twelve o'clock. We returned later this afternoon and found the recently uncovered fresco from the 13th century that our book described. We walked from one side altar to another — all of them have windows. There were several people at prayer, so we moved about as quietly as we could.

After supper, we came back to the hotel and talked about what we had seen and it inspired a discussion about ritual, religion and myth.

We are packing for Gordes tonight. We will go to Gordes by bus tomorrow, stay until Sunday when we will return to Avignon to take the train to Nice on Monday morning.

Gordes

17 November, 1971. Wednesday

We left Avignon this morning at 10:20, travelled as far as Cavaillon, then changed to another bus for the short ride to Gordes. From Avignon to Cavaillon we could see hills or low mountains in the distance. On the trip from Cavaillon to Gordes we began to ascend; we must have passed through six or more very small towns along the way. We were headed toward one of the small towns built on a hillside that we had been seeing from a distance.

Entry to Gordes was beautiful, for as we ascended a winding mountain road, we could see the houses on the face of the hillside and the plain below. The bus stopped at the top of the mountain in the town square in front of the Chateau that houses the Vasarely Museum. We saw a sign just off the square that points to a 12th-century Abbey ten kilometres away.

We walked down the first street to the left, that begins a descent of the hill, to La Mayanelle, the hotel-restaurant Niki had recommended. We have a room with full bath (the nicest room we have had on this trip) that faces the street. Nelson is disappointed that the room does not have a hillside view (those rooms cost more than this one and they are all taken), but he will not suffer; this town is so small and picturesque from every angle that we can see it from outside.

I asked about the Abbey and how to get there. There are no taxis in Gordes and no tour to the Abbey at this time of year, but the owner said that she would arrange to have someone drive us there tomorrow morning. No English is spoken here; I do what I can with my French.

At about 1:30, we went out for a walk. We followed a paved road that led downward, then turned sharply into another that crossed the face of the mountain and turned downward again to become a steep dirt path. We walked this path with some difficulty, but the view was wonderful; we stopped every few feet to take it in. This path leveled out finally and we looked up to see the back of our hotel. This, then, is the view from the hillside rooms. We continued along to find that the path ascended and became a stone walkway with broad flat steps that wound in and around the buildings. We followed a path off the stone steps that took us to the edge of a grassy cliff where we looked out over the wide valley to the hills beyond. There was no guardrail or stone wall here; it felt like a straight drop and we both became uncomfortable about that, so we returned to the stone walkway. The path led us to the entrance of the Chateau where there is a fountain. We saw that the Chateau would soon be open, so we went into the little cafe across from it and had a coffee.

So much detail! But I write it all, so I can recall every step of that walk.

I don't know anything yet about the Chateau — when it was built, who built it, or who owns it now. I don't even know who is responsible for housing the Vasarely collection here — probably Vasarely himself. I would like to know who decided on the method of exhibiting the work, for it is the most comfortable large exhibit I've ever visited. Most of the work is housed in electrically operated serial cabinets and there are chairs everywhere. One can sit down in front of the cabinets or sit to study a large work hung on the wall.

The Chateau has three levels. On the first level, there is a large, long room with a carved stone fireplace that adorns an entire end wall, floor to ceiling. The [Renaissance] fireplace has thirteen empty niches [for figures of Christ and the 12 apostles] and two wooden doors, one at each end. This room had two large Vasarely tapestries hung on the window side and four more on the opposite wall. There were two large painted works (black paint on aluminum) on the wall opposite the fireplace. We sat looking in this room for so long that a lady keeper came in to tell us there was more to see upstairs.

The upper levels are reached by a spiral stairway within one of the building's corner towers. The stairs have been recently rebuilt and the slot openings around the tower have been closed off but for a circular piece of glass. One can look out these "windows" and get bird's-eye views of the town and the landscape from the various positions inside the tower.

On the second level is Vasarely's recent work — the work with which I am most familiar. The serial cabinets begin on this floor. The cabinets are double show-cases, each about 30" square and just as deep and both sides are filled with small original paintings mounted in deep matts that are the size of the case. The viewer has two works side by side to view, then one slides over the other and a third piece comes forward; the third passes over the second and a fourth piece is exposed and so on in that manner. Some of the cabinets are operated by pushing a button, but most of them are automatic, set to leave plenty of viewing time between each move. One could view everything in a pair of cabinets, then view it all over again, and again. A large amount of work can be seen in a small viewing area; there are six or eight double cabinets, back to back. We sat and viewed most of them.

Large paintings and tapestries are hung on the walls and on movable partitions. Sometimes two paintings that are the same size are hung back to back. There are two rooms on this second level. The smaller room has black and white paintings, tapestries and multiples; the larger room has colour works.

Vasarely's earlier work is on the third level. This floor has two rooms as well. The large room has eight viewing cabinets housing works from 1940 to 1950 (as far as I could tell). We looked at four of the cabinets and at the large works hung on the walls. One of the cabinets was titled the "Fausse Route" and we saw a book with the same title giving the dates, 1933-1947. The small room housed a tapestry of one of the early "stone" pieces and paintings from 1933, 1936, perhaps to 1940. The paintings were figurative to abstract, early investigations that seemed poorly directed, but I suppose, had to be painted. The inclusion of these works is an unusual aspect of this collection. The painting of three Chinese faces and another large-eyed portrait were the worst looking things. It is heart-warming on the one hand, but incredible on the other to see that Vasarely could ever have been so naive.

The place is called The Vasarely Didactic Museum and one can see why. I was impressed by a particular subtlety of the colour in the small paintings that I have not been aware of in Vasarely's work before. It may be that I've seen too many reproductions, but it seems as well to be lacking in his prints. I pointed this out to Nelson and he said that he was aware of it, too.

We have talked about what we saw at the Chateau, about culture and visual heritage in relation to the Vasarely work, about the landscape, about frescoes. We have been chewing over ideas about illusion and reality.

After leaving the Chateau, we followed another road, found a pastry shop and bought some chocolate and some cookies. On another route back, we bought some juice and apples. We had supper in the very elegant dining room here in the hotel.

18 November, 1971, Thursday
This morning we went to L'Abbaye de Senanque. It was the hotel owner's husband who drove us across the plateau and down the other side of the mountain to the Abbey in the valley. On the plateau, the driver pointed to what looked like cone shaped piles of small stones; he called these "boris." They were like small huts, for we could see they had openings (doorways). The drive down the mountain is beautiful. One can see the entire valley enclosed by mountains on the other side. One sees the Abbey from above; the stone roofs on the stone buildings meld with the landscape perfectly. Our driver was as excited by the view as we were.

When we arrived at the Abbey, there seemed to be no one about. Our driver found the keepers who live there and was told that the guide was in Paris, so the good man began to show us around himself. He took us into the dormitory, explaining in French that this was where the monks slept (sleeping gesture) on the floor (plancher) on straw mats (maïs). I was able to follow what he was saying and tell Nelson. He showed us a room that I understood to be for reading and writing. Beside it is another room with a fireplace, the only heated room in the Abbey. Then he took us along one side of the cloister and into the Church. At this point, the keepers arrived with a girl who spoke English to continue the tour and our good driver was free to return to Gordes.

The girl, Elizabeth, is the niece of the guide who is in Paris. She is from the United States and has been here since July studying at the University at Avignon. She is bilingual, but strangely, cannot translate from one language to the other. We continued the tour in English, but Elizabeth knew little about the Abbey and answered, "I don't know" to most of our questions. It was frustrating. She got us a brochure about the Abbey in which there was a folded page printed in English. She led us to a room where there was an exhibit of plans and drawings, symbols and quotations from poems and manuscripts, but she could tell us nothing about it. I thought I saw the order of the Golden Section in one piece and there was a reference to "Le Nombre" in another. I wanted to know the reason for this order and its meaning in Cistercian architecture, but there was no literature on the exhibit. And somehow, I was making a connection to Vasarely's geometry.

Nelson and Elizabeth stood and talked in the cloister while I roamed around. The Abbey is overwhelming by its purity and simplicity; it is completely unadorned. The oldest structures have barrel vaulting and there is ribbed and groin vaulting in two of the rooms. The Church is bare, austere; everything is about silence. Only the cloister seems adorned. It has four arches on each side; the arches each contain two pairs of pillars, each pair having differently decorated capitals. The pillars and the gardens in the centre are in keeping with each other, but as I looked at the capitals, I wondered, *Who did this? If this is not by one hand, surely it is from one mind.*

Elizabeth drove us back to Gordes and agreed to pick us up again in the afternoon to drive us to some nearby places.

So we went at 2 p.m. We drove down the mountain from Gordes by yet another road and across the valley below to enter a range of red stone, red earth hills (colorado) to the town of Roussillon. The town is built of the red stone. The colours are red, orange, even yellow earth — it's an incredible sight. The buildings, the streets, stone walls, fences have the same colouration and the lush dark greens of foliage are their perfect complement. Even now, I question my own eyes, so rich and fantastic were the colours of nature. It is that special red of the frescoes, the red of Vasarely, brilliant and low-keyed at the same time. No wonder I see this colour in tune with the earth. Here it *is* the earth.

We drove on along winding roads; little by little the red disappeared from the rocks until they became warm greys and whites. We drove to Apt. This town

seemed quite large. It is built on a broad shelf on the hillside, making it appear larger, more visible than Gordes. In Apt, the streets can run parallel, not on the zig-zag
of Gordes. Still, we could see the valley beyond, and further ascent of the mountain. We drove to the town's centre; I saw signs for a museum and several other sites,
and postings for campers and tourists. We passed through some of the narrowest
streets and I saw two towers that were part of an early rampart.

We began our return by another route. Elizabeth was not sure of the way, so
she followed the signs for the Abbey. We must have passed through six or seven
small villages, each a cluster of stone houses. There were new houses built along
the way, some quite finely styled, but all built of stone. Between the Abbey and
Gordes we saw more small stone huts; they are everywhere it seems. Elizabeth said
they are prehistoric houses; people had lived in them. She called them "Gauloise."
We saw some that were quite large and rectangular, but most were the smaller cone
shape. They are built with a white flat stone. The same stone is often used for fenc-
ing.

I asked Elizabeth about the Chateau at Gordes. She said that Vasarely owns it,
then added that Vasarely and Pompidou are good friends. She told us that when the
Chateau opened as the Vasarely Museum last year, Pompidou visited Gordes to see
it, arriving by helicopter on a Tuesday. The Chateau, like every other museum in
France, is closed on Tuesday. The Chateau was opened for him and Elizabeth
thought it was a great joke, "He was in there all by himself." I can think of no better way to view the exhibition.

We learned that Gordes is busy with tourists in the summer, that there are
more European and British travellers than American. Many of the homes on the
hillside are owned by summer visitors. People rarely come (or stay) this late in the
year. This accounts for our solitude. Whenever we have been out, morning or afternoon, we have been alone on the streets. Gordes is very quiet, peaceful and inti-
mate.

At Gordes, Nelson gave Elizabeth some money for her gas and her time. She
took it reluctantly, but with good grace, and we said goodbye. We walked to a spot
where we could look down on the valley and still see part of the hillside. Nelson
says that he will need at least two days to absorb what he has seen before he will
even be ready to write a postcard.

19 November, 1971. Friday
The mistral blows hard today, disturbing the shutters and sending leaves whirling
in the air. This morning, we walked to the Church on the hillside below the
Chateau and went inside. It is quite a sight. Except for the ceiling of the central
nave, the interior is entirely painted. Whole walls are painted to imitate marble; the

altars, made of wood, are painted to resemble various inlays of stone; the chapels are painted with the repeat patterns of tiles; the statues are painted. At the front, on the flat wall on each side of the main altar, two figures are painted to appear to be stone statues standing in painted niches. The pulpit is painted to resemble inlaid marble. I have never seen anything like this. It is a bright and lively interior; its simple structure is made elaborate by this tasteless decor.

We followed a road that runs steeply up the hill from the square opposite the Chateau and came to a graveyard. The fence was stone; the metal gates were locked. We could see crosses and ornamental stones above the barrier and, by only turning around, we could look out to a magnificent view of the valley. The sun was breaking through cloud, in and out, warm when it appeared, but the wind was cold. We came back, passing the hospital, to a little restaurant in the square where we had a coffee. Conversation among the group of men at the counter (farmers?) seemed to be entirely about the mistral.

This afternoon I went to the Chateau again. By moments, the wind is so strong that it could blow me off the mountain, so Nelson walked with me up the hill. He returned to the hotel to do some writing and came back for me at quarter to six. I had the place to myself; only four people passed through quickly in the first half hour of my visit. Aside from the guards, I was alone.

I went up to the third level to begin with Vasarely's early work. The earliest piece, two interlocked animal forms, is dated 1936. The Chinese portrait is 1940; the portrait of the woman with large eyes is 1945. Each of these pieces deal with stripes or a linear pattern and broken areas; they anticipate later works and that would account for their inclusion. I looked again at the "Fausse Route" cabinet (mostly works from 1947); these works, too, anticipate later concerns. I saw a "Graphic Period" cabinet (1936-1939) that I had not seen before; these works are pictorial: realisms, trompe-l'oeil, perspectives. They are masterfully done, but rigid. As realisms, they do not seduce the eye. I'm tempted to think that Vasarely was not a good painter of "things"; he either lost interest or found his real subject elsewhere.

Then the cabinets of the "Denfert Period" and "Belle-Isle" (late 1940s to mid-1950s) that show elements of landscape and the stone or pebble shape in highly varied but orderly patterns. (I think the *real* subject begins here.) These works and the "Crystal Period" (1948-1960) interest me most; I relate to them, think I understand them.

I looked at all of the eight cabinets on this floor. The guard anticipated my moves by switching two of the cabinets on automatic for me and turning the others off. I was his only customer and I was being thorough.

I went down to the second level where there are six cabinets in the large room. I began with the first one again, but having seen four of the cabinets earlier, I moved to one of the two I hadn't viewed before. (The guard on this floor accommodated me, too.) The new cabinet was "Planetary Folklore" (1960-1964). Some unusual images. Although I am familiar with the square and the circle in Vasarely's work, I felt I was seeing something different in this series. One impression: the circle speaks of air, the square, of earth. It was like a revelation, but here it is only a few words.

Of course, I got saturated. From time to time, I would simply stop trying to absorb what I was seeing and let the images pass my eyes. It was a restful exercise, for soon something would crash through to my consciousness and I would look with concentration again until I could not sustain my own curiosity and my mind went back to sleep, leaving my eyes to record what they could. I was sitting comfortably in a chair; it is a grand way to view so much work. One need only turn one's head to find a tapestry or a large painting to view.

Nelson greeted me with "L'hiver est arrive — Il neige." Snow flakes had been falling (or blowing) as he walked to the Chateau. He told me later that while he walked, he kept trying to think of the French word for snow, then a young boy whipped by him on a bicycle singing, "Il neige, il neige." So Nelson said his line to the downstairs guard who coolly shook his head and said, "Il n'y a de neige en Gordes." Nelson repeated his line; the guard repeated his. It was dark and windy when we left the Chateau. Whatever snowflakes had fallen were gone. The guard will never know.

20 November, 1971. Saturday

This morning we woke to such a fierce sound of wind that we were sure there would be three feet of snow outside. It was too cold to open the shutters to see, but on going down for breakfast we looked out a window on a green sunbathed landscape. The mistral, it seems, can't blow out the sun.

Before noon, we walked to the Chateau fighting the wind all the way up the hill and were almost blown away by it at the top. I bought a copy of the exhibition catalogue (English edition) and a few reproductions on postcards, then we returned to the hotel. It is impossible to stay outside in that cold wind.

The catalogue is as well assembled as the exhibition. It surveys the evolution of the work and is divided into the various "periods" which overlap each other by their dates. For each period two works are reproduced. The essays are made up of Vasarely's quotes and I suspect that the paragraphs that connect these quotes were written by Vasarely, too. No author is attributed for the major part of the catalogue, only for the few pages about the history of the Chateau. I found some answers to my questions. I had gone through the catalogue by three o'clock when Nelson walked with me back to the Chateau. (I'm afraid to try walk alone in the wind.)

I went back to the second level and looked at the cabinet "Black and White Period" (1951-1963), then at the two cabinets of "Tribute to the Hexagon" (1964-1971). These last I had seen before, but because of the catalogue description, they were more meaningful. (The hexagon, from which the cube emerges.)

I went into the small room to see the large black and white paintings. There were two cabinets in that room; one houses more small black and white paintings and ink drawings, linear works that are disturbed by "waves." The other cabinet has work from the early "Graphic Period" (to 1939); it is placed here, I think, because the paintings strongly herald later concerns. At this point, Nelson arrived. We viewed a cabinet together, then walked back to the hotel for an early supper.

In our room now, Nelson is reading Gael Turnbull and he is writing. He seems happy about the writing he has done over these past two days. We have talked about the link between the landscape at Gordes and Vasarely's work. Perhaps we will never separate the two again (a not unhappy thought). It was not long ago that I couldn't "like" Vasarely's work; I'm not sure I like it now, but I have a new respect for his vision and his particular madness.

So much of what we have seen has been enlarged by these four days at Gordes. The landscape, the Abbey, the Chateau and Vasarely seem to have come together to give a fresco remembered from Avignon or a wall from Mainz new meaning. This is impossible to explain.

21 November, 1971. Sunday

This morning at Gordes, we woke to a cool, dull day. After breakfast, we packed, paid our hotel bill and with about two hours before bus time, we went for a walk. The mistral was not about, but the air was cold and soon, snowflakes were falling. We could hear them; they made tiny points of sound in the still air when they fell on the green leaves and grass.

A church bell rang — once.

Nelson walked up a hill path and discovered two boris.

A fire whistle blew causing no activity at all except a weird siren echo.

We got cold, so returned to the hotel to warm up, then went to the square to wait for the bus. It was beginning to snow more heavily. In the 20 minutes we waited (the bus was late), we watched the crevices of the tiled roofs and stone walls fill up with snow and our beautiful view disappeared behind a veil of white. And we just about froze.

We were in Cavaillon before we began to feel warmed. Luckily, we did not have to change or wait at Cavaillon, but came through to Avignon on the same bus. We went to a restaurant to eat, then to the hotel. We are spoiled, now, by the openness and freshness of Gordes and the hotel there.

We have checked trains to Nice at the railway station. We leave at 9:30 a.m. tomorrow.

Nice

22 November, 1971. Monday

It was dull, but not too cold, when we left Avignon this morning. On the way to Arles we could see hills in the distance; at Arles, the sky began to clear. We travelled flat land to Marseille, passing a huge lake, a beautiful blue-grey; the landscape seemed unusually green, considering the temperatures.

It was at Marseille that we got our first look at the Mediterranean Sea. Between rocks and hills we got glimpses of a sea of the richest blue-green. We lost sight of it between Marseille and La Ciotat, but were compensated by hills and valleys of lush landscape with rich red earth appearing here and there, then cool white rock.

To Toulon, the côte d'azur, we were in a landscape/seascape, wanting to look out both sides of the train at once. From Toulon to Fréjus and St-Raphaël, we went inland far enough to lose sight of the sea. There was mountain on both sides; perhaps we rode quite high and were not aware of it because the train was on a plateau. The view was beautiful: ranges of hills and mountains, dark green growth with yellows here and there, that brilliant red earth and red rock appearing again and again, distance seen through the most delicate purples. We did not talk much.

St-Raphaël, Juan-les-Pins (pine trees among the palms), Cannes (a big place where every building we saw was a hotel), Antibes, then Nice — all along the way we saw the incredible sea, its changing blues and the sky so blue, sometimes grey, and the red rocks and cliffs with lush greens on top, pushing out into the water. The water's colours change from turquoise to rich ultramarine and at the shore, it laps cobalt. One wonders if a cup of it might still be so blue.

We reached Nice at 1:30 p.m. We are at Hotel Thiers. We settled in and went out to eat. The sun disappeared and it began to rain, so we are back at the hotel.

23 November, 1971. Tuesday

This morning, we walked to the water. We went down avenue Jean-Médecin, passing Nice's Notre-Dame, then through a garden park to La Promenade des Anglais where we sat on the wall and looked at the sea. The sea was its lovely patterned blue; the pebbles on the beach were bright white in the sunlight. We walked east along the promenade to a place were some people were sunbathing. There was a screen that reflected the sun on the group that was gathered at this sheltered spot.

We saw a girl arrive wearing coat, hat and scarf, then watched her strip to a biki-ni and join her friends. There were about twenty people sunning there; only three or four went into the water. In our coats, we were warmed by the sun.

We walked back to the gardens where there is a small amphitheatre (stepped stone seats on the grass). There is statuary, white stone, but it struck me as quite crude.

We returned to the hotel by the same route, but on the opposite side of the street. Nelson is put off by the commercialism here. The place looks clean and pol-ished; there are few tourists here now, but even without them, this place seems like a playground.

We went out this evening to look for a VO [voice-over] movie. We didn't find one. Instead, we found ourselves at the Notre-Dame Church, so we went in. The interior was dimly lit; the rosary and vespers were being said. There was a small congregation. We sat in a pew at the back of the church. The nave was tall and dark with stone pillars rising to ribbed vaulting. There were stained glass windows in each of the side altars, but with the sun gone, they gave no colour or light. There was a crucifix to the left of where we sat; we watched people come to light can-dles and pray there, each touching or kissing some part of the figure of Christ. I was moved by these various forms of devotion and by the subdued appearance of the Church.

We are at odds with this place and with each other; we have talked about what to do next. The things I want to see (like the Matisse Chapel and the Maeght Museum) are a bus trip out of the city. The history of this coast (prehistory, Greek, Roman) seems inaccessible; searching for it would mean not going to Italy. And Italy (Rome) is where I wanted to go before returning to Paris and London. Nelson dislikes Nice in spite of the perfect Mediterranean. Of course, he would have stayed in Gordes forever; he wants to return to Paris now.

We have about three weeks before we must be in Paris; our Eurorail passes will run out then. Rome is 12 hours from here by train, but even I would rather not go directly there. Another complication: Italy is having strikes in all kinds of services and the railway is threatened. We can't risk being stranded in Italy with our rail passes either useless or out of date and we could easily run out of money.

We have decided to go as far as Pisa and make some decision there. We will make reservations tomorrow to leave on Thursday. Tomorrow morning, we are going to take a bus tour of Nice.

24 November, 1971. Wednesday
We did the bus tour of Nice this morning; there were six of us on the tour. The sky was overcast the whole time, giving us a different landscape.

We went along the Promenade des Anglais to Quai des Etats-Unis to pass a War Memorial built into the side of the hill. The Memorial has a modern domed appearance, plain lines and no figuration except for a frieze in bas-relief near the bottom. We passed the harbour and went on up the mountain to a pink palace of Eastern design called "Chateau de l'Anglais." We were told it was built by an Englishman 100 years ago. It is very ornate. There seems, in fact, to be a lot of pretentiously ornate architecture in Nice — homes and hotels as well as public buildings. It shows itself off against the landscape instead of melding with it. We stopped on the hill to view Nice and the harbour; the hills in the distance were blue, muted by the mist.

We drove on upward to the Roman town of Cimiez. It is a recent excavation; we saw remains of an amphitheatre and other ruins. Nearby there is a grand hotel where Queen Victoria stayed on her visits to Nice. It is now an apartment building and although it retains its past glory, it looks as if it is melting like the icing on a wedding cake — dusty memories there. We stopped at a church of the Franciscan cloisters. The church has been recently restored; I was not impressed by the paintings on its porch. Inside, there were two altar pieces in the side chapels; one was a pieta, the other a descent from the cross. They were made by two brothers in a family of artists in Nice (named Bréa, 15th or 16th century); I was impressed by these. The main altar was ornate with gold; the entire apse was like a gold panelled screen. The ceiling was entirely painted in an Italianate style.

We walked through the cloister — simple and austere — then outside through a landscaped garden to a wall at the perimeter where we looked down to the valley at a polluted Nice, then up at another mountain where an observatory stood. The mountain was shelved with roadways.

We drove on to Gairaut, through fields of carnations (not in bloom), past olive groves (this is the time of harvest) to stop at an artificial waterfall which is, we were told, the town's water supply. The waterfall's symmetry is almost disturbing in this setting, but it was nice to look down the mountain and walk in the quiet.

We drove back to Nice to the Russian Orthodox Cathedral. This church is of a pure Byzantine style of the 16th century and it was built by Czar Nicholas II in 1902 in memory of his uncle (his father's older brother who would have become Czar) who died in Nice at the age of 26. He died in 1865; a Byzantine chapel was built on the site of his villa in 1867 and later replaced by this Cathedral. The church is built in the shape of a Greek cross; it has a central dome from which the four short arms extend. The icons took my attention; paintings covered with pearls, gold and silver (only the faces and hands were visibly painted). There were no statues here, but the paintings hung on, or were set into, the walls, and they even decorated the gold screen behind which the service is carried out. The icons were laid out as small altars, one on each side of the main altar. An altar to the left was called "the tomb of Christ." It becomes central at Easter, we were told, when the whole church is draped with black cloth.

We were delivered right to our hotel; it was a good tour.

This afternoon we went to the station to inquire about the train to Pisa (the train to Rome) and we went to the bank and bought lira.

Pisa

25 November, 1971. Thursday

We left Nice this morning at 9:55. We followed the coast for almost the whole trip; most of the morning, we stood at the train windows on the Mediterranean side to watch again the variation of blues that cross the surface of the water and the patterns close to shore. At Monte Carlo, a palace on the hill — Monaco. Then Menton, the last place in France. We passed through a tunnel and were in Italy. Before entering the tunnel, the sea was streaked with blue, purple, green and yellow; when we came out of the tunnel the phenomenon was gone. We were at Ventimiglia where we stopped for customs and passport checks. From here on, there was a change in colouration. The prettiness of the landscape and architecture disappeared. Trees were a darker green; the air seemed amber coloured and a fishing village looked like a fishing village. After San Remo, the distant mountains became higher, more pointed and angular, beyond the soft rolling green. Then Genova, a big town with three station stops and after Genova the tunnels became more frequent. My map shows La Spezia, Sarzana, then Pisa. We passed these places and many more. Between La Spezia and Sarzana the train slowed down and I saw we were beside a flatbed car of what looked like chunks of ice. But no, if it were ice it would be melting in the sun. It was marble! There were lots filled with marble slabs, marble blocks, trucks loaded with marble chips. I told Nelson that we were at Carara; the plane face of that mountain was not snow or ice, it was pure white marble! It is here that Michelangelo got the marble for his sculptures.

For a long time we sat looking left and right, mountains on one side, the sea on the other, until we were saturated by their physical presence. Palm trees, cactus, persimmon trees. The houses took on a weathered look; clothes lines hung from every balcony.

The tunnels increased until we were in them more than we were out. The landscape in daylight came as a shock and was gone before we could take it in. Then we emerged from under the mountain to a broad plain; the mountains became distant; we could no longer see the sea. As we approached Pisa, I could see the top of the leaning tower beside a church spire — this was it.

Our train tickets allowed us to travel first class, so we were alone in a compartment most of the trip. The second class cars were packed; people were standing. At almost every stop, the Italian trainmen got out and there was shouting and animated talk among them. One got the impression that they all had to get off the train to discuss which way the train should go.

We arrived here at 4:30 p.m. It was after five by the time we found this room. We went out to walk around and found a restaurant where meals were served at 6:30 (not like in France where service starts at eight o'clock), so we have had a good dinner, not too rich for our palates. Our room is drab, but it will do for one night. We will go on to Florence tomorrow.

Florence

26 November, 1971. Friday

This morning after breakfast out (no breakfast at this hotel), we checked on trains to Florence. We learned there was a train (second class) at 12:12 p.m. and another at 12:45. We were at the track at 12:12, but the little train was so crowded we waited for the next one. It brought us to Florence (Firenze) in an hour.

Our hotel is well situated in the Piazza San Stefano, near the Uffizi and not far from the Pitti Palace across the Arno. Our room has stone floors and walls that give off perpetual cold and it has a little portable heater that we hug for its little warmth.

We walked to the Uffizi today. We crossed the Ponte Vecchio. This is an incredibly beautiful place. One need only stop on the street, look in any direction to see art history unfold.

Tonight, we ate at a restaurant in a street just past the Palazzo Vecchio — a long, leisurely meal. And we were warm, for we sat near an open fireplace. We walked back to the hotel through the Piazza della Signoria where the replica of Michelangelo's *David* stands.

27 November, 1971. Saturday

This morning, we went back to the Piazza della Signoria, only a short walk from the hotel. At 11:30, we went into the Uffizi; we came out at 3 p.m.

We saw 13th century Sienese and Florentine art and work from the 14th to 16th century. Giotto, Cimabue, Botticelli, Piero della Francesca (two small portraits in profile) and a Uccello (horses, men with lances) come immediately to mind. Filippo Lippi, Van der Goes, Dutch and Flemish paintings. Raphael, a tondo of the Holy Family by Michelangelo, Andrea del Sarto, about six paintings by Titian, Veronese, one painting by Vasari — these off the top of my head.

I am running out of words. My entries are growing shorter because of it. Here, there are so many highlights I can't begin to write about them; here, *everything* is a highlight.

The Gallery is beautiful inside and out (built by Vasari). It has three corridors that give fine views of the city as well as the structure of the Gallery itself. The corridors house sculpture and tapestries; we looked at these swiftly as we walked through. It was cold inside; I wonder about the effect of such temperatures on the art.

Before leaving, we entered the restored area of a chapel. Work was being done on a lower section to open a crypt. There were some small paintings there, fragments of wall paintings and a large Annunciation by Botticelli.

I am reading the catalogue for the Gallery. I want to go back tomorrow. Our hotel room does not seem so cold; either we are adjusting or the little heater is doing well for us.

28 November, 1971. Sunday

We went back to the Uffizi this morning, staying until it closed at one o'clock. Then we walked to the Duomo. On our way, we stopped at a church. It had niches all around the outside, statues in each, put there by the guilds. The interior was being restored, but we saw two chapels (altars), its windows, the frescoes on walls and ceilings.

At the Duomo, we looked at the blue and white cathedral, Giotto's campanile and the baptistry. Ghiberti's doors, those facing the church, are magnificent. We stood for a long time looking at the ten panels of scenes from the Old Testament and the small figures around them. The little portrait heads intrigued me. They look out of their round portals, up, down and at each other. As I stood there looking at them, I thought some of them were looking at me because those that were higher on the door seemed to be in higher relief. I wondered how tall Ghiberti had been; perhaps he was no taller than I am.

We walked back to the Piazza della Signoria to the Palazzi Vecchio. The galleries were closed, but we looked at the lower court at frescoed ceiling and walls, decorated pillars and the fountain at the centre.

We went to a restaurant for a sandwich and coffee and bought some chocolate. I am reading about what we have seen. We can retrace our steps; there is so much to absorb.

29 November, 1971. Monday

We visited the Museum of the Duomo today where we saw sculptures by Donatello. We saw the rooms with the "singing galleries," the one done by Donatello, the other by Luca della Robbia.

There was a room of paintings; some were tiny mosaics. We saw a silver altar with precious inlay; it had little silver figures in little niches and scenes that covered the surface. This altar is known as the Altar of St. John and it was made by the collaboration of several artists. It is a stunning surprise to the eye, not just for its richness, but because it demands contemplation. Like Ghiberti's doors, it took a lifetime to make, so it wants a lifetime in return from a viewer.

One room has thirty-five or thirty-six sculpted relief panels that were taken from the outside of Giotto's campanile. These were made by many sculptors over a period of about two hundred years. There were diamond shaped and hexagonal pieces; they depicted biblical and mythological scenes, scenes of various crafts, of harvests, of boats and the sea. The scenes were most often about the people and their work. I really enjoyed seeing them.

30 November, 1971. Tuesday

We spent most of the day at the Uffizi, and this evening we have been reading our books. At the gallery, we revisited some of the rooms we had seen, and tried to look at all those we had not seen before.

We saw two pieces by Leonardo da Vinci; one was unfinished. We saw Rembrandt, Peter Paul Rubens, Holbein, Steen.

We returned to the painting by Paolo Uccello. It is fascinating; it seems modernist in its foreshortening of figures and horses, and especially of the landscape in the background. Before leaving the gallery, we stopped to see the sculpture of the sleeping hermaphrodite.

I have learned that the painting by Uccello, *The Battle of San Romano*, is part of a three part painting. It was painted for Pietro de' Medici and was hung in his bedroom at the Palazzo Medici. The three parts are separated now; one is here, one is in the Louvre in Paris and another is in the National Gallery in London. I want to see the other two paintings and since we will be returning to Paris and London, we can look for them.

That railway strike is still threatened; it is making us uneasy.

1 December, 1971. Wednesday

We went to the train station this morning and made reservations for Milan for Friday. Then we took a taxi to the Accademia to see Michelangelo's *David*. On entering the Accademia, one can see the *David* at the end of the long room; it stands on a pedestal in a niche-like alcove. There are about six of Michelangelo's last works along this room; they are unfinished figures only partly released from their marble blocks. Some were rough-hewn, but others were polished, still held in their rough-hewn blocks. I have seen these works in photographs and have wondered if those that are polished are, in fact, finished works. Seeing them now, I am even more convinced that may be true. While looking at these pieces, one can't help looking toward the *David*. The room is narrow; there is nowhere to go except to the *David*. It is a dramatic installation.

There were five or six people looking at the *David*. We joined them and looked at the sculpture. I thought: *This is a sculpture, not a painting. Why are we all looking only at the front of it?* There is enough space in the alcove to walk around the sculpture, so I did (then, one of the other people did, too). The pedestal must be about five feet high (as tall as I am) and I believe the *David* is supposed to be 17 feet tall. It is magnificent, up close and from a distance. There is some dispute among art critics about the proportions of the *David* (it is an early work); the hands and feet are said to be too big. If that is so, it is not something that disturbs me; it may only be a matter of size. I had a strong impression about the size; that is, if *David* were to step down from the pedestal and become life-sized, he would be about as tall as I am. (I had a similar impression at Ghiberti's doors.)

There were four rooms of 13th and 14th century paintings, works influenced by Giotto (Daddi, Gaddi and Cione).

This afternoon, we walked to the National Museum at the Bargello. There we saw a room of 12th century Tuscan sculpture. The figures were flat-faced, simplified, and often seemed playful. There was also Florentine sculpture of the same period that was more sophisticated. We saw the famous *Mercury* (Giambologna).

We found Donatello's sculpture: his two Davids, his Saint George, a cupid, two Saint Johns and several busts. Donatello's figures are small and highly refined.

We looked at some ivories and at plates and bowls by Urbino, who did the Uffizi ceilings. We saw only a small part of what the museum offers and we will not have time to return. We'll see the Pitti Palace tomorrow.

2 December, 1971. Thursday

We went to the bank and found that we could not cash our travellers' cheques. We were directed to the American Express Office. We went there and had no trouble (our cheques are in Canadian dollars); we received 600 lira for $1 Canadian, as usual. We were told that the US dollar is down to 590 lira. A young man who came in at the same time we did would not cash his cheques which were in US dollars. He went away in disgust. We don't know what has happened to the American dollar. The *Daily American*, which is printed in Rome, has not appeared today.

We went to the Pitti Palace today. Even from the outside, I knew it would be impossible. It is huge — magnificent, but huge. We went up to the Modern Art Gallery. It housed 19th and 20th century paintings; I remember one Giorgio de Chirico and two Pissarro paintings. The rest were uninteresting. The decor of the rooms is of greater interest and from the windows, we looked out at the Boboli gardens.

We returned to the ground floor where we looked at inlaid tables, gold goblets, and furnishings made of silver and gold. The walls and ceilings of the rooms were completely frescoed. It was fantastic; some rooms show painted pillars, scenes, people in landscapes. It was a surprising environment and we spent most of our time looking at the effects of this decoration. It was visually exhausting.

Outside, we went to a strange open-faced building. It was a grotto, decorated with paintings and statuary. We passed a fountain (fat man riding a turtle). We could not go further, so came away.

The newspapers are reporting more strikes. I hope the railway keeps working at least until we get out of Italy.

Milan

3 December, 1971. Friday

Our train left Florence at 10:28 this morning and arrived in Milan around three o'clock. Before leaving the Milan station, we made our reservations to Paris for Monday.

On the train, we watched a new array of landscape; there were mountains and underpasses to Bologna. The tunnels were the longest we have passed through yet; we nearly came to a stop in one of them and we came out of another to find snow on the ground.

After Bologna, the land began to flatten. Parma was the last stop I remember; then a long ride over flat land with strange vine-like trees, irrigated fields and rows of tall poplars. Those poplar trees told me we were in Lombardy. The scenery changed as we moved north; the towns became more industrial.

Milan has the appearance of a modern cosmopolitan city. We are in a pensione not far from the station. We have eaten and now we are looking at a city map.

4 December, 1971. Saturday

We took a cab to the Duomo. It's the largest Gothic cathedral in Italy. It's overwhelming, even a bit frightening; inside, it's like being in a forest. As one walks the naves, the pillars seem to move in the way tall trees seem to move as one passes.

There are three large stained glass windows at the back of the apse. Each is made up of small panels depicting biblical scenes and scenes of the life of Christ. I could not see the depictions from the pews and when I stood closer to them, the height of the windows put the top-most panels out of sight.

The huge pillars have figures in niches as capitals. The figures were too high to be fully seen, but the effect is impressive. It is dizzying. Looking up to such a height, I thought I would fall over on my head. The ceilings in the four side naves were vaulted and carved with an intricacy that made me think of tree tops in a primordial forest.

The whole structure is sober and solid with stone (there is no painted decor), but the size is almost a fault because so much detail is distant — the windows too tall, the statues too high. The inside of the church is restful; one loses the sense of one's own presence in it.

The outside of the church is crowded with statues. By comparison, the Duomo in Florence is more of a unit with its blue and white marble. The statues on the inside and outside of the Milan Cathedral number in the thousands.

5 December, 1971. Sunday
We had no plan for today; we slept late and rested. We went out for a walk and found a place to have coffee and ice cream. We watched the after-church people come and go, families with children who came in to buy ice cream to take home. The children are beautiful; they have a timid doleful look that is very appealing.

Paris

6 December, 1971. Monday
The train left Milan at 3 p.m. About an hour later we passed a huge lake. We went into the Italian Alps, then Switzerland. The train stopped at Brig, again at Lausanne and after that it was too dark to see more.

Switzerland was covered with snow; the windows of the train were frosted. The mountains, when we could see them, were rock faces only inches away from the window.

We had dinner on the train. I was surprised by the service; it was so regimented that one had to eat fast (and everyone did). We sat in the bar car from Dijon to Paris. It was a pleasant diversion since we could see nothing outside.

We arrived in Paris around 11 p.m. and took a cab to the hotel. We are warm and comfortable in a fourth floor gable room at Hotel d'Isly.

Paris is grey and dull, but the weather is mild. On the drive to the hotel, I felt quite excited about being in Paris again — crossing the Seine, passing Notre-Dame. Perhaps that's the charm of this fickle city.

7 December, 1971. Tuesday
Nelson walked to the Canadian embassy to see if we had gotten mail. While he was gone, I looked out of the window at the roofs of Paris and down into the streets below. Nelson returned with eight letters! We spent an hour reading them.

We were tired today, so we made no effort to go anywhere. Nelson read newspapers. I went out only to buy bread, cheese and paté. We ate in our room.

8 December, 1971. Wednesday

We went to the Louvre today. We went directly to the second floor to see paintings. We first looked at French paintings, then moved on to a room where Leonardo da Vinci's *Mona Lisa* was hung. There was a cluster of people in front of the *Mona Lisa*, so we really didn't get to look at it. The people all wore earphones and were concentrating on what they were hearing; most of them were not even looking at the painting. One girl had her back to the painting; she listened while looking at her shoes.

We looked at the Italian rooms — works from the 13th to 16th century. We found the Uccello painting, the second piece of the triptych. The painting is pale; it has so little paint on it that, in some parts, it is difficult to see the figures. The painting in the Uffizi is strongly coloured with that warm umber that seems to even colour the air in Italy. This painting would make a pale companion to it.

We saw a room of paintings by Rubens that were all in praise of Marie de' Medici. There were twenty large allegorical paintings. They portray this queen as if she were the Queen of Heaven. I couldn't look at these works as painting because I was too distracted by the treatment of the subject. (This is the first time that has happened to me.) Finally, Nelson said, "This is degenerate art." I agree that it is degenerate *something*, but I'm not sure what.

We saw paintings by Van Dyck, Bruegel, Géricault's *The Raft of the Medusa*, many works by Poussin, Courbet, Delacroix and an Ingres. Paintings were often hung two deep, making it difficult to see some of them, or to concentrate on a single work. It was frustrating.

We moved slowly, overwhelmed by how much there was to see. The halls are incredibly long; it is tiring. In the end, I think we saw a great deal of what we had come to see.

Tonight we bought some little anchovy pies and ate in our room again.

9 December, 1971. Thursday

Today we went to La Hume to look at their new books. Nelson looked at English language literature while I leafed through the most recent issues of *Art International, Art Forum, Studio International* and *Art and Artists*.

We came back to the hotel and Nelson stayed here to work on poems. I went out to look at the galleries nearby. I went along rue Jacob to rue du Seine, along rue des Beaux-Arts and rue Bonaparte. I saw a lot of empty work. At Galerie de Seine, I saw a show by César Domela, works from 1955 to 1971. The works were abstract, collages using plastic and wood, constructions (reliefs) really. I wasn't very impressed by the works, but I've never heard of this artist; I want to look him up.

I bought food on the way back and we ate in our room.

10 December, 1971. Friday
We went to the BEA office on the Champs-Élysées today and arranged to fly to London on Monday. When we left the office, I looked one way at the Arc de Triomphe, the other toward Concord. The trees along the boulevard were decorated with gold strips; they looked elegant and gay, but we just stood there, both of us, feeling sad at the thought of leaving.

We walked to rue La Boétie to the Galerie Denise René. We saw a show of drawings, paintings and collages by Le Corbusier (works from 1922 to 1963). It is an interesting collection and I'm glad I saw it.

We took a cab, intending to go to the Place de Saint-Germain, but got out on the boulevard at the Denise René Left Bank gallery. We went in and found that a new portfolio of Vasarely prints, the Gordes portfolio, was hung. There were three lithographs, three engravings and six silkscreen prints. The show was a treat to see; the works were meaningful and nostalgic to us. There were also two large Vasarely paintings.

We walked to the Church of Saint-Germain-des-Prés, went in and just sat for a while.

11 December, 1971. Saturday
We went to Montparnasse today. We took a cab to rue Daguerre where we met Jan Pachucka again at Atelier 17. We went out for coffee and talked about what each of us had been doing since we last saw each other. Having told Jan about our stay at Gordes, I mentioned that we saw Vasarely's Gordes portfolio yesterday. She asked excitedly, "Did you buy it?" When I said no, she groaned at the missed opportunity. (She has *no* idea!) When we left Jan, we promised to see each other in Toronto.

Then we walked to rue Froidevaux. Niki and George were holding an Open House — a studio show of their jewellery and some woodcut prints. Niki told us that the show in Toronto, on now at Bernie Taylor's, was having sales. She showed us the poster that Bernie had done for the exhibition. It showed the naked torsos of a male model facing the camera, a female model whose back was to the camera, wearing jewellery on an arm, on ears and around their necks — the female model's pendant necklace hung down her back. I thought the poster was good, both elegant and saucy, but Niki and George thought it was "not in good taste." (I was amused by that.)

We went to visit briefly with Claude Yvel and Chérie in their studio, then returned to say goodbye to Niki and George, promising to see them in Toronto in January.

We took the Métro, so went into the station Denfert-Rochereau. We were on the platform, waiting for the train. Nelson was leaning against the wall and because I was tired, I turned my back to the tracks and faced the wall. The wall was tiled; all the tiles were cracked, some horizontally, some vertically — little landscapes, little figurative shapes. Revelation! *This* is the source of Vasarely's "Denfert Period." I was standing in Vasarely's shoes.

12 December, 1971. Sunday

This afternoon, we walked along the Seine and onto Pont Neuf. I'm sorry to be leaving Paris, but excited about seeing London again.

London

13 December, 1971. Monday

The flight was uneventful, but a bit of an ordeal for both of us. Nelson especially was uncomfortable on this flight and I had no comfort knowing he was suffering. It was the cab ride to Orley airport that scared me; I think our driver was trying to break the sound barrier.

We are back on Bernard Street at the Edinburgh Hotel; we have the same room and it costs less now (off-season rates). After settling in, we went out for a walk, ate at the Milk Bar, then returned to the hotel with newspapers and an *About Town* magazine. After much pondering, we went to a movie. We saw *Modesty Blaise* — it was the kind of diversion we needed.

14 December, 1971. Tuesday

This morning, we went to the Air Canada office on Regency Street to make reservations for our return. We were able to get seats on a flight direct to Toronto on the 22nd, a week from tomorrow. Flights were booked solid on the 19th, 20th and 21st. I'm not unhappy about waiting until Wednesday; I'll probably feel reluctant to leave when the time comes.

From there, we walked to the Marlborourgh Gallery where we saw a show by Adolph Gottlieb, works from 1958 to 1971. The same young man was there as on our last visit. He greeted us cheerfully, said that he had looked for us at the International Book Fair in Frankfurt. I told him we had looked for him, too. It turned out that the Marlborough Gallery booth had been in one of the smaller buildings that we didn't visit. He gave me a copy of the catalogue for the Gottlieb show. Nelson gave him a copy of *Round Stone*; he looked at it, and said, "Oh, you don't want to give me something like this." (He was serious.) We assured him that we did.

We took a cab to Compendium Bookstore. Nick Kimberley was out so we browsed. I found two books to buy and Nelson bought the books that had been set aside for him in September.

This evening, we went to a movie — Monty Python's *And Now for Something Completely Different*. Great fun.

15 December, 1971. Wednesday

Today, we stayed at the hotel, slept, showered and only went out to eat. I found a couple of paperback mysteries in the lounge, brought them to our room and we each read one. Then we traded books and each began the other until we read ourselves to sleep.

16 December, 1971. Thursday

We finished reading the mystery books this morning. When I returned them to the lounge, I found a copy of John Steinbeck's *Tortilla Flat*; I have begun to read it.

We went to an afternoon movie; we saw *The Anderson Tapes*. It was full of adventure, but disturbing at the end.

We walked to Better Books (Charing Cross Road) and met Lee Harwood this time. He is very friendly and seemed delighted to meet Nelson. Andrew Crozier (Ferry Press) and Ian Tyson (Tetrad Press) came in and there was talk about poets and small presses in Toronto, in London and everywhere else. Poets and small press publishers know about each other whether they meet in person or not.

We went with Lee Harwood for tea at a place in Soho. The place had large wooden tables with benches. It was full of young people and so noisy that talking was difficult. Harwood invited us to a poetry reading tonight.

We came back to the hotel and after we had eaten, I tried to persuade Nelson to go to the reading. He is (we are) whipped, saturated after these months. So we are reading our books. I have finished *Tortilla Flat*.

17 December, 1971. Friday

We went again to Better Books this morning. We had another talk with Lee Harwood and a girl named Judy in the quiet of the bookstore.

This afternoon, we went to Canada House to pick up mail and then went into the National Gallery. We wandered; I was too tired to absorb what I was seeing and I still feel a strong regret about that, but I was on a mission. We found the Uccello painting, the third part of the triptych. I was dumbfounded. It is brightly painted; the horses and figures are stiff, rigid; nothing about it belongs with the other two paintings. Is this the result of restoration? Did an English restorer forget where Italy is?

We saw Leonardo's cartoon. It is the preparatory drawing for a painting by Leonardo da Vinci showing the Virgin, the infant Jesus, St. Anne and the child, John the Baptist (a similar painting is at the Louvre). The drawing is large; it is alone in a fairly small room. It is well lit, but the rest of the room is dark — a bit too dramatic for me. Still, I thought it was wonderful to see and looked as closely as I could (there was a barrier) at the drawing hand that made those lines, following them as if I were drawing them myself. *Is this Leonardo's hand or have the lines been enhanced by a restorer?* It was an awful thought, a terrible moment. It passed. The cartoon is beautiful; in it, I cannot doubt Leonardo's presence.

18 December, 1971. Saturday
Today, the Tate.

Toronto

26 December, 1971. Sunday
We have been back for four days. The flight from London to Toronto took eight hours. I had the good luck to sit beside a girl who was good company, but not too much company. Nelson sat on the other side of me coping with his apprehension by reading most of the time. The trip was not as hard on him as the flight from Paris to London.

Christmas is past. We have both been sick with colds and I have not been out since we got back. Nelson went to the bookstore to see Marty; I have seen no one yet. I've been doing laundry and cleaning this place. Nelson has been dealing with the mail; there was a huge stack of it waiting for us.

29 December, 1971. Wednesday
On Monday morning, I got our first phone call. It was Jack Pollock. He had so much news that I could hardly take it all in. He told me he has bought two houses (a duplex) on Dundas Street across from the AGO. He is going to turn it into his new gallery. He plans to feature both Canadian and international work.

He said he got a monkey for Christmas. A friend gave it to him as a gift. He won't keep it for very long, but will give it to the zoo.

Eugen Gomringer (concrete poet, art writer) was at Pollock's house and particularly liked my painting. Pollock showed him his copy of *Points of Attention*; he said Gomringer was interested and liked Nelson's poems.

Pollock then said that "in good time" he wanted to represent me, show my work in his new gallery. I was not ready for that and did not respond. It was as if I would not let myself hear it. But yes, I will be able to work toward something. On Tuesday, I called Pollock back to say that I was quite excited about the possibility. He invited us to his place for New Year's Eve; he said it will be a quiet gathering.

Yesterday, I went out for the first time since we've been back — to the bank for Nelson and over to Markham Street to see the exhibition of Rosenthal Porcelain at Pollock's. The works are made in editions; the artists were commissioned by Rosenthal to do a work in porcelain. I am not familiar with most of the artists, but there are some fine pieces in the show — there is a small, delicate Henry Moore and the Gomringer vases (with a poem embossed on them) are a delight.

While I was there, Niki Rolfe and George came into the gallery. Niki's mother was with them and I was introduced. We all went to Mrs. Pollock's coffee shop to talk; it was a reunion.

Last night, I called Carol to let her know we were back. She was extremely depressed and cried on the phone. Her state of mind is no better now than it was in September. I congratulated her on her sale and she told me a sad story about that. I wished her good luck with her CC application and heard what a fiasco that was. She told me (again) that she was going to quit painting. About that, I said nothing.

I have been working on drawings. I am drawing free-hand square shapes, packed and stacked on a square page. I'm not sure what these pieces are about but they are exciting to make and exciting to see. Each piece has a different rhythm. I think about Gordes and the Mediterranean. I will pursue this until I have exhausted it or it turns into something else.

31 December, 1971. Friday

bpNichol visited us yesterday. He must have stayed three hours, bringing us up to date on what has been happening since September and the progress of his own work. We told him some things about our trip and what we have been doing since we got back. bp asked about buying one of my paintings. I told him yes, he can look and take whatever time he needs to choose what he wants. He knew about Gomringer's compliment about my painting, for Pollock had told him about it when he was at the gallery. bp said he bought one of the Gomringer vases from the Rosenthal show.

I have been working further on my drawings. I'm really excited about what is evolving [*Graphite Drawings, Series 4*. 15" x 15"].

I received a letter from Dora Stewart at the AGO Rental Gallery, saying that my painting, *Colour Lock #9*, has been damaged ("defaced"). This is disheartening. I have tried to call, as the letter asked, and was told no one will be at the rental gallery until January 3rd. I don't know what my position is in this situation. The terms of the contract are clear (the gallery is liable for damage), but the letter says they want to return the painting to the studio "for inspection and restoration if possible." I don't know if I should accept the return at this point. If I attempt to restore the painting myself will that jeopardize the positions of liability?

We go to the New Year's Eve gathering at Pollock's tonight.

1972

1 January, 1972. Saturday
We went to a New Year's Eve party at Jack Pollock's house last night. Pollock, Bernie Taylor, Mrs. Kritzwiser, Margaret Jones (a teacher), Donna Rolfe, Niki Rolfe and George from Paris, and a friend who is a librarian were there. Other people came and went in the course of the evening. We had dinner, then sat about talking. Near midnight, everyone went outside to the back of the townhouse. Bernie passed out sparklers and little firecrackers to everyone. At the stroke of midnight, Pollock took off like a madman, ran up and down the roadway, leaping in the air, wild with joy, shouting "Happy New Year" at the top of his voice. It was wonderful to watch him.

5 January, 1972. Wednesday
Yesterday, the "defaced" painting, *Colour Lock #9,* was delivered from the AGO Rental Gallery. I called the gallery and spoke to Mrs. Stewart. Today, I wrote a letter to her giving my assessment of the damage. The painting had been out on lease to a company where someone, using a pencil (graphite), printed the word "ugly" at the centre of the face on the unpainted canvas that separates the colour-shapes. I am going to try clean and restore the painting myself. Maybe I need to talk with that lawyer after all.

18 January, 1972. Tuesday
The accountant who helps us with our income tax returns sent his assistant to make an "advisory" visit tonight. The CC bursaries will be no problem. The young man was shocked to learn that Nelson had quit his job at the U of T Library to take a writing grant; he didn't know that a person can't hold a job and a CC grant at the same time. It turns out there is a problem with the book, *Points of Attention.* Nelson can't pay me out of the sales of the book for the prints because "a man can't pay his wife." He can *give* me the money, as if it were housekeeping money, but he must declare the amount as his own income. I can't declare it as my income

even though I file as an artist. Imagine! We can deal with this, but I see a bigger problem ahead with the Nichol prints, the collaboration. We thought Nelson could distribute them through Weed Flower Press. That's not going to work.

I am working on the damaged painting using only dry methods to remove the graphite. I continue to make drawings. Every one is the same; every one is different.

1 February, 1972. Tuesday

Yesterday, Kay Kritzwiser was here to interview us for an article she will write for *The Globe and Mail*. We talked about Weed Flower Press books and about our time in Europe — at book fairs, at galleries. Today, a photographer came and took photos.

During the interview, Mrs. Kritzwiser described the evening at Jack Pollock's house with Eugene Gomringer. She told me that Mr. Gomringer walked about looking at each of the works that were hung, then returned to my painting and said "This is the best piece in the collection." Wow.

11 February, 1972. Friday

Pollock cancelled on the 7th when he was going to talk with me about representing my work. Today, he set a new date — 22nd February.

I'm working on the damaged painting using the tiny blade of my stencil cutter to loosen the graphite between the threads of the canvas, then I remove it with an art gum eraser. It's slow, but it's working. I continue to draw.

20 February, 1972. Sunday

Went in to the Pollock Gallery on Monday to pick up the key to my Markham Street studio; I left it with Pollock while we were in Europe. I asked about the two unframed drawings and the sleeve of slides [for Binghamton] that haven't been returned. They couldn't be found. Pollock had Dan Kuhn call Binghamton to track down the drawings. On Tuesday, Dan got a reply from the private gallery in Binghamton — there were no drawings there and no slides. Dan searched the gallery for them. Not found.

On Friday, I got a phone call from the lawyer. We talked about the painting damaged by the AGO Rental Gallery and he advised me on how to proceed. Today, I finished work on the painting; the graphite is all removed; the painting is restored.

21 February, 1972. Monday

I called the AGO today and spoke with Mrs. Stewart; I asked for $200 for the job of cleaning the painting. I have written a letter to formally request this amount.

22 February, 1972. Tuesday

Pollock called to say he had found the key to the studio; I went to the gallery to pick it up. He intended to come here today and did; he arrived at 5 p.m. He talked for over an hour. He said that he would delay representation until the 1972-73 season when he will be in the new gallery space. In the meantime, I am to say nothing about it; he doesn't want to cause hard feelings with Aggregation, or appear to have "stolen" me from them. He said he wants a three-year contract and that lawyers will be used for both sides. There is little else to put here for all his talk; he talked around all this giving no specifics, not even a generalization, about the terms of an agreement. I don't feel I learned very much.

His earlier plan to publish a portfolio of prints by Canadian artists (he had asked me to contribute a print in an edition of 50) has been abandoned. I am not unhappy about this. I thought he was dreaming anyway.

24 February, 1972. Thursday

We have covered the restored painting and set it aside to return it to the AGO Rental Gallery. With the easel-boards free again, I can move on to a painting. I have looked over all of my prints [*Colour Lock Prints #1-12*] as well as the six prints in the Nichol collaboration.

I've sent slides to Michael Greenwood, curator of the Art Gallery at York University, and asked for a studio visit. Pollock suggested it; he said Greenwood was interested in my work.

I'm not writing very much in this book these days. I'm busy.

I've read Barbara Rose's *Readings in American Art*, have begun the book on Moholy-Nagy; also, I read James D. Watson's *The Double Helix*.

26 February, 1972. Saturday

Yesterday, we stretched a piece of canvas on the easel-boards for a 6 x 6 foot painting and I applied the first acrylic size to it. Today I applied the second; the surface is prepared. I am working on sketches toward two 6 x 6 foot paintings and more 5 x 5s.

Since January, I have made thirty-five new drawings. From one of the drawings, I cut a profilm stencil and made a print using one colour. I made five prints in five different colours using the same stencil, but I did not pull an edition. I liked what I saw [*One-Colour Prints, Cut #1*. 15" x 15"]. Now I have cut another stencil [*Cut #2*] from another drawing and I'm printing it in my Markham studio. I'm aiming for four one-colour prints, each a different colour, pulled from the same stencil in editions of 8 or 10.

Nelson and I have talked about combining his poem, "Our Arms Are Featherless Wings," with a small silkscreen print.

A week ago, I received a phone call from the Winnipeg Art Gallery's Art Rental asking me for some of my work. They had visited the AGO Rental Gallery and saw my work there. I am to receive a letter describing their rental program.

I checked back in these books and found that the two drawings that are missing were delivered to Pollock's gallery on 30 March, 1971, for the show at Binghamton. There is still no news about them. The two 4 x 4 foot paintings that Pollock put in the group show in the private gallery in Winnipeg have not been returned yet.

1 March, 1972. Wednesday

Today, I began work on the 6 x 6 foot painting by taping the boundary and mixing colours. I made a low red (for three shapes that collect), a blue-purple (for three shapes, dispersed) and a yellow-green (three shapes, dispersed and balanced). I applied the red shapes.

Dan phoned to say the paintings from Winnipeg will be delivered to Pollock's tomorrow.

2 March, 1972. Thursday

I'm applying the yellow-green shapes. It's raining, so the paint is slow to dry.

Dan called to say the two paintings are in the gallery now and one of them has a crease on the surface. I'll go see it tomorrow; I may be able to correct it by applying a damp sponge to the back of the canvas.

I read Louis Untermeyer's *Lives of the Poets*; I'm reading a copy of *Form* magazine on Theo van Doesburg and Neo-Plasticism.

3 March, 1972. Friday

I applied the three blue-purple shapes today. The painting is finished [*Colour Lock, Second Series #11.* 72" x 72"]. I am pleased with it. I'll leave it on the boards for a few days so I can look at it.

I went in to Pollock's to see the paintings. The "crease" had simply disappeared, but there are marks on the canvas edge of the face of one painting that I will have to remove. Tonight, we carried the paintings to the studio. At the gallery, I talked with Pollock and Margaret Jones, and met Tom Seniw.

8 March, 1972. Wednesday

We stretched a piece of canvas on the easel-boards for a 5 x 5 foot painting today. I have begun to prepare the surface.

On Sunday, I cut stencils for the print for Nelson's poem, "Our Arms Are Featherless Wings," and printed it at the Markham studio on Monday and Tuesday

— a four colour print, 5¼" x 5". Today, I looked over all of them and selected 100 prints. We will make a folder for the print and poem. I am working on sketches for three more small prints. Nelson has taken the poems to Coach House to be typeset.

I received a letter from Michael Greenwood; he returned the slides and asked me to call him in May to arrange a studio visit. I also got a letter from the Winnipeg Art Gallery's Art Rental outlining the program, but their contract was not included (I had asked to see a copy of the contract). They want the two paintings. I am to send them collect; works are returned pre-paid. I guess I'll send them.

I successfully cleaned the marks off the painting returned from Winnipeg. This time I worked wet — I washed it. Scary, but it worked.

I am working evenings with Nelson at the Village Book Store helping him catalogue Marty's books. Nelson suggested that I should be keeping a written record of all of my work. I have begun a Record Book in which I'll list all my paintings, drawings and prints.

14 March, 1972. Tuesday

I completed my painting today [*Colour Lock, Second Series #12*. 60" x 60"]. Risky colour, new composition. Three "brown" shapes collect at top left; three orange-red shapes are dispersed centre and right; three purple shapes are dispersed at three corners.

About the Mark Prent show at Isaacs Gallery for which Isaacs has been charged with showing "disgusting objects": Pollock told me he met Mark Prent; he thinks Prent is strange, so strange that he believes Isaacs will have a hard time defending him and the work. I was appalled by Pollock's idea of "not normal."

I visited Carol Martyn at her studio on Sunday. I've had a call from Jim Gordaneer.

I've cut stencils for a print for Nelson's poem, "A Star Is Smaller."

15 March, 1972. Wednesday

I called Deakin Fine Art Transport about sending the two 4 x 4 foot paintings to Winnipeg Art Rental. They will pick them up tomorrow or Friday.

I called Mrs. Stewart at the AGO Rental Gallery to see what was happening with my damage claim. A couple of weeks ago, she called me to propose a plan of her own. Instead of asking the lessee to pay the $200 for damage, she wanted to offer them the painting at $200 *less* than the price. I thought this was absurd, but didn't say so; I simply asked her not to do it. I said that I wanted her to follow the agreement by asking the lessee for the payment for damage and told her not to offer them the painting at all. She seemed really disappointed that I didn't like her idea.

Today, she told me that since we last spoke, she has checked with two restorers about the painting and the claim. First, she wanted to know if my $200 charge was fair; both restorers supported it. She told each of them about her plan to offer the painting to the lessee at a price reduced by the amount of the fee and they both told her not to do that. They pointed out that, not only would I lose my fee, I would be losing part of my price. One of the restorers told her not to try sell the painting to the same firm that damaged it (and pays the fee) unless they request it; instead, collect the restoration fee from them and sell the painting to someone else. She told me all this as if it would be news to me.

So now she is willing to ask the lessee for the fee. *But*, she said, if the lessee *wants* to buy the work, she will ask the full price, plus the fee *with an adjustment (reduction) of not more than $100.* What could I say? I have to be grateful that someone has straightened her out. I couldn't have done it; she would never have accepted the same arguments from me. She hasn't been in touch with the lessee yet.

16 March, 1972. Thursday

Deakin picked up the paintings for Winnipeg Art Rental this morning. This afternoon, I worked at the Markham studio. I began the print for "A Star Is Smaller." Pulled one colour.

When I got back, Joe Nickell was here signing the copies of his book, *The Changing Air*. We got into talking about Allen Spraggett's book, *Probing the Unexplained*. Joe, a poet and magician, is hostile toward parapsychology and the occult — "all hoaxes," he says. He reviewed Spraggett's book for *Books in Canada* and totally condemned it. I have read the book; I told Joe that I thought he had been too hard on it, had taken it too seriously. Spraggett was not advocating; he was reporting. Joe adamantly disagreed with me.

Much talk tonight. Nelson doesn't want to go back to work at the U of T Library when his CC grant tenure is over. He wants to start his own bookselling business.

18 March, 1972. Saturday

I finished the print for "A Star Is Smaller" yesterday. Coach House has finished typesetting the poems; we saw the galley proofs.

Today, I saw the Larry Poons exhibition at Mirvish Gallery. I spoke with Alkis again. He said he would come to see the new work. This studio visit has been on then off since January. That's how it is. Dealers agree to see the work, project a date, cancel, make a new date, cancel again. (Artists are not a high priority.) Then they will tell you not to get discouraged.

24 March, 1972. Friday

I have made fourteen small drawings (5¼" x 5") toward a print for Nelson's poem, "Dry Spell." Today I chose one of them and cut the stencil from it for the print. I have begun to work on a large drawing — 22" x 22" page.

I received a notice about the formation of a Society for Colour in Art, Industry and Science. There will be a symposium in Ottawa on the 15th and 16th of May. Milly Ristvedt gave them my name and address.

Last night, we went to the AGO to see Mike and Kim Ondaatje's films, *Sons of Captain Poetry,* and another, a comic adventure about a robbery and a chase over the countryside that played like the Keystone Cops. In the Walker Court, the sound was worse than it had been at the Merton Gallery last year. A third film called *Genesis* (don't know who made it) fared better; it had music, but no narration.

27 March, 1972. Monday

On Saturday, I printed a one-colour print for "Dry Spell." Yesterday, I spent the whole day on my Record Book, a binder in which I'm listing all of my work — paintings, prints, drawings and the book covers I've done. I've included the work done in Mexico (1964), but no student work. I'm entering the paintings I showed at Gaslight Gallery in Kitchener (1966) and those made in 1966-67 even if I mark them "destroyed." Nelson spent the day at the Village Book Store cataloguing Marty's books.

Today, I placed an order for paint; I drafted two letters to look for teaching jobs — one to Neddeau at Central Tech, another to Sullivan at Northern Secondary. I began a second large drawing on the square page, but stopped about halfway through the work. The drawings are unsuccessful at this size (22" x 22"). I have destroyed both drawings.

I went out and wandered for a while, then saw Carol Martyn at her studio.

28 March, 1972. Tuesday

Today, I numbered and signed all of my prints for poems: "Our Arms Are Featherless Wings" has an edition of 80 and 15 AP; "A Star Is Smaller" has an edition of 80 and 10 AP; "Dry Spell" has an edition of 80 and 30 AP.

30 March, 1972. Thursday

I stripped the staples from the painting on the boards and rolled it. We stretched a new piece of canvas for another 5 x 5.

Alkis phoned and made an appointment to visit the studio on Tuesday, April 4th at 2 p.m. I am to call and check with him at noon that day.

1 April, 1972. Saturday
I worked on my new painting today. I mixed colours — a light brown (low orange, rather than low red), a red that I leaned toward red-orange by adding yellow oxide, and a blue to which I added raw sienna. I taped and applied the red shapes.

Nelson was book searching today; he is buying stock for his own book business.

3 April, 1972. Monday
I applied the "brown" shapes to my painting yesterday. Today, I applied the blue shapes and the painting is complete. In this one all three colours are paired [*Colour Lock, Second Series #13*. 60" x 60"].

Jim Gordaneer called yesterday. He asked if I knew how to remove waxed crayon from an oil painting. It seems that a visitor's child got creative with her crayons while the adults weren't watching and added blue crayon to a blue area in one of his paintings. Jim thinks I know everything ever since I removed the graphite from my painting. Aside from scraping carefully, I could think of nothing that would remove the crayon without damaging the oil paint.

I've moved things around in here and set out my paintings for Alkis' visit tomorrow.

4 April, 1972. Tuesday
I phoned Alkis at noon today. He postponed his visit until Thursday; I am to phone him again at noon that day.

I finished reading Henry Miller's *Black Spring*. Read some short stories from *Gringos and other Stories* by Michael Rumaker.

6 April, 1972. Thursday
Deakin called yesterday to arrange to pick up the restored 4 x 8 foot painting. They came this morning and delivered it to the AGO Rental Gallery.

Then I called Alkis and *I* cancelled today's visit. I did it so I could feel I had control over my own life and that was good, even if it was stupid. Alkis was probably relieved. I said I'd call again in a couple of weeks.

I'm reading Thomas Merton's *The Seven Story Mountain*.

12 April, 1972. Wednesday
We spent the weekend in Kincardine. I had to clear my work out of the room I used as a studio while I lived at home. There were *hundreds* of paintings stored there, work that I made in Mexico, at college, at Doon, and while I was in high school. We destroyed most of it. I kept only what fit in the two crates I brought

back from Mexico and a few things that I can store here. It was a depressing, soul-destroying experience, but it had to be done. I tell myself that it will be liberating.

So now I am rearranging my storage space for paper, works on paper, prints and small paintings. Nelson has built a bookshelf for new books and he has set up his back porch "writing room" again. I have done housewifery these past few days.

13 April, 1972. Thursday

I worked at my Markham studio today. I pulled new prints using the stencil for "Dry Spell"; it's still on the screen. I pulled seven one-colour prints (5¼" x 5") in editions of 6 and 10. The seven colours: blue, purple, blue-purple, yellow, yellow-orange, orange and red-orange.

14 April, 1972. Friday

I pulled eight more one-colour prints from the stencil in editions of 10. The colours range from reds to "browns" to purple.

15 April, 1972. Saturday

I pulled five one-colour prints in editions of 10. Blues through to a greyed blue-violet.

16 April, 1972. Sunday

I worked at Markham pulling nine more one-colour prints. The colours range from blue-green to yellow-green, then an orange.

For some reason today, I looked at the paintings I keep over there and saw that one of the 4 x 8s was missing. Where is it? I stopped at Pollock's on the way home and asked him if he had sent one of my 4 x 8 foot paintings along with the two 4 x 4s to Winnipeg while we were away because I am missing a painting. He said he knows nothing about it.

17 April, 1972. Monday

I worked at the studio pulling nine new one-colour prints in editions of 10. I pulled one white and eight coloured greys: yellow-greys, orange-greys, red-greys and purple-greys. I have made a total of thirty-eight one-colour prints using the same stencil. Today, I washed the stencil off the screen. I'll look over all of these prints. This work has been about mixing colour and *seeing* colour.

Pollock told me today that all the work has been returned from Winnipeg, but that he has a large crate from that show in storage at Len Deakin's. He is going to have the crate opened to see if the missing 4 x 8 painting is in it.

22 April, 1972. Saturday
I went to the galleries today. I saw Jack Chambers' show at Nancy Poole's Studio, the Yves Gaucher show at Marlborough-Godard, Charlie Pachter's "streetcars" at Isaacs and Murray Favro at Carmen Lamanna Gallery.

Yesterday at Pollock's Dan and I searched the gallery for the two missing Binghamton drawings — nothing. Pollock will be moving, so Dan said he'd watch for them when they pack for the move. No one has called Deakin yet about opening that crate.

I saw Carol this week. She has offered to arrange for us to spend a few days in Stratford at her family's house. Someone who is working at the Festival Theatre stays there alone and Carol said there is lots of room. It sounds nice. Nelson likes the idea; he wants a break from the city.

25 April, 1972. Tuesday
I visited galleries today. At Dunkelman I saw the Dubuffet show and at Jerrold Morris, Picasso. Lillian Morrison has a show by Andy Kingissepp. At Gallery Moos, I saw Lynn Chadwick's sculptures. Then I went to Mirvish and saw the Hans Hofmann show. I was most interested in the Hofmann and the Dubuffet.

Yesterday, I stripped the staples from the painting on the boards. We rolled it and stretched another piece of canvas. I laid the first application of acrylic size on it tonight.

28 April, 1972. Friday
The Toronto Antiquarian Booksellers Book Fair (the first) is on at the Westbury Hotel. Marty has a booth. We went on Wednesday and again yesterday. Today, Nelson is at Marty's bookstore while Marty does the Fair.

At Pollock's this afternoon, I was introduced to Joseph Calleja. His show of kinetic sculpture was being installed. I spent this evening writing catalogue information on cards for Nelson's stock of books. A tedious job.

1 May, 1972. Monday
The Calleja show opened on Saturday; I went in to see it and spoke with the artist and his wife. John Leonard's large painting of Pierre and Margaret Trudeau along with related drawings (some made for, some after the painting, I think) were hung in the small upper gallery. It was a good opening, well attended.

On Sunday, Nelson and I went to the opening of George Henderson's new Whizzbang Gallery on Markham Street. Original comic book art. The original drawings (some paintings) are made large scale (then reduced in reproduction), so they show the overdrawing and even the white-out where changes or corrections have been made. Some have the artist's or editor's notes pencilled on the margins.

Yesterday I wrote letters and made phone calls all day. I wrote to the Canada Council for application forms for a project cost grant; to the Winnipeg Art Gallery's rental gallery for confirmation or a decision on my paintings; to CAR for a copy of the report to the Legislature; to CAR Toronto for a fee and payment schedule. I called Mrs. Stewart at the AGO Rental Gallery and she told me that a $200 cheque for the restoration fee was in the mail.

Today I wrote to Saskatchewan for *The Structurist* and to the Munsell Colour Co. for a list of their publications. I continue to make cards for Nelson's books.

We are taking the train to Stratford at 6:40 p.m.

7 May, 1972. Sunday
We got back from Stratford last night. We arrived there on Tuesday evening and met Cynthia MacLennan at the house. We had coffee and generally got to know each other. Cynthia is in charge of the costume department at the Festival Theatre. She is the person who translates a designer's drawings and ideas into wearable costumes.

On Wednesday, we walked around and amused ourselves. On Thursday, Cynthia gave us a tour of the costume department at the Theatre. It was fascinating to see the designer's sketches, then to see how Cynthia and her people solved the problems of making costumes, sometimes faking materials to create an authentic appearance. For instance, she showed us a suit of armour made of material stiffened with glue, then painted to look like metal. Cynthia is working very closely with this year's designer to realize what seem to be pretty vague sketches of the designs. Discussion and rapport between her and the designer are important. She has worked with many designers and sees each of them as having their own "signature" or style — as we say of painters. She showed us the props department, for it is often an extension of her own department.

Friday evening, Nelson and I went to Rothmans Art Gallery in Stratford for the opening of two exhibitions: the Robert Downing Retrospective and an exhibit of Marcel Duchamp's works from the National Gallery. Downing's show was of particular interest: I like his "cube" sculptures, but I'm less interested by what he is doing with plexiglass. Robert wasn't there, but John Bennett gave a short talk about the artist and the work. Brydon Smith from the National Gallery gave a talk on Duchamp. The exhibit was a good one; there were some works I did not know Duchamp had made and it gave me a chance to see the Duchamp holdings at the National Gallery.

We had dinner out several times. Cynthia was horrified; she thinks the restaurants in Stratford are too expensive. We put a little money in the kitchen "kitty" when we left for we paid nothing to stay there — Carol wouldn't hear of it.

The letter from the AGO Rental Gallery was here when we got back with the cheque for $200 and there was a letter to the CAR membership from Judy Gouin announcing her resignation.

Today, we prepared Nelson's first list of books for sale. He will mail it tomorrow.

9 May, 1972. Tuesday

I begin to mix colours for my painting. I want a green, an orange and a red.

I received a letter from the Winnipeg Rental Gallery saying that the Selections Committee was concerned about the fact that the paintings do not use an outer frame. Surely they saw that when they saw my paintings at the AGO Rental Gallery. They have asked me to "accept responsibility for any soiling or damage" to the edges of the paintings. I can't do that — it would give them license to damage the paintings and I would have no protection at all. I don't know how to reply. I'll have to think about it.

11 May, 1972. Thursday

I applied the three green shapes to my painting today. They are alone on the canvas now, close together, playing off each other. That play will change as each new colour is added.

Dan called to tell me that the missing 4 x 8 foot painting has been found. Pollock *finally* called Deakin; the crate was opened today, and there it was with the other large painting that went to Winnipeg. I didn't know Pollock had sent three paintings; I had set out two for him, but he had the key to the Markham studio. He had forgotten that he had sent it.

I wrote a letter to Winnipeg Rental Gallery asking again for a copy of their contract. I can't decide what to do until I read the terms of agreement.

14 May, 1972. Sunday

Yesterday, I applied the orange shapes to my painting and today, the red. The painting is finished [*Colour Lock, Second Series #14.* 60" x 60"].

Milly Ristvedt came by on Friday. She is involved with a new artists' co-op that is starting in Montreal, Véhicule, and is gathering work for an exhibition. She wants me and Carol to put paintings in it. My 4 x 8 foot painting was delivered to Pollock's that day; Nelson and I went over and walked it to the studio.

Nelson had bought a stock of Ryerson Poetry Chapbooks (RPCB) from Marty. Today, we made cards for all the titles.

16 May, 1972. Tuesday

We stretched a new piece of canvas on the boards today and I began to prepare the surface. I went through all of the small one-colour prints (5½" x 5") to try to group them by their colours. They are book prints and I want them viewed that way, one print at a time, one after the other, by turning them like the pages of a book. I want to put title, edition and my signature on the back of each print so the eye will not "read," but will receive each colour, hold it and adjust when the print is turned and the eye receives the next colour. This may work, if I can find the right order.

Nelson got his first order for a book from his first List yesterday. I received Vera Frenkel's letter to the CAR membership that explains her resignation as rep. She writes a good letter. Otherwise, I spent the day reading the RPCBs for Nelson. Some of these books are "desirable" and the price for them is established; others are by less known poets, so I searched the authors and read the books to separate the "inspirational" poets from those with other things to say. Nelson will list the RPCBs as his second List.

Today I went to the Mirvish Gallery to see the Hofmann show again.

18 May, 1972. Thursday

I began my painting today after so much thought and so many sketches. I mixed colours: a green toward yellow, a red and a blue, then applied the green shapes. The colour did not dry evenly, so I will remix and rework these shapes. I feel very unsettled.

Yesterday, I read all of Nelson's poetry books: *Room of Clocks* [Weed Flower Press, 1965]; *Beaufort's Scale* [WFP, 1967]; *Sparrows* [WFP, 1968]; *Force Movements* [Ganglia Press, 1969]; *Water-Pipes and Moonlight* [WFP, 1969]; *The Pre-Linguistic Heights* [Coach House Press, 1970]; *Round Stone* [WFP, 1971] and our book of poems and prints, *Points of Attention* [WFP, 1971]. Beautiful.

20 May, 1972. Saturday

Yesterday, I applied the red shapes to my painting. Today, I remixed the red to a red toward orange and reapplied the colour to those shapes, then applied the blue shapes. I am uncertain about the result. The blue surface is disturbed and I want to rework the green.

Nelson has had almost $100 in orders for books, so far. He is going to call his business "William Nelson Books" and will open a bank account in that name.

21 May, 1972. Sunday

I've decided to change the blue in my painting before I rework the green shapes. I can't see what has failed here, but I seem to be losing this one.

I received a letter from Winnipeg Rental Gallery this week with an "official receipt" for my two paintings (the titles are wrong) and two copies of the artists' contract. The letter tells me to sign one copy and return it and keep the second for my files. Both copies are *blank*! Now, what do I do; fill them out myself? Who is running this gallery? The letters come from someone different every time. I'm drafting a letter about the edges of the paintings.

30 May, 1972. Tuesday

A frustrating week since last writing here. I finished the letter to Winnipeg and mailed it today with the signed copies of the contract (I filled out the contracts myself). They can reject the works and return them if they don't like what I have written about the care of the paintings.

I reworked the blue and the green on my painting. I can do no more to the surface. I'm still uncertain. I stripped the staples and rolled it to clear the boards for Michael Greenwood's visit last Friday, but Greenwood cancelled.

I've gotten estimates for stretchers and for frames. I'm preparing an application for a CC project cost grant ($1000).

A week ago Sunday, we spent the evening at John Robert Colombo's with a Bulgarian couple — he is a poet and she is interning in medicine. John talked about his trip to Russia as a Canadian poet/ambassador, about Vosnesensky and the group of keepers who were their constant companions there, and what John called "phoney cloak and dagger stuff." I thought some of his stories made the Bulgarian couple uncomfortable — especially the one about eating at a huge workers' cafeteria, from which he blithely showed us the tin spoon he *stole* for a souvenir. (That made *me* cringe.) Peter Dorn (Heinrich Heine Press, now in Kingston) and his wife arrived later. Nelson asked John for a manuscript for Weed Flower Press. John showed him three and has sent copies.

31 May, 1972. Wednesday

Today, I worked at the Markham studio. I pulled two more one-colour prints (a blue and a blue-green) using the same stencil I used earlier for the grey and the yellow prints [*One-Colour Prints, Cut #2.* 15" x 15"]. I pulled 10 prints of each colour, then I removed the stencil from the screen.

4 June, 1972, Sunday

I have cut a new stencil from one of my drawings and yesterday I put it on the screen [*Cut #3*]. Today I pulled a one-colour print through it — grey. The variation of colour in each one-colour print is due to the irregularities of the hand-drawn squares and the spaces between them. Each colour varies, too, because of the *character* of the colour itself. I am going to make more prints with this stencil with different colours: the form will not vary; what variation occurs will be due to the colour.

bpNichol came on Friday with his Ganglia Press material. Nelson is going to buy some of it outright and take some on consignment. Much of it needs to be collated, or trimmed, or folded. I am going to complete the covers on three of the "rare" Nichol titles. That night, I collated some of Earle Birney's *Pnomes, Jukollages and Other Stunzas* [Ganglia Press, 1969] while Nelson cut and folded a bunch of the *5¢ Mini Mimeo Series*. I'm still collating.

Michael Greenwood came on Friday afternoon. I showed him my paintings, some drawings and prints. He was interested in the book, *Points of Attention*; we showed him other WFP books for which I had done the covers and when he left, we gave him a copy of bp's *The Other Side of the Room*. It was a good interview, Greenwood is easy to talk with and he seems to like my work. He agreed to support my application for a CC project cost grant.

9 June, 1972. Friday
On Monday, I pulled a yellow-orange print using the third stencil. On Tuesday, I mixed and pulled a red print and a "brown" print; on Wednesday, I pulled a red-purple and a blue-purple. Yesterday, I counted them, numbered and signed each edition [*One-Colour Prints, Cut #3*. 15" x 15"]. My editions are 7-10 with 1-3 AP. I'm really happy with these prints.

I have finished the lettering on the covers of the Nichol titles that bp left incomplete. I imitate his drawing hand. bp brought one completed copy of each title and I worked from those. I did the hand lettering on sixteen copies of *The Langwage The Langwedge* [Ganglia Press, 1966], on four copies of *Portrait of David* [Ganglia Press, 1966] and on fourteen copies of *The Chocolate Poem* [Ganglia Press, 1967]. It was fun.

I have talked with Pollock about the CC project cost grant. He will support my application.

Nelson is working at Marty's most days now; we work on Nelson's book stock at night.

11 June, 1972. Sunday
My stretchers were delivered yesterday: five 60" x 60" and four 72" x 72". Today we unrolled the last three paintings and put them on stretchers. I have them where I can look at all of them. I'm happy with two of them, but I can see now that the last painting I did is a failure. I will strip it off the stretcher and roll it up again.

16 June, 1972. Friday

I am working on sketches for a 6 x 6 foot painting. I want a new subtlety of colour on this big painting as well as a new contrast. I am still looking for the order, the placement of the colours.

bp came by twice this week; once, to bring a batch of poetry magazines that Nelson is buying from him for stock and again to talk with me about a writing project that he and Steve McCaffery are doing called TRG (Toronto Research Group). Their collaborations will be published in *Open Letter*. They are going to do a TRG Report on "narrative" and bp asked me to contribute an article. He wants me to write about visual art as narrative. He thinks I can do this! I'm not so sure.

Today, I talked with Lois Steen. She will take slides of my new paintings when I get them all on stretchers.

I am thinking about printing a series of books using my silkscreen equipment. I could combine letterpress and silkscreen, like Nelson's poems and my prints, or print some of bp's concrete images. I want to call it Seripress. A silkscreen print is a serigraph; ergo Seripress. Nelson likes the idea of me starting my own little press.

18 June, 1972. Sunday

We stretched a piece of canvas on the easel-boards for a 6 x 6 foot painting yesterday and today I finished preparing the surface.

I finished my application for the CC project cost grant. I'll mail it tomorrow along with my letters to Greenwood and to Pollock. I typed up some points from the notes I made for the article "on narrative" then threw it away. It was garbage.

I've been setting up files — correspondence to galleries, CAR, CCA, etc. I'm going to reorganize my slides, too, to be sure I keep a complete set of slides for myself.

Nelson worked at Marty's today until 8 p.m.

19 June, 1972. Monday

I taped the edge of my canvas this morning and began to mix colours. I applied the first colour, a blue that I lowered and softened with raw sienna. I went on and applied the second colour, a blue-green. The third colour is a low yellow; I have it ready.

20 June, 1972. Tuesday

I applied the yellow shapes today. The painting is complete [*Colour Lock, Second Series # 15*. 72" x 72"]. It works.

22 June, 1972. Thursday
Yesterday, I stripped the staples from my painting and we put it on a stretcher. I like what is happening here. There is subtlety in the combination of the blue and blue-green shapes and the low yellow shapes contrast with them.

bp visited today. He wants Nelson to print a Ganglia Press index for him. I told him about my idea for Seripress and we talked about the six Milt the Morph prints. He wants me to add two more prints to the series: one, a print of the Colour Lock, like the 4 x 12 foot painting he saw, and another of the contours of those shapes, like the drawing I made for him to work with. They will become a portfolio of prints from Seripress. He asked me for a title; I said, *The Adventures of Milt the Morph in Colour.*

25 June, 1972. Sunday
So much bad weather. Wind and rain — hurricanes in NY State. Not only has the small skylight been dripping, but the bathroom ceiling is leaking now. I went over to Markham yesterday to check the windows in the studio.

I have been writing letters and doing housewifery. I am working on sketches toward the Colour Lock print for the Milt series. I am reading *The Dawn of a New Era: 1250-1453* by Edward P. Cheyney.

27 June, 1972. Tuesday
My order of screen wash and solvent was delivered yesterday, so I've been cleaning screens at the Markham studio these past two days. Today, I cut the stencils for the two prints for the Milt series.

Mrs. Stewart called yesterday from AGO Rental Gallery. They want to return my two graphite drawings and look at slides of two 5 x 5 foot Colour Lock paintings for a new consignment. I'll go down tomorrow.

Dropped in at Pollock's yesterday. Pollock told me about the dinner party he had at his house for Wattenmaker, the new curator at the AGO. Pollock and his other dinner guests are skeptical about this man (he did his thesis on Jean Hugo, an artist who painted screens and who nobody seemed to know of, or care about). CAR is up in arms because Wattenmaker is another import, an American.

30 June, 1972. Friday
I went to AGO Rental on Wednesday to deliver my slides and pick up my drawings. I learned that someone from Women's College Hospital has shown an interest in my work and is looking for a painting for a particular space at the hospital. Mrs. Stewart thinks that the two 5 x 5 Colour Lock paintings, hung side by side,

could hang in the space. I told her about the 5 x 10 foot painting, *Colour Lock #15*. Yesterday, I mailed her a slide of that painting to show to the woman who is selecting for the hospital.

I saw Jim Williamson at AGO. He will call me about the children's classes. Now that the CC bursary is over, I need teaching jobs.

Lois Steen is going to make my slides in exchange for some of my work — her idea. I pay for the film and processing.

Yesterday I worked with the small (5¼" x 5") one-colour prints again. I ordered them into a "1st sequence" of fourteen prints, a "2nd sequence" of thirteen prints and a "3rd sequence" of eight prints — thirty-five prints in all, each in an edition of 10. Three prints are left out-of-sequence.

Today I put the "frames" stencil for Milt on the large screen at the Markham studio. Went in to Mirvish to see the group show: Olitski, Noland, Poons, Stella, Frankenthaler, Motherwell, and Bush. At Pollock's they were in the process of hanging works by Claisse, Max Bill, Vasarely and others. I'll go in again when the show is up.

4 July, 1972. Tuesday

I tried to print "frames" on Saturday, but the humidity was high and the screen stretched, so I stopped printing. I have not gone back to that job.

I wrote to the Winnipeg Rental Gallery to find out if they have decided about the paintings. This business has been going on for over five months with no contract.

Nelson is spending time book searching, mainly Canadian literature. He found a book for me: *Art under a Dictatorship* by Hellmut Lehmann-Haupt. I was not aware of just how thorough Hitler's campaign against "degenerate art" had been. Disturbing.

Today we stretched a piece of canvas on the easel-boards for another 6 x 6 foot painting.

10 July, 1972. Monday

I went over my sketches for the new painting today. I'm about ready to begin. I have been cataloguing books; Nelson has built some new bookshelves. He is working regularly at Marty's — sometimes, long hours. Marty will be moving the Village Book Store from Gerrard Street to Yorkville Avenue— from one "village" to another. Nelson saw the new place last week.

I received the entry forms for the Vancouver Art Gallery's jury show called SCAN (Survey of Canadian Art Now). The jury will select slides — not works *from* slides, but *slides*. The gallery will keep the slides for a slide archive.

15 July, 1972. Saturday
I have finished my painting [*Colour Lock, Second Series #16*. 72" x 72"]. The colours: three blue-green shapes (collected at top right and centre), three low red shapes (collected at bottom left) and three orange shapes (paired at top left, the third at bottom right). The orange was hard to find; I mixed, then adjusted it several times. I applied the orange last. I like what I see happening.

bp came by yesterday with the manuscript for the *Gronk* index, stayed and talked a while. I went out to Mirvish Gallery — a new Bush painting is in the show. I went in to see Pollock's show, too.

I am reading bp's *Martyrology* [Coach House Press].

16 July, 1972. Sunday
Winnipeg Rental Gallery has returned one page of the contract, signed and dated, with a note written on it saying *they forgot*. The paintings are accepted and consigned (for better or for worse). No mention of my letter.

Nelson book searched yesterday and came back with a book on Kandinsky for me. Mr. Wenn [the landlord] came up from the store. Water has finally run down two floors and is leaking into the store, so maybe the leaks up here will get fixed now. I showed him the skylight, the bathroom ceiling and the stove and sink while I was at it.

23 July, 1972. Sunday
It has been too hot to work this week. I tried drawing and was unsuccessful, so I have been reading, writing letters, cataloguing books and addressing envelopes for Nelson's next List. I finished completing copies of bp's *A Vision in the U of T Stacks* [Ganglia Press, 1966] and sorted and folded more of the *5¢ Mini Mimeo* series.

I heard from the AGO Rental Gallery. They want the 5 x 10 foot Colour Lock painting (for Women's College Hospital) *and* the two 5 x 5 foot paintings for a new consignment. They have revised the terms of their contract. Earlier, all transportation costs were paid by the gallery; now, those costs will be shared — I will pay to deliver works to the gallery, they will pay for returns to the studio.

I've read Brigit Patmore's memoir and the book on Salvador Dali. Read *Reflected Lights* by Frank Panabaker — really enjoyed it. I read a book on the History of the Church; it is about Catholicism and was written by a Protestant. Incredible. A revelation for me about Protestantism. I guess I should have known what I was getting into because someone had painted the cover of this book *orange*.

I went to Marty's with Nelson this afternoon. I read while he worked. I looked through a copy of Dan Kuhn's book, *The Pustulate Youth Excruciatingly*

Groaned. It's a big book — too big for "perfect" binding. (That word fools people.) We ate tonight in Chinatown.

30 July, 1972. Sunday
Sharkey [Art Presentation Associates] picked up the three paintings for the AGO Rental Gallery on Thursday. Nelson helped him carry and Sharkey told him that my work is well constructed. While they were taking the 5 x 10 out, he said, "You'll get your purchase on this one." It was delivered directly to Women's College Hospital (a rental for 3 months) to hang in the main entrance lounge. The gallery paid the transportation for it; I am billed for the two 5 x 5s that went to the AGO gallery — $12.

No real work this week. I'm cataloguing books. I saw Carol; Jim visited. bp came by; he said he has a couple of visual poem sequences for Seripress. He's going to bring them next time.

Nelson bought a fifteen-volume set of Oscar Wilde (1909). I read *The Life of Oscar Wilde* from it. I've sent seventeen slides to Vancouver for SCAN.

4 August, 1972. Friday
Yesterday, bp brought me his drawings for Seripress, two sequences: *Aleph Unit* and *Unit of Four*. He also brought a typewritten page of his thoughts about doing the Milt prints. He wants me to write a page, too — my thoughts about the collaboration. The idea is to use them as an Introduction for the portfolio. I don't think I can say anything he hasn't already said and he has said it better than I could have. I began the layout for bp's drawings today — size of page — and have begun to cut the stencils.

I saw Carol today. I dropped in to Pollock's. Jack talked again about representing my work, but nothing is clear.

6 August, 1972. Sunday
Lois Steen came today to look at the paintings to be photographed. She wants to do what she calls "a dry run" on Friday.

I've written to CC Art Bank to inquire about this new purchasing program.

Nelson and I talked about the situation with Pollock. He still insists on secrecy and that has become awkward because he talks to people about my work — people tell me about it and encourage me to ask him to do a show. On Friday, he described another unrealistic plan. Even if he could do it, I wouldn't consider it. Then he said that I was going to have to "make a commitment to the gallery" — as if *I* were the hold-up. When I told this to Nelson, he said: "Make a commitment to *what!*" He has listened to Pollock and knows he has said nothing yet. I sour on the whole thing. I expect there will be no "representation" and no show.

10 August, 1972. Thursday

I called Alkis at Mirvish Gallery on Tuesday and asked him if he would look at my new work. He said he'd come Wednesday at 2 p.m., postponed to today, and miraculously, he showed up this afternoon. The purpose of my call was to ask if he would write a reference for my application for a CC bursary. He declined, saying he would explain when he visited. It seems that he and David no longer write for artists, because, he said, "the Canada Council doesn't like us" — no artist they have supported has received a grant. He said that a letter from the Mirvish Gallery is a liability to an artist; they can be more helpful by not writing.

I showed him twelve paintings, one of the drawings, the twelve Colour Lock prints and eight one-colour prints and told him something of what I was doing in this work. Alkis is always polite, but I could see he was cool toward the work. He said he found the paintings "monotonous"; it was the similarity of form, not the colour, that he was focused on, and he suggested that I should try to vary the shapes that I was using — maybe add some rectangles. I handed him a sleeve of slides of the first Colour Lock Series of paintings and he said, "Oh, you've already done that!"

It was not a bad interview; the talk was easy. Alkis is fair and has a helpful attitude. He talked about Pollock briefly — I didn't have to encourage him, just listened. I don't talk about Pollock, but I listen carefully now when other people do.

I called Rybak yesterday and ordered more stretchers: two 6 x 8s (each made in two pieces, 6 x 4) and three 4 x 12s (also in two pieces, 4 x 6) — ten pieces altogether.

16 August, 1972. Wednesday

Lois came to do her "dry run." She does not move or help to move the paintings, so Nelson and I put them into position for her. I'm happy to do the moving; it makes me feel better anyway. She talked a lot over each one, so even this short session took a long time.

The sleeve of slides that was lost somewhere in Pollock's gallery has surfaced. They called; I picked them up. It's hard to hang on to slides; people keep them, lose them, or just forget to return them. My slides have to be "originals," not duplicated — colour can change dramatically in duplication. Lois wants to do eight to ten shots of each painting.

bp came by yesterday. I showed him what I wrote for the introduction for the Milt prints. I watched him read it and when he finished, he gave me such a puzzled look. He said nothing, so neither did I. In my own words, I had written all the same ideas that he had written. *He's the writer; I'm not.* Today, bp returned with a new piece of writing and a new idea for the introduction. We will combine the two, his and mine (which is mostly his, too) in alternating paragraphs — the use, or lack of, capitals and punctuation will distinguish the author of each part. Maybe I should feel guilty about what I did, but he solved the problem overnight. That's fast work compared to what I've put into making the prints and the job's not done yet.

I ordered two small screens and some black ink today through Open Studio.

26 August, 1972. Saturday
Rybak delivered my stretchers yesterday. I gave them a cheque for $75 and another, post-dated to September 25th for $78.53. I saw Lois and gave her $40 to buy film.

On Thursday, I went to Marty's with Nelson, to the new store at 118 Yorkville Ave. I went to Nancy Poole's and to the Marlborough-Godard Gallery where there is a show of Canadian printmakers — Barbara Hall has a piece in the show.

It's too hot today to do anything. I read a book on Jackson Pollock that Lois loaned me.

29 August, 1972. Tuesday
I got the project cost grant from CC! The letter and the cheque for $1000 were in today's mail. What a relief! The "project" is to buy stretchers, photograph new work and have new drawings framed; I have two of these things underway and now the pressure is off about how much I can do. The framing is going to be the biggest expense.

I phoned Michael Greenwood and Pollock to say I got the grant and to thank each of them for their support. Greenwood has agreed to write for my application for a bursary. Dennis Young (now in Halifax) will also write, and I'm going to ask Mrs. Kritzwiser.

Lois photographed fourteen paintings last night — a long night of work. I set up each painting for her, then ran out of the room to do something — like make her a coffee — to keep her from talking to me instead of shooting. She came by today to get a copy of Nelson's *The Pre-Linguistic Heights* for her nephew, Ron Gillespie. She will photograph the drawings and prints tomorrow night.

4 September, 1972. Monday
Hold-ups in all directions. My screens were delivered and they are defective. Open Studio will have them remade — it will be another week before I can think about printing.

The photography drags on. The drawings were over-exposed and have to be done again. I have learned that these slides have to be mounted by hand (using an iron); Lois will come tomorrow and we will begin that job together.

The show Milly is doing for Véhicule will have no insurance and the artist pays transport; I worry about the handling of my work. Milly wants a donation of *slides*, so the gallery can start a slide archive. I don't really care about this show, but Carol is anxious about "getting in" — as if it were a jury show. I wrote to Milly with some questions. I'm going to check transportation costs.

The Vancouver Art Gallery accepted my slides for SCAN. They will pay $1 per slide — $17 (big deal). I've entered four one-colour prints in the Canadian Printmakers' Showcase at Carleton University. They are the first prints I've sent anywhere. Some people seem to think that a print of one colour is not a print at all. So often, people seem blind to my work.

I worry about Pollock. So far, he has talked about three different ways to represent artists: one is to pay an artist a monthly salary in exchange for what he produces; another is to buy outright an artist's complete production. These are dreams. He has not told me what *his* terms are, or will be if he represents me. He is still interested; the show won't be until 1973, so there is time to work things out. He asked me for a piece of my work for the opening of the new gallery. I declined and it was okay with him. He will be opening with Josef Albers on the main floor and his "stable" on the second floor. I want to talk with the lawyer about the dealer/artist relationship. I need advice.

Doug Fetherling was here yesterday. We haven't seen him in a long time. He is doing research for a biography of Maxwell Bodenheim. He's pretty excited about it.

Nelson's bookselling takes up a lot of his time. His Lists are doing well, but the sales are far from earning us a living. The job at Marty's is not helping, because Marty doesn't pay him regularly — Nelson can work for four months without any pay and Nelson will not ask him for anything. I am money-scared all the time.

5 September, 1972. Tuesday

I called Deakin. Two paintings to Montreal will cost $20-$27 (so $40-$50 return). A truck will be going before the end of the month. I had lunch with Carol. We talked about the Véhicule show.

I dropped in to Pollock's. A group show is hung — Thelma Van Alstyne and Paul Fournier are featured. The show doesn't look good. The paintings are crowded; the gallery seems dark and the walls are dirty. Upstairs, the boys were packing for the move.

10 September, 1972. Sunday

We mounted slides this week. Lois spent an afternoon here and I worked further at it on Friday and yesterday. Lois spent a couple of hours here yesterday, too. She told me that I was running up quite a bill with her (while she was sitting down to a coffee and I was at the ironing board mounting the slides); she estimated between $250 and $300 then changed that to $200-$250. Her original estimate was $80 and $2 an hour for mounting. (My calculation was about $150.) I will trade my work to this amount. Last night, Lois photographed the drawings again. Thank goodness this job is over. I haven't been able to work in the studio while the photography was being done.

I heard from Jim Williamson about the Saturday kids' classes at AGO. I will be teaching Scholarship II this year. Classes start October 14th; I'll be paid $25 a class.

Milly didn't answer my letter about the show at Véhicule; rather, she phoned Carol (not me) and told her what to tell me in reply (Carol loved this). I've written Milly to withdraw, saying I can't afford the transportation right now. That's finished.

12 September, 1972. Tuesday

Last night Lois came and we finished the mounting. Then she worked out her fee for me. I didn't know (because she didn't tell me) that she would charge me $1 per slide (and there are so many!). The total came to $445.50. I was stunned; we had agreed to make a dollar for dollar trade. Then, she said she wouldn't accept the prices on my work because they were too low. We looked at small works (that's what she wanted). She chose a framed drawing [*Graphite Drawing, Series 1, #9. 1970*] and a copy of *Points of Attention* (one of my copies; the book is out-of-print now). We looked at the series of twelve Colour Lock prints. She was looking at #9 and #10 of the series, trying to choose between them, and I told her to take them both. She seemed quite satisfied and I am, too. We are settled.

Yesterday, we stretched a piece of canvas on the boards for a 4 x 12 foot painting. Today, I looked at my new drawings (15" x 15") and chose twenty-three to be framed. I am reading Peggy Guggenheim's *Out of This Century*. Strange book, strange lifestyle; I begin to understand the John Dos Passoses of the world.

14 September, 1972. Thursday

I'm working on sketches toward 4 x 12 foot paintings. I have sketches for six paintings this size, but I cannot let myself make that many. In June, I made two paintings this size, but I will put only one of them on a stretcher (the other is rolled and will stay rolled). I have two more stretchers. I am looking for *two* paintings.

We received an invitation to the opening of The Pollock Gallery Limited — the pre-preview. Dress is to be black and white; this is Pollock's way of bringing attention to the colour in Albers' paintings. I don't know what we'll wear. We have lots of black, but it's not quite presentable.

bp came by yesterday. Nelson paid him some money for his books, then went off to work at Marty's. I expected bp to leave when Nelson left, but he stayed and visited with me. He read to me from a novel he is writing (called *Journal*), because there's a line in it that he says I said: "It is always the same story." When he finished, I commented on the form, the structure of what I had heard and he sprang to his feet, took my hand and said, "You get it!" He left me his manuscript of "John Cannyside" to read. I'm surprised that bp was willing to talk about his writing with me and I'm pleased he left me his manuscript.

17 September, 1972. Sunday

I mixed colours yesterday for my painting. I was able to establish a low red, a blue and a blue-green. I mixed a low yellow-orange, but I'm still not sure of it. I was able to apply the three red shapes. Today, I adjusted the blue-green and applied the three shapes. So far, I'm pleased with what is happening.

19 September, 1972. Tuesday

I finished my painting yesterday. I worked a long day, from 11:30 am to 7:30 p.m. I applied the blue shapes and the low yellow-orange shapes. This is *Colour Lock, Second Series #17* (48" x 144"). I have entered it in my Record Book. I'm happy with it.

I have placed an order for canvas and another for paint. (The paint will be about $60.) I'm trying to reach Mrs. Kritzwiser for a reference for my CC bursary application. I am working on the application forms today.

I have read "John Cannyside." I'm very impressed with it; it has made bp's *The True Eventual Story of Billy the Kid* [WFP, 1970] clearer to me.

21 September, 1972. Thursday

I spent yesterday afternoon with Nelson at the Village Book Store. I looked at some of Marty's art books: *Maria Chapdelaine* with the Gagnon illustrations, a book on Canadian landscape by Robson and a book of Andrew Wyeth's paintings, among others. Looked at all the early numbers of *Canadian Art* magazine. We brought home Emily Carr's *Book of Small*, a book on Homer Watson and Lorne Pierce's *Remembrance* about poet Marjorie Pickthall.

I'm preparing twelve slides to send to CC Art Bank.

bp called. We talked about "John Cannyside."

24 September, 1972. Sunday

I have been working on drawings these past few days. After a slow start (and a waste of paper), I arrived at a piece that was promising, a nice thing of itself, by drawing horizontal lines across a page. In the first few drawings, the lines have a lot of variation and suggest "landscape"; they are nice things, but not very exciting. I tightened the lines, drew with less variation and got a stronger drawing. The first works were small; I'm working now on the larger page. The lines are difficult to draw, to sustain; each line must flow without interruption and I must draw slowly.

Phone call from Carol. We had an uncomfortable talk. She is not invited to the opening of Pollock's new gallery on Thursday night and she knows that we are. Mrs. Kritzwiser wrote about this "exclusive" pre-preview (invitation only) in yesterday's paper.

1 October, 1972. Sunday

I reached Mrs. Kritzwiser and she said she did not need to visit the studio to support my bursary application — just send her the form. Okay by me. I have mailed all three forms and yesterday I completed my part of the application. I'll mail it tomorrow, then forget about it until next April; rather, until December 1st, when the regional jury looks at original works.

I have been working on drawings (horizontal line) over the past week. I'm also working on sketches toward another 4 x 12 foot painting.

We went to Pollock's opening wearing our best black. (Pollock told me, "Put on your black slacks and a black turtle-neck and *come!*") Everyone wore black and/or white except for one woman who apparently forgot. Mrs. Pollock (Jack's mother) was there wearing an elegant black gown trimmed with feathers that Jack bought for her. She sat sedately, but self-consciously, on a chair (throne) in one of the main galleries for the whole evening. When Nelson went over to her, he knelt down to speak with her and they clasped hands like long-lost lovers — I thought she was going to throw her arms around him. Marty was there wearing a rented tux. Lister Sinclair was there and Marty remarked that he had finally gotten himself a new set of teeth.

Albers was not there, but Pollock announced that he was going to phone him in Orange, New Jersey. A speaker phone was set up for the call; everyone gathered round while Jack dialed and dialed and we all listened to the rings. No one answered. Bernie was sweating buckets on Jack's behalf until Jack finally gave up. Then everyone went back to talking to each other. The place was hot and crowded and noisy, but everyone seemed to be having a good time. Nelson and Marty went outside to talk. I may have been the only person who looked at all the paintings upstairs and down. The gallery was only barely finished for the opening; the staircase to the second floor was being installed right up to the opening hour.

8 October, 1972. Sunday
My "final report" to CC for the 1971 bursary is in the mail and I have completed the biographical information form for the National Gallery. I've begun to write my "interim report" for the CC project cost grant. I called the lawyer, Mr. Miller, and I have an appointment to see him on Tuesday.

I have seen the Albers show at Pollock's twice since the opening. I learn by looking at this work. On one of those days, Pollock talked with me for some time; this prompted me to make the appointment with Miller.

I have set aside my drawings (the horizontal line). I have entered all nineteen drawings in my Record Book as *Graphite Drawings, Series 5.* The small drawings are 11½" x 15", the large ones are 22½" x 29".

I've chosen the drawings I will have framed: twenty-two drawings (15" x 15"), four prints (15" x 15") and thirteen drawings (22½" x 29"). Pollock said I can frame through him. I expect the cost to be between $500 and $550.

Yesterday, we stretched a piece of canvas on the easel-boards for a 4 x 12 foot painting; this will be the last painting I will make in the Second Series. The surface is prepared, I know where I'm going with the colour; I will begin mixing colours tomorrow.

I've been making sketches toward new paintings (a new series) and I'm making progress. I will work with new colours, new forms, new sizes and shapes. I have enough canvas to begin when I find the sketch that will start this work. I only need *one* to begin.

Aggregation Gallery opened in a new location this week. In her column, Mrs. Kritzwiser wrote all about the gallery; only one short paragraph was about the exhibition — pity the artists. Carol had a large painting stretched, framed and delivered to the gallery for the opening show, then Lynne and Dave didn't hang it! She's furious. She should have given them a smaller painting.

12 October, 1972. Thursday
Nelson read at the ROM last night. John Robert Colombo has organized this series of poetry readings and Nelson and David McFadden read last night. Hans Jewinski, a policeman, poet and collector, came with a stack of his books to have signed by both poets. I talked with Hans and his girlfriend Tricia. I was sorry I could not talk more with David and Joan [McFadden]; this is the first time I've met Joan.

On Tuesday, I saw the lawyer, Mr. Miller. There is little encouragement in what I learned and most of it was so oblique that I have had to deduce by implication. Essentially, I was told to take what I could get; or, "Make the best deal you can." Miller was not surprised by any of the problems I raised. It seems that contracts, or terms of agreement, are rarely in writing; dealers want to be free to change terms at will. It is in an artist's interest to go along with this because *artists are a dime a dozen* and an artist can easily be replaced.

Mr. Miller had asked me to bring slides of my paintings. When he looked at them, I knew he was not interested. Still, he talked with me for about two hours. I was surprised he was willing to spend so much time with me — surely, lawyers are busy people. There were long silences in the conversation, as if he were deciding how much he should tell me. In this slow, relaxed manner, he actually told me quite a lot. In the end, he said he would advise me on any contract I can get, but he expects that I can work this out for myself. If he (or his office) has to do any work for me, it can be on a "work for work" basis. That was a concession on his part; clearly, he doesn't like or want my work, but he will do this for me as a favour to my doctor. They are friends. The law offices are decorated with paintings and sculptures.

There's one thing Mr. Miller said that's still reverberating. He said that some artists just can't get along with dealers. I have to wonder if I'm one of them.

13 October, 1972. Friday

I finished my painting today, *Colour Lock, Second Series #18*. This one: four colours, each repeated three times. The colours are a red, a green, a yellow and a blue-purple. This painting and the last one work well; I am happy with both of them.

I talked with Jim Williamson today. The AGO children's classes begin tomorrow.

Carol is in Montreal tonight for the opening of Milly's group show at Véhicule. Then she is flying to Paris for the weekend. She said she wants to buy perfume at the duty-free store in the airport. She works for Air Canada, so she can do this.

18 October, 1972. Wednesday

Saturday was the first class with Scholarship II [high school students doing a second year of classes with the AGO, on scholarship]. It looks like a good group. One student, now 16 years old, was in the first class I taught as Jim's assistant in 1962-3, while I was a student at OCA. He was 6 years old then. We recognized each other. Gordie White and I will work together.

I went into Pollock's after class. Pollock is going to NY this week to see Willem de Kooning and he'll visit Albers. He said he will settle this season's exhibitions after this trip.

I received the screens (remade) from Open Studio — a good job this time.

26 October, 1972. Thursday

I have pulled the two additional prints for the Nichol collaboration — the "frames" and the Colour Lock print. I pulled "frames" on Tuesday. Yesterday, Nelson helped by staying with me in the Markham studio to carry each page (colour) printed from the press to the drying table. I printed all four colours; we were at the job for eight hours. The title page, the introduction and a colophon page have yet to be printed. Nelson is going to talk to a binder about making a portfolio.

3 November, 1972. Friday

I finished a new painting today — the first work from the new sketches [*Colour Lock, Third Series #1*. 60" x 60"]. Lots of hesitation about getting into this and it's too soon to know what I've got. Exciting colour activity — five shapes, four colours: two different reds, a green and a blue that is repeated in two shapes. I'm anxious to go on to another painting, but I want to look at this one for a while.

Frameguild Mouldings picked up my drawings yesterday. They'll return them here when the framing is done. The bill will go to Pollock; he'll pass it on to me.

16 November, 1972. Thursday

Frameguild delivered on Tuesday. Such a pleasure to see this work properly framed — aluminum strip frame with no mat, no visible mount.

I have been working on mural proposals for the Windsor Public Library (a competition). I have prepared two proposals and I'm working on the cost structure. I called Robert Downing for some advice about costing — he is full of information. He and Sally will visit us here next Tuesday.

I have a new piece of canvas stretched on the easel-boards for another painting. I have prepared the surface. It waits.

1 December, 1972. Friday

I finished my painting a week ago [*Colour Lock, Third Series #4*. 60" x 60"]. I was uncertain about it for several days. We put it on a stretcher and I am pleased now that it is working. I will go on. I have a new piece of canvas on the boards for a 48" x 64" painting.

I received a letter from CC Art Bank returning my slides. They'll be in touch again in a month or two to arrange to view works in the studio.

The Windsor mural designs have been sent, and I've had a reply acknowledging receipt. Robert Downing and Sally spent an evening here. Robert talked about Pollock (everyone does); he called him "ruthless." Downing told me that to get into a gallery, an artist should just take some of his work in and leave it there. He said this puts the commitment on the dealer's side, then the artist can tell him what to do. I don't like the sound of this and I doubt that it would work for me. I'm not six feet tall and a former cop.

We are busy with Weed Flower Press books. Nelson is doing *Praise Poems* and *Leonardo's Lists*, both by John Robert Colombo, *Eleven Early Poems* by Doug Fetherling and *The Ova Yogas* by David McFadden. He is looking at poems by Ants Reigo.

17 December, 1972. Sunday

I have been in a terrible state of mind. I've done no real work for two weeks. I feel harassed and I worry about *everything*.

I got a phone call from Len Deakin last month about the Winnipeg Art Gallery. The rental gallery had just paid his bill for shipping my paintings in March, but they didn't pay all of it. They sent a letter telling him to bill me for half the cost of the crate. He wanted to know if I knew about it; I didn't, so he read me the letter. *They wrote him, but they didn't write me!* Deakin was not kind in his comments about galleries that have *him* "charge the artist" when the artist hasn't been told. This bill went out months ago — all the more reason for him to be suspicious. We laughed about it and I told him to send his bill to me and I'd take care of it. I paid Deakin, then sent a copy of the bill to Winnipeg with a letter asking for remuneration (as per their contract!). It's not the $21.28; it's the principle. They had every opportunity to tell *me* about this, but they got Deakin to do it instead.

I spent a day at the AGO Rental Gallery cleaning two of my paintings. I got a call saying that the canvas' edges were finger marked, so I went down with my art gum eraser and a brush and cleaned the paintings right there in the gallery. Mrs. Parkin wrote me saying that I had done such a good job that the gallery will keep the paintings; the consignment will be extended until January 1974. They seem to rent my paintings a lot, but I wonder if it's worth it.

And Pollock. Poor Jack, he says he *hates* his new gallery now. His backers have told him that he's *a poor businessman*. (He calls me and tells me these things!) He has just learned that the international prints that he's been accumulating are "inventory," an *asset*. (He didn't know this?) He says running the gallery "just isn't *fun* any more." Sometimes he's so open and sounds so innocent that it breaks my heart. Jack has pushed my show ahead to the 1973-74 season. I don't know what I'm going to do.

1973

1 January, 1973. Monday

The New Year begins. We had ice cream and ginger ale at twelve o'clock last night. Nelson is working at the Village Book Store today; he worked there yesterday, and will be there again tomorrow. Over the past week, we did a lot of work on WNB [William Nelson Books] and Weed Flower Press.

The new year is looking dim for me with a lot of work ahead just to survive and no prospects for my work. Two things: Marlborough-Godard Gallery has my slides (Eve Baxter asked me to bring them in, but it is Mira Godard who will look at them.) and the CC Art Bank people are supposed to visit the studio in January or February. Both of these things are long shots.

Pollock has finally told me that the artist pays him a $300 fee for a show and he takes 40% commission on sales. The artist shares transportation costs and supplies him with slides. That 40% commission applies to sales in the gallery, in other galleries and in the studio — this is what he calls "representation." No word on promotion or insurance.

That "in the studio" bothers me. I don't want a dealer to think he has rights to this place or the work in it. I work in the same place I live and I don't live alone. We both do a lot of work here and I don't want a dealer to think he has access, can bring clients here to view work, or any of the other invasive nonsense I hear about from artists. I want to *consign* works to a gallery for an agreed period of time. It can be an exclusive agreement, but *everything* is not included.

My work has been at a halt for the past month. I have been worried about not being able to show my work. I can't go looking for another gallery now; Pollock has made that impossible.

The Winnipeg Rental Gallery wrote that my work is the first they have received from out of town and they didn't expect to pay crating costs. (How was I to know that?) I have written a nasty letter.

2 January, 1973. Tuesday

I began to work on a new painting yesterday. The canvas was stretched and the surface prepared three weeks ago. I mixed and applied three colour areas: a blue-green, a blue and a blue-purple all in the top half of the painting (the blue shape is at centre). Today, I mixed and applied two shapes (wider than high) at the bottom: a red-purple at the left and a yellow-green at the right [*Colour Lock, Third Series #5*. 48" x 64"].

While I was working yesterday another work this size began to fall into place in my head, so I made some notes and sketches. This work is starting to find its form. I feel good about it.

I've been thinking about the two mural designs I submitted for the competition in Windsor. (They were rejected.) One of them relates to the Colour Lock, Second Series; the other belongs with this new work. I would like to make them as paintings. I am making sketches to find the essential *size* for these works.

4 January, 1973. Thursday

I am really pleased with my new painting. The last two, or first two of this new series, that I made in November, were clouded with uncertainty while I worked and even when I saw them completed. I'm excited about this one and I want to go on.

Nelson is preparing his List #8. I have addressed all the envelopes for the mailing. We both worked on quotes last night — we have to keep William Nelson Books rolling.

Today, Nelson visited Helen Ball; she's a poet. She called yesterday to see if he would buy some of her books. She is 75 years old. She called again today to speak to me because, she said, we have the same name, "Mrs. Ball." She sounds delightful. Rowley Murphy, who taught at OCA, is her brother. I was able to tell her I'd studied there with him. She's very proud of him and misses him terribly since his death.

7 January, 1973. Sunday

We've brought WFP mail up to date over these past few days and Nelson's List #8 has been mailed. I've made a card file of the WNB mailing list and will make a WFP mailing list today. Nelson is working at Marty's.

We rolled my last painting and I have a new piece of canvas stretched on the boards. I think I am newly aware of colour mixing and I can see it in the last painting. It's because of the "minus colour theory." I'm not using this theory, but having read about it, I'm more conscious of what is happening when I mix colours.

9 January, 1973. Tuesday

I received the invitation to Pollock's next exhibition. It's the show of "master drawings" that he talked about with me. He was going to show Canadian and international drawings together and he said he wanted a piece of my work for it. Here's the show and there are no Canadians in it.

It's pretty obvious that Jack is in financial trouble. His backers want him to focus on international art and especially, to move that huge stock of international prints. I know he's at odds now about showing my work. I suspect he's being encouraged to just drop me since he has made no formal commitment to me. But he's proud of his honesty and he says he "promised" me a show, and he will do it. I'd like to let him off the hook. I want to ask him to do a one-time show of my work — one show, "in and out," a simple consignment for the duration of the show and no commitment afterward — no representation. I have to think this through.

17 January, 1973. Wednesday
I completed my painting today [*Colour Lock, Third Series #6*. 48" x 64"]. In this one, a green shape and a purple (toward blue) shape are at top and a low yellow-orange (higher than wide) lies between them. The two shapes below (wider than high) are a red-purple at left and a yellow-green at right. These two colours are different intermixtures than in the last painting though the words are the same. I think I'm making a great deal happen in this and the last painting.

Dr. Herbert Ives' "minus colour theory" is described in *The Painter's Eye* by Maurice Grosser. I read this book years ago. I was impressed then only by how unworkable the theory is, but on reading it again, I am struck by the *why* of it. The fact that each colour (pigment) is not pure, but reflects other parts of the spectrum along with its hue, has given me a more subtle awareness of intermixtures. What Ives does with his theory is try to create *pure* colours by mixture. What I'm doing is almost the opposite; I am making those low value colours that occur when the naturally impure pigments are intermixed. Ives can't mix pure colour using pigments because he can't mix a *white* by this method. The natural outcome of mixture lowers a colour, greys it, or even makes a *black*. I think theory has to come out of the painting experience. It can't be imposed on it.

I put the idea of an "in and out" show to Pollock. He leapt at it. It will get both of us off the hook.

28 February, 1973. Wednesday
Everything just gets harder. I have been so confused about Pollock and now the Gadatsys are giving me a hard time.

In January, I went to the opening of Jim Gordaneer's show of drawings at the Gadatsy Gallery in Yorkville. It is a new gallery that shows only drawings and it's run by Stephen and Julianne Gadatsy. The space is good. I showed them slides of my drawings, then they came to the studio. My drawings are framed and ready to be shown, so they offered me a March date (17th-30th). Their terms are direct: no fee, shared costs on printing, postage, an ad in *The Globe and Mail* and the opening (food and wine). The work is consigned to the gallery for the duration of the show.

If they keep any of the works it will be on a new consignment. I wanted to do it; I need to get some of my work out where it can be seen. I told Pollock about it and he doesn't object. He will show my paintings in May.

Jim's main objection to the Gadatsy Gallery is that the space is not divided. They hang a one man show with three walls of other works encroaching on it. This is awkward, even embarrassing, especially at an opening. I talked with Stephen about adding a partition (two feet wide) to act as a divider between the two spaces. It would give the main gallery a bit more space and it would end the confusion. He liked the idea and was going to do it, then changed his mind. To explain, he told me that he was only hanging my work to bring new people to the gallery so he could sell the other artists' work. He doesn't think my work will sell; in fact, he doesn't even like it — he said it was dull, not interesting.

Today, Stephen called to tell me he has decided to put in the partition. So I will hang the show as planned, but it will have to stand on its own strength with no help from the gallery. I'm not feeling very happy about it.

The Winnipeg Rental Gallery answered my letter with payment for the crate, plus the rental earned on one of my paintings, and a letter that put me in my place. The consignment was ended and my paintings were returned. Today, I wrote a letter to say that they arrived in good condition. That's finished.

5 April, 1973. Thursday

I've just read the last entry. The show at Gadatsy did pretty well on its own. Stephen said he wants to do another show next year.

I put forty-two drawings and four one-colour prints in the show. A drawing and two prints sold at the opening, (a surprise for all of us), another drawing sold in the second week, then Stephen and Julianne bought a drawing for themselves. Because everything had been paid by the end of the exhibition, we settled the show on the last day. Total sales were $390; when the 40% commission and 50% of expenses were removed, I was still ahead. I was given a cheque that day for $137.25 — it's the first time I've received money, instead of owed money to the gallery, at the end of a show. Stephen drew up a statement — all very business-like. The gallery is keeping six drawings on consignment for 5 months. The rest of the work is back here in the studio.

On the day of the opening (Saturday, 17th March), there was a heavy snowfall. I was sure *nobody* would come to the show, but the gallery was full for the greater part of the afternoon; people kept coming and going. It was a good experience and the work looked good in the space.

15 May, 1973. Tuesday

Last Friday, the CC Art Bank jury walked into the Pollock Gallery to look at my work. Of course, it wasn't there. The work for the show hasn't gone down yet. (Art Bank didn't write or call *me* about this!) Jack phoned to tell me that he had sent them here, that they were on their way and he was very specific: "Show them the work *that will hang in the show,*" (as if I didn't understand English). Then he called me right back again to say: "It will be nice to see *a red sticker in the show.*" (Okay.) The three jurors arrived: Luke Rombout, Vera Frenkel and Walt Redinger. I did, in fact, show them all of the paintings that were going to be in the show. (Nelson was out, so they had to help me move them.) They were interested in my drawings and prints so they looked at those, too, as well as a copy of the portfolio, *The Adventures of Milt the Morph in Colour.* They seemed to like my work: the drawings, the prints, and only Vera reacted badly to bp's drawing hand on the Milt prints. They were ruminating over the paintings when Nelson came in and in all innocence said: "There's a big one in the hall here that we'd like to get out of the way." They were interested, for they had walked past it and I hadn't shown it to them, so we brought the 5 x 10 foot Colour Lock painting (1970) into the room. (This painting, returned to the studio from Women's College Hospital after a three-month rental period through the AGO Rental Gallery, will *not* be in the show at Pollock's gallery.)

The Art Bank jury has the artist leave the room so they can openly discuss what they have seen. (Some artists object to this.) I sat in the kitchen with Nelson. Luke Rombout came in with a list of works they will consider for purchase and asked me from whom Art Bank was to purchase them. I told him that the Milt portfolio has to be purchased from Seripress; the set of twelve Colour Lock prints from the Pollock Gallery; the drawings and the painting, directly from me. I explained that my show at Pollock's was an "in and out" show and the painting they chose was not part of the show. Art Bank purchases are finalized in Ottawa; I will hear from them.

Later, I called Pollock to tell him what the jury had on their list. If they buy the prints, there will be a red sticker in the show. I told him I had shown them the paintings that were going to hang in the show, but they chose an earlier piece instead. He was silent, but I know *he's thinking.* We'll see. (Nelson had no idea that he might cause a problem when he mentioned the 5 x 10 foot painting.)

Deakin will take the work to Pollock's on Friday; we will hang the show. It opens on Sunday and will hang until June 7th. Pollock's terms: $300 fee, 40% of sales and I pay all the transportation. Let's get it over with.

17 May, 1973. Thursday

I have typed up a consignment sheet for Pollock to sign tomorrow. It states the terms we've discussed and agreed on with the exception of the $300 fee (he should write that down for me; I'll sign it). It states that in the event of sale, the gallery's commission is 40% *of the listed price*. It *also* states that the artist will receive 60% *of the listed price*. I've attached the list of works and their prices: eight paintings, five framed drawings, thirteen framed prints, plus the number of prints available unframed. The consignment is from May 18th to June 8th.

Everything I've written is standard practice, but it's seldom written down. By writing it, I'm trying to block some common practices that are never discussed. That 60% line will prevent the dealer from lowering a price to whatever a client will pay, then taking 40% of *that*. I risk having no sales by doing this, but I want to have this show over, clear and clean, by 30 days after the show comes down.

I have written so little on these pages recently. Exhibitions are a terrible distraction. I have been unable to paint for over two months. The last painting I made used coloured greys (tonal tints?) with intense colours [*Colour Lock, Third Series #7*. 48" x 64"]. It is a new kind of colour. Now, I want to work with colours *up from black* — I don't know how to say this. I have sketches, but I don't know when I will begin.

We are going to move on July 1st to a new place at 686 Richmond Street West. Gernot Dick and Colette Whiten are moving out. Gernot has bought a house and we will take the studio/living space at Richmond. We have 14 days to move out of here.

I was awarded that Canada Council arts grant and have received the first installment. And I have begun Seripress! In April, I registered the name and opened a bank account for the press to make it *my* little business, separate from Nelson. *The Adventures of Milt the Morph in Colour* is the first title released — half the edition sold in two weeks! Now I'm printing bp's two sequences, *Aleph Unit* and *Unit of Four*.

11 June, 1973. Monday

The Art Bank purchase came through from Ottawa for everything on the list. Eva Quan at Pollock's called to tell me she had received Art Bank's purchase order for the twelve prints (unframed); I delivered the prints to the gallery with an invoice.

That sale to Art Bank ($400) was the only sale in the show. It gives me $240 credit against the $300 fee. I told Eva to send me a statement and I'll send the $60 owing. She will simply have to write down that fee.

Deakin's bill for transportation will come directly to me. The framing costs for the show were $167 — I've paid that already.

I did my best with the consignment agreement I had drawn up. Pollock read it and signed it, saying that it was all "standard." Then he gave it to Eva and she noticed that the $300 fee was not mentioned on the consignment. I said that if they would write it down I would sign, for I intended to pay it. She saw the 40/60 split on sales and asked Jack about interior decorators. Jack told me he had to take 10% off the price for these people. I told him to handle his clients as usual — he had 40% to work with, but I would still need 60% of the listed price of any work sold. Jack got a bit hysterical about this and began to speak to Nelson, not to me. But I'd told Nelson before we went to the gallery that if Jack did this, appealed to him (not me), he was to listen, say nothing, then turn and look at me — *I will answer*. Nelson thought this whole conversation went smoothly because Jack could find no loophole. I felt wiped out by it; when we got home, I was exhausted. I'm not proud of winning that round. I like Pollock.

The show opened on the 20th, a Sunday. It was the holiday weekend. Few people came and those who did were people who got the announcement from me. Pollock printed lots of invitations, but I don't believe he sent them to his mailing list. Alan Foster, who is on both our mailing lists (he bought one of my drawings from the show at Gadatsy), told Pollock: "Next time, don't open on a holiday!" Pollock looked embarrassed.

Kay Kritzwiser wrote a favourable review in *The Globe and Mail*. Sol Littman from *The Toronto Star* saw the show; Pollock told me his response to the work was good, but he didn't write a review. In the end, I think quite a few people saw the show.

The show didn't look good; the space was disappointing. I knew the show would hang on the upper floor in two rooms — one of them is the print room — and I could not change that. (All the shows by Canadians have been on the upper floor in the new gallery.) Several people told me about the "other stuff" and the "clutter" in the rooms. bp thought I should complain; he said I was not being treated well by the gallery. Stephen Gadatsy was there when some people showed an interest in my prints. He told me that Jack turned their attention to the other prints and multiples in the room and in the print cabinets. Stephen thought this was unfair and I should complain. I made no complaints. No one who saw the show and spoke to me about it failed to say something about the gallery: the bad lighting, the cluttered space, the uninterested staff, even the unfinished windows. Everyone knows the renovations cost half a million dollars; Pollock has been shouting it all over town.

I'm not sorry I hung the show. I had Mr. Robinson take slides and photos of the installation; they look uncluttered, better than the actual show. I have to hope that in the long run the show will be of some value to me.

12 June, 1973. Tuesday.

The Adventures of Milt the Morph in Colour is doing very well. Neither bp nor I anticipated that it would sell so well. There are eight copies left now (of an edition of 25) with three or four sales pending. All the costs of production have been covered and have been paid. Now, all money will be divided 50/50. I have accounts receivable of almost $900.

I've finished printing the pages for the next two titles from Seripress, bp's *Aleph Unit* and *Unit of Four*. I was glad to have this work to do between my shows; glad to be able to accomplish something. Typesetting is next. Nelson Adams at Coach House will do it — he did the typesetting for Milt.

bp has brought me some of Steve McCaffery's work for Seripress. I'm not sure I can work with it; I'll let it sit for a while.

Dennis Young was in town during my show at Pollock's. Jack told me he liked the work and he told Jack that he was glad I got the CC grant — he referred to me as "someone who deserved it." (I wonder if he really said that, or if it was Jack who said it.) Eve Baxter told me that Mira Godard was "not favourably impressed" by my work; she felt that my work had not developed enough. I'm not upset by this; in fact, I'm relieved.

Paul Fournier told me he saw the show. He called my work "uncompromising," said the show was "a painter's show." (I think that means that it's *for* other painters.) Jim Gordaneer saw it and called to tell me which paintings he liked best — #10, #11, #4 and #17. We had a good talk.

I met Judy Currelly last week; Carol arranged it. Judy saw my show and said that #10, the 6 x 8, was the painting she liked best: "the colour and the placement in that one were perfect." I am glad to hear these things.

Colette Whiten saw it. She liked the prints best. She seems to be confused by paintings. She told me that she doesn't know why anyone would paint, that she can't "see" paintings because she doesn't know what she is supposed to be looking at. She says she's not interested in other artists' sculptures — "it has nothing to do with me." Strange. We talked about her work at great length.

Carol Martyn, Lois Steen and Ron Gillespie saw the show and were enthusiastic about it. I was there when Lois and Ron looked at the work; Ron took a long time looking at everything, then said to me, "You're a dangerous woman, Barbara Caruso."

I am making a list of public and university galleries. I want to send them slides. I'm going to avoid commercial galleries for a while. I want to work through this period of the CC grant undisturbed.

18 June, 1973. Monday

We are packing. Nelson bought one hundred cartons just to pack his books. Right now, there are over fifty cartons of books stacked in the front room. All my framed drawings are wrapped in bundles and most of my materials are packed. The paintings are covered and stacked. Nelson will have Ernie Cox (Cox Cartage) move the books; I will get Deakin to move my work to the new place.

I have a list of galleries. I'm going to send slides and background information to these places, if not to get a show, at least to make myself and my work known to them. I have prepared four sleeves, each with fifteen slides; I'll attach to each sleeve a list describing the slides and enclose four reviews and a biography. I intend to send the slides to four places at once. When a mailing is returned, I'll send it out again to a new place. I will only have to type a new covering letter each time. If I do this by rote, I'll do it. If I have to think about it too much, I probably won't.

I went into the Gadatsy Gallery. Stephen told me that Shelley Shaw was in asking about a show: three people — Shelley, Lynn Hutchinson and another woman named Ingrid. He will probably do the show. We talked about Shelley's "womanism."

Carol called. She thinks she may lose the third installment of her CC grant. Air Canada has called her back to work (part-time) and she can't afford not to go. She'll let me know what happens.

Lois Steen got a CC short-term grant, at last, after five refusals. I'm glad she got it and I hope she can make good use of it. She may be one of those people who become so overwhelmed by the commitment to work with even a small grant that they can't do anything until the grant period is over. bp said that happened to him.

My work is at a standstill until we are moved. The Windsor murals may become paintings yet. The new studio will be large enough to work them. I'm going to have new easel-boards, 9 feet high and 20 feet long — five 4 x 9 sheets of plywood attached together. It's going to be grand. I've given up my print studio on Markham Street; I'll be able to print in the new place, too.

Nelson wants to put out a List (American Poetry) just before we move so there will be some money coming in as soon as possible. I'm hoping to get paid by Art Bank soon.

23 June, 1973. Saturday

I've mailed slides etc. to 1) Doris Shadbolt, Vancouver Art Gallery; 2) Maurice Stubbs, McIntosh Gallery, University of Western Ontario, London; 3) Kenneth

Saltmarche, Windsor Art Gallery and 4) Fernande Saint-Martin, Musée d'art contemporain, Montreal. I also finished writing a final report on the project cost grant I got last August and mailed it to CC.

bpNichol came by last night. I was able to give him a Seripress cheque for $250 — money received for the Milt portfolio. He wants me to write another article for TRG, or just for *Open Letter*, this time on the first and second series of Colour Lock paintings. bp plans to take some time out from Therafields to get some writing done, or as he put it, "to write a few novels."

Doug Fetherling came by earlier with some books for Nelson. Doug has bought a property near Barrie, Ontario, so needs money. He will take over Kildare Dobbs' job at the *Star* for the summer while Dobbs is on holiday and Doug's working at the CBC. His book on Ben Hecht is about a third done in draft; he says his POCA [Province of Ontario Council for the Arts] grant is all used up.

5 July, 1973. Thursday
We have done such a lot this week. We took over the studio at Richmond Street on Sunday while Gernot was still moving the last of his things out. The place looked so dirty, it was depressing. Nelson moved all the lumber from Bathurst Street and began to build bookshelves. While he was building, I washed some floors, painted a cupboard, washed the bathroom and some windows. Yesterday, we washed the entire studio floor and today, Deakin moved my paintings. Three men (with Nelson helping) moved over fifty stretched paintings, the rolls of canvases and all the small framed works.

Colette and Gernot left us their hot plate. We will use it.

8 July, 1973. Sunday
Yesterday, Nelson finished building the storage rack for my paintings. I designed it; he built it. It is a few inches over 8 feet tall, so it will house the 5 x 5, 6 x 6 and 6 x 8 foot paintings. It has a roof (flat), so I can store stuff up there, too. He built a packing table for himself and a paper and print storage cabinet for me. We have spent a lot of money.

Mr. Cox will move the books tomorrow.

12 July, 1973. Thursday
The books are in. The phone is in. We are in. We've spent two nights here now. We are unpacking slowly — at least, it goes slowly. The weather is hot. There's a lot to be done.

Nelson bought me a bouquet of flowers today — carnations: eleven pink and one white. This place is going to be fine.

14 July, 1973. Saturday
Last night, I typed invoices and Nelson packed the orders received on his last List.
We've gotten a good start on the work that has piled up.

Carol called yesterday. She told me about her interview at Aggregation. She
said she paid her bill (under $200 owed after her last show); it was less than she
expected. Then she told Lynne and Dave that she was leaving the gallery. They gave
her no resistance.

16 July, 1973. Monday
My slides have come back from Windsor with a letter from the curator, Ted Fraser,
and this morning, I got a return and letter from Doris Shadbolt in Vancouver. Both
letters are promising; both said they are already familiar with my work and they'd
keep me in mind for future shows. I will mail the slides out again to the Agnes
Etherington in Kingston and maybe to Alvin Balkind, the new curator at the AGO.

It's mid-morning; I'm slow to get started today. We have done so much over
the past two weeks. Nelson is working at Marty's today.

18 July, 1973. Wednesday
I went to Yorkville yesterday to see Nelson at the Village Book Store and to visit
some galleries. Marlborough-Godard was showing Kenneth Lochhead, paintings
from 1965 to 1967. It's a good show; some nice colour work. At Nancy Poole's
Studio, I saw prints by Kim Ondaatje, prints and paintings by Jack Chambers. The
prints are little more than reproductions. Kim has screened a white veil over the
reproduction of a painting to make the print unique. This is an attempt to make
works available at a low price, but it changes the whole concept of the printmak-
er's art. They are nice things to look at; I wonder how well they are selling. Gadatsy
Gallery was closed; they have shorter hours in July, but I could see that five of my
drawings are hung.

Jim Gordaneer visited last night. A good talk.

Today, I got a reply from Maurice Stubbs at the McIntosh Gallery at UWO.
He returned the slides and offered me a show at the gallery for the 1974–75 season. He wants a reply now and will make more specific arrangements at a later
date. I'll follow up, of course; this is more than I hoped for from my mailings.

19 July, 1973. Thursday
I've written to Stubbs in London. I have two more packages of slides ready to mail
to 1) the Burnaby Art Gallery and 2) the University Gallery in Edmonton.

Last night, I looked through the first eight issues of *The Structurist*. Jim Lowell
had them listed in his most recent catalogue and I bought them. I read most of Eli

Bornstein's articles and some by Charles Biederman. Following Bornstein through those eight years reveals a passion and excitement in his writing that has disappeared in later issues. I have ordered the next four issues and placed a standing order for future issues.

20 July, 1973. Friday
The boards were delivered today (five 4 x 9 foot sheets of plywood, good one side) — $115.58. Ordered the 2x4s for the support.

I read Douglas Woolf's *Spring of the Lamb* and Charles Reznikoff's *By the Waters of Manhattan*. Nelson is working a half day at Marty's today. He will get paid soon.

3 August, 1973. Friday
So many changes since last writing here — some things accomplished. My easel-boards are in place; I have a studio at last.

I have been working on new drawings over this past week. I have some nice things happening. I'm working with a contour square (drawn through a stencil) on the 15" x 15" page [*Graphite Drawings, Series 6*]. I've begun to work now on a 15" x 30" page.

I've applied for a Vendor's Permit. I've ordered a supply of paint.

I received payment from CC Art Bank, but they mixed up the sales tax on the orders; I have to write them about it. I received a letter from Edmonton telling me they were *copying* my slides and will reply later when they return them. (That's dumb. Don't they know about copyright?) I've written to Montreal about the slides I sent in June; there's been no reply or acknowledgement. The Hamilton Art Gallery is also slow to reply.

Jim and Tessa Lowell visited here on Sunday. I think they think we're crazy to live in this area and in a place like this. Nelson is so proud of all our work, the set up and the space. He was really disappointed by their reaction.

bp has been here a couple of times. He delivered my copies of *Open Letter* [Second Series, No. 5. Summer 1973. Issue on Narrative.] and returned the drawings that are reproduced (poorly) in it with my article, "Telling About Line Telling" (part of TRG Report 2). The last time, Ellie came with bp and we learned from her that she had been a nun for seven years. (She was surprised that bp had not already told us.) It explained how they met at Therafields, and why bp disparages religion and religious institutions.

19 August, 1973. Sunday
My drawings have moved into something I want to call a "spatial-temporal

dimension." I have three drawings (15" x 30"); they involve an idea I've been pondering ever since I read about Theo van Doesburg in *Form*. There, a space-time continuum defined objects in space. I'm making it a planar event in these drawings; I suspect that Mondrian may have seen it this way.

Now I am working with the diagonal, drawing the square with continuous diagonal lines. The drawings have no significant margin. The 1:2 ratio of the page is retained in the drawing, but nothing moves off, or outside, the page [*Graphite Drawings, Series* 7]. I compare these drawings to the prints in the Milt portfolio (15" x 30") where the page is 1:2, but the 4" margin makes the printed image 1:3. There is something important about this; it's a new recognition of the energy of the entire plane, of the "margin" and the activity of line, of the page and of the drawing on the page.

22 August, 1973. Wednesday

I've moved on to more new drawings. I've made three drawings that overlap square contour shapes and three drawings that use straight lines to form one large square shape on the square page: in one all horizontals are drawn; in another, all verticals; in the third, all obliques [*Graphite Drawings, Series* 8. 15" x 15"].

Now, I'm drawing the field of the page with loose hatched lines. The square shapes are drawn loosely or they are controlled. I could call this "tone," but it's not that; tonalities are not the subject of this work. It's not about "positive/negative" either; rather, these drawings are about *surface tension* [*Graphite Drawings, Series* 9. 15" x 15"].

I called Stephen Gadatsy yesterday. We talked about sales in the studio. He said they would not be relevant; he deals only with works consigned to the gallery. I needed to know this, to have it understood.

The Gadatsys did "split costs" for my show (no fee); those costs were defined at the start and did not change over the duration of the show. At Aggregation, Lynne and Dave charge a fee and they split costs; those costs were defined at the start, too, but they would change — I could not guess what would be included as an expense. Pollock charges a fee of $300. All of the galleries take a 40% commission on sales. Most often, there are no sales, or sales are so low that the artist can't clear the debt to the gallery with his 60%.

If there were sales, significant sales, I wondered what the artist's 60% would be worth. I have calculated: at a $300 fee and 40% commission, the first $500 in sales belongs to the gallery. At $1000 in sales the artist has paid his debt and has $300. — less than one-third of sales. It would take $3000 in sales for the artist to reach 50%. At $10,000, the artist receives 57% of the sales. To gain 1.5% more (58.5%) there must be *another $10,000* in sales. In dollars, that would be a lot of money, but most shows would not be worth that much even if the whole show sold. The artist's 60% of sales (if there are any) is his credit against the debt that is built into the dealer's system.

I am not considering the artist's costs for framing (his responsibility), not even the cost of transportation (sometimes shared) in my calculations. Only the bare bones agreement with no tricks.

Milly Ristvedt says that the best deal for an artist is when a dealer charges no fee and no costs, but takes 50% of sales. Then, the dealer *has to work* for sales; he can't just hang a show, do nothing, then collect from the artist. I don't think anyone does that here.

23 August, 1973. Thursday

My paint was delivered today — $71. I prepared my entries for the Ottawa print show; the prints and forms are ready to be mailed tomorrow.

Carol phoned today. She was in a snit about not being married. She said that all the women artists she knows are married and she thinks she's at a disadvantage because she's not. I didn't see the point of it. It's hard to talk her out of this sort of thing. She read me an interview with Aaron Milrad from *The Globe and Mail*. In it, Milrad talks about the absurdity of commercial galleries having no contracts with their artists. This is more to the point.

28 August, 1973. Tuesday

I received a reply from the accountant at CC Art Bank re: the sales tax. It seems they can't believe that artists will collect and remit sales tax so they pay it directly on the artist's behalf. I have written and asked them to send it to me. I don't know why they are ignoring invoices. When Judy Currelly sold her painting to Art Bank, she sent them an invoice showing the price of the work plus the sales tax and they didn't send her the tax either. She took the amount of the tax out of her price and sent it in. She said she didn't know what else to do.

I talked with Barbara Hall. She is leaving next week for six months in Florence, Italy; it's part of her CC grant. She is entering her prints in the jury show in Burnaby. I'm entering that one, too.

I have a stencil, cut from a recent drawing, ready on a large screen. I want to make one-colour prints, but it's too hot and humid to print today. I have set aside the new drawings (15" x 15"). I tried to continue this work on a larger page and it was not successful. More and more, I see that *size,* the *right* size, is extremely important.

31 August, 1973. Friday
My slides came back from Burnaby Art Gallery today with a letter from Sheila Kincaid saying that she may be in Toronto this winter and will visit the studio to view my work. She said she is considering a show for 1975. Promising.

Carol called today to tell me she had bought some stretchers from a young artist who is moving to England. She got fourteen stretchers; they are 4½ feet high, 13 feet long and 3" deep. She wanted to know if I wanted some of them. (I don't use 3" deep stretchers; mine are 1¾" deep.) The boy she bought them from wanted $100 for the lot. She told me she offered him $140, then they settled at $150. It's so like Carol to haggle in the wrong direction. But she knew he needed the money and it's a lot of lumber. He was having trouble finding someone who wanted stretchers that size. [Earlier in the year, Carol had moved her studio from Markham Street to a larger, more accessible studio space on Queen Street West.]

It's still too humid for me to print. The newspaper reports that temperatures have not been this high in 14 years.

2 September, 1973. Sunday
I have slides ready to mail to Brydon Smith at the National Gallery in Ottawa. I am preparing the prints and entry forms for Burnaby. I've written to CC to request the second installment of my grant.

11 September, 1973. Tuesday
Last week, I pulled a "red" (red + yellow) one-colour print, but only eight were perfect. Yesterday, I successfully remixed the colour (a match on the second try) and pulled it again to make an edition of 20. Then, I mixed a lower tone of red (red + yellow + blue) and pulled another edition of 20 through the same stencil.

Today, I have been writing letters to the galleries in Hamilton, Montreal and Edmonton, asking that my slides be acknowledged or returned. It is discouraging to have to do this.

14 September, 1973. Friday
My slides came back from the Hamilton Art Gallery on Wednesday. Glen Cumming wrote that he will visit the studio to see my work for a show "possibly after 1974." I've replied. The return from the National Gallery had a reply from Pierre Théberge. It's a really strange letter.

I am mailing these slides out again to 1) Moncrieff Williamson at the Confederation Centre Gallery in Charlottetown, PEI and 2) Gerry Moses, the curator of the Imperial Oil collection. Jim Gordaneer told me to approach Moses; he gave me the name and address.

I've pulled two more editions of "red" one-colour prints through the same stencil. One is an intense red (red + red), the next is lowered (red + red + blue). Of the four "red" prints, all are intense reds. The first moved toward orange, the second toward violet, but all of them read as *red hues*. Today, I pulled another red (red + red, greyed); it could be called "brown." I want to pull one more colour, a red that is *up from black*.

I decided to work with "red" because I was not successful with it last year. It is a strong, positive colour, but I got my weakest prints with it. I was too timid, so I begin again.

I realize, as a result of this work, that the eye is not stable. The colour printed on the page is stable, but the receptors in the eye fluctuate, so the colour fluctuates as the eye moves. It is the eye that varies, not the colour.

17 September, 1973. Monday
I pulled the last "red" print *up from black* (red + red + black). Nice. I have numbered and signed all of the prints and wrapped them, leaving out one imperfect print of each of the six reds so I can continue to look at them. I think about the colour, about perception and about these prints as art. It begins to come together.

I've cut a new stencil. I am going to print *yellow hues*. The square shapes are larger than those for the "red" prints. I'm out of paper.

On Saturday, Nelson put together the stretchers for the 4 x 12 foot paintings. Last night we put *Colour Lock, Second Series #8* on one of them. I made this painting in June, 1971, and rolled it. I've waited a long time to see it again.

23 September, 1973. Sunday
I received a reply from Charlottetown acknowledging receipt of my slides. Mr. Williamson is "out of province" until the end of the month, but I'll hear from him when he is back. On Tuesday, Gerry Moses phoned to say he had received the slides. He is going out of town, but will call again on the 30th to arrange a visit to the studio.

Then, on Friday, I received a call from Professor Alasdair Dunlop, director of exhibitions at the University Art Gallery in Edmonton. He was here, in town, before his letter with my slides reached me. He came by at 2 p.m. to see my work. I showed him paintings, drawings and prints and he proposed a show of about fifty drawings (framed) and prints (sent unframed, but the gallery will frame them; they use the same frame I do) for a month-long show in December 1974. I will choose the works. We discussed everything and all went smoothly until we came to the crating. He said he would pay part of the cost; I asked him to pay all of it. He said he could not go over $100. I said I would get an estimate. When he gets back to Edmonton, he will write me a letter confirming the details of our agreement.

The crating is always a problem. He explained that the gallery believes it should not pay for crates because they don't materially benefit the gallery; the crates are returned to the artist. My position is that the crates are an essential part of the transportation of the works and are of no benefit to me either. No one, not even Deakin, saves or stores this kind of crate (called a "one-way crate"); it's a waste of space. I called Vera Frenkel about this question on Friday evening. Her position is the same as mine; she said that she fights to get the galleries to pay for crating, but she doesn't always win.

I went in to the Gadatsy Gallery this week. Stephen extended my consignment to March 30th, 1974. I have put off having a show in the spring. Stephen is promoting the gallery as a show place for "unknown" artists. That rankles.

Seripress is moving along. bp's *Unit of Four* has an edition of 90; *Aleph Unit*, an edition of 70. Nelson has taken the typesetting to Nelson Adams at Coach House. Adams will also print the two folders with Nelson's poems, *Our Arms Are Featherless Wings* and *Dry Spell*, and I'll tip in my prints. I want to have the flier out on these four titles by the end of October.

4 October, 1973. Thursday

Connie Keyser, an art consultant, called me earlier this week. She came today. She is considering two paintings (I gave her the slides); they are each $850 and her commission is 10%. She said she will have a decision about them by November 1st.

Last night, Steve McCaffery came by with his work. There must be two hundred sheets of concrete poetry (letter images), all on 8½ x 11" pages. I asked if there was an order to the pages — he said, no. I asked if he could make any choices amongst them — he said he couldn't. So I've kept the lot and will go through it. I'm surprised that he has made no decisions, has nothing in particular in mind from this great pile of stuff.

7 October, 1973. Sunday

On Friday, I began to work on my painting. This is the fourth of four paintings this size (48" x 64") conceived at the beginning of this year. When I finished the first two paintings in January, I decided that the next two would use greys and then blacks. I made the third painting in February. In March, I stopped this work to hang two exhibitions, make prints, get Seripress off the ground, move, etc., etc., and I've mulled over this one with colours *up from black* ever since. At last the painting is complete [*Colour Lock, Third Series #8*] and to my over-anxious eye it is very exciting to see.

The painting has three "black" shapes: a yellow-black that appears to be green-black, a blue-black and a red-black that approaches purple-black. These colours are rich and dark and they contrast with each other because of their hue. They are hues in their lowest value ranges. There are three shapes of intense colours: a blue, a purple and a red. The blue shape and the purple shape as intensities are low in value. The red, which I applied today, is light weight, or "airy," but low enough in value to lay on the surface with the dark shapes. I'm happy with this painting.

8 October, 1973. Monday
I've been working on the sketches for projected paintings in this series. I've made several changes. I want to make two more 5 x 5 foot paintings. Originally, my sketches for the four 5 x 5s involved only intense colours; now, I'm going to add blacks and greys, so painting #2 will have one grey and painting #3 will have two blacks. These works all have the lightest or brightest shapes at the bottom; I will continue to do that — it's about *gravity*, a colour-gravity. I have no better word for it.

I have sketches toward two long paintings, 4 feet high and 11 or 12 feet long. They are still unsettled in spite of all the time I've spent over them. But I'm going to work on the two 5 x 5s next. I want to stretch two pieces of canvas on the easel-boards at once (I have room to do it) and work on them one at a time. I'll leave the first painting visible while I work on the second one. It may sustain a context; I'll try it. For so long, I've had only my test sheets to look at after a painting is finished and rolled up.

I've looked through all of Steve McCaffery's work. I've chosen two things for Seripress: the piece bp brought earlier, *H: A History*, and a series of three pieces, "Moon." I'll call Steve to get his approval.

10 October, 1973. Wednesday
Yesterday, I went to Pollock's to see the Anni Albers show. The drawings and some earlier works using gouache stand out in my mind. I liked her prints. There were three tapestries; I know so little about weaving that I couldn't see her "hand" at work in them in the way I see it in the other works. I was least impressed by a series of linear works, both drawings and prints. Some spoke of weaving and the more complex they became, the less interested I was. I would have to spend more time with them, for I feel that the key to the "hand" in the tapestries is in these works. I am not sensitive to it.

The colour prints were either very good or bad to my eye. One print was blind stamping in relief on gold paper. I didn't like it at all. It had several red stickers (sales). The order of the image seemed buried under the glare of gold. Perhaps this piece was a move from tapestry to print, for the gold paper is treated as if it were fabric — and it is not. I liked best the ink drawings that show a pencilled grid.

14 October, 1973. Sunday

On Thursday, we stretched two pieces of canvas on the easel-boards for 5 x 5 foot paintings and I prepared both surfaces on Friday. Then, I called Carol about her 13 foot long stretchers. I saw them in her studio last Wednesday; they are not 3" deep, but 1¾" — the size I use. I'm going to take two of them (she has fourteen and no plan for them yet).

15 October, 1973. Monday

I have begun the first 5 x 5 foot painting. Today, I mixed and applied a low grey-green shape (centre top), a blue shape (top right) and a purple shape (top left). The blue and the purple shapes are higher than wide, like columns, or pillars, of colour on each side of the almost square grey-green shape. These three colours fill the top half of the painting and they are all low in value. I am after a red and a red-orange for the two square-like shapes in the lower half of this painting. The colours are not mixed yet. I won't be able to paint tomorrow.

Gerry Moses phoned today. He is still on holidays, but is in town, so he can come to see my work tomorrow at 3 p.m. I'll cover this painting with a sheet for his visit.

I mailed a cheque for $20 to Carol for the stretchers. She charged me less than she paid for them! When I protested, she said that she wouldn't sell them to me at all if I wouldn't pay just what she asked.

16 October, 1973. Tuesday

Gerry Moses arrived on time. He is a congenial person and I enjoyed his visit. I showed him *Silence #2*, a 5 x 5, *Lock #2*, 4 x 12, both from 1969, and *Colour Lock #13*, a 4 x 4 (1970). Of the second Colour Lock series, he saw #14 (5 x 5) and #16 (6 x 6). I showed him the suite of twelve prints, three drawings from 1971 and about eight more from 1972.

He was most interested in the graphics. They were more immediate for him. He gave himself to the paintings and did not express any reservations, but I could see that he was having problems. We looked at *Colour Lock, Second Series #14* again and I described the possible route a viewer's eye might take (and why) over the surface. This helped and it opened up the conversation. We had coffee. I gave him a copy of *Open Letter*.

Moses has done fine printing; he has been a member of the Guild of Hand Printers and his printing has been in *Wrongfount*. He is "Willow Green Press." I introduced Nelson to him as "Weed Flower Press" and he was interested in what Nelson was doing with a Gestetner to produce books of poetry. Nelson showed him *The Other Side of the Room* by bpNichol and our book of poems and prints, *Points of Attention*.

Before he left, he looked at the drawings again. He said he wanted to buy a piece of my work for the Imperial Oil collection. He said the new budget begins in the new year so he will be in touch with me. Nelson was disappointed that he didn't buy something today, but I was relieved that he didn't. As much as I want and need sales, I hate to give up a single piece. I was also able to relax and enjoy the talk once I knew there would be no purchase to deal with today.

We've returned all the works to their places and taken down the sheet. I can go on with my painting tomorrow. I have thought about calling this work by another name, but in the end, I suspect I will call it *Colour Lock, Third Series* and number each painting.

17 October, 1973. Wednesday

I finished my painting today [*Colour Lock, Third Series #2*. 60" x 60"]. I mixed and applied the two "red" shapes: one, a low value red square shape at bottom left; the other, a red toward orange which is higher in value, but is also lowered by the inter-mixture. Even as I worked today, I found myself giving new thought to the next painting.

Each of the 5 x 5 foot paintings has a red shape, sometimes two. In the first 5 x 5 (#1) made last November, two square "red" shapes fill the bottom half of the painting. In #4, made following #1, there is a large (wider than high) red shape and two different low orange shapes (higher than wide) at left and at right of it. In this new painting (#2), I have a red and a red-orange, both low in value. The next painting (#3) will complete this transformation of raising and at the same time lowering reds to orange.

I'm excited about these paintings. I wish I could find better words to describe what is happening. This writing is a kind of "run-off," but the words say so little.

I want to put #1 on a stretcher (it's still rolled) so I can look at #1, #2 and #4 at the same time. I want to see them before I begin #3, to see their relatedness and their singularity. Each one must be strong as a single work.

It's strange that this is occurring. In the Second Series, I worked throughout with a relatedness of order (each work was a separate, single piece). Here, I have worked against that order, breaking with that kind of relatedness and now, it seems I've created a new one.

I have been writing, both here and in my notes, about these paintings, some ideas about hue, hue value, weight and gravity. I can't sort out what it is I'm after, but it has to do with the one-colour prints and with these paintings. The idea of "gravity" began last November when I did painting #4 of these 5 x 5s. I know the word is wrong, but it is involved in my decision to put low value (or "cool") colours at the top of the paintings and reds and oranges at the bottom. The darker shapes and columns of colour are heavy and I wanted to *hold them up* with the larger, but lighter weight reds.

Red is such a complex colour. Albers works with it and when he does, he *works* with it and its related colours: purples, browns, reds, oranges and some orange-yellows. There's a broad range of colours that will still say "red." Somewhere I wrote that if someone were to create a one-colour theory, that one colour would be *red*.

18 October, 1973. Thursday

Today I went to Mirvish Gallery to see the Olitski show. One painting was huge; most were small. It's difficult to hang small works well in that gallery. Even the largest piece was not hung well; it had two small narrow paintings at each end and I kept thinking of a couch with two lamps on end-tables. Olitski is using gel on some paintings; it leaves a roller tread. Some were spray painted. Most of the work was dated 1973, although some were from 1972. The 1972 works have a drier surface, more pleasing on close inspection. The gloss and greyed coloured gel in the 1973 paintings looks like a sugar coating on some works on close viewing; from a distance they look good. Olitski's works are a pleasure to see, but in a show like this it seems he's a *factory*.

The edge work was sometimes pencil thin on the new works. The edge line, drawn with spray, or brush stroke, or drip, is always so attractive. The frames didn't bother me as much this time; they are the same gold-edged frames that were used in the last show where they seemed to compete with the delicate edge work and overwhelm its colours. The large paintings always come off best in a show like this; still, to come upon a small one in a small room in a group show can be a good experience, too.

I went to Hughes-Owens and bought a set of Rapidograph pens. They are better than the ones I had at college. I'm going to use them to hand print the text of Barbara Godard's translation of Paul Chamberland's "I Have No" for Frank Davey's *Open Letter*. bp told Frank I could do it because I have "forged" *his* hand lettering. I'll imitate Chamberland's lettering. I've found the alphabet; I'm practising his hand.

We put the first of the 5 x 5 foot paintings on a stretcher. I am looking at the three paintings, #1, #2 and #4 now.

21 October, 1973. Sunday

I've been busy since the last entry. I'm ready now to start the next painting.

My slides came back from Moncrieff Williamson in PEI. He will consider my work for a 1975 group show, if not for a one man show. He thought he could see my work at Aggregation gallery when he came to Toronto, so I've written to correct that; he will have to visit the studio.

I've sent out two more sleeves of slides to 1) Owens Art Gallery at Mount Allison in New Brunswick and 2) Winnipeg Art Gallery. Yesterday, I set up two sleeves of slides to send to Alvin Balkind at AGO. That's ready to mail.

I finished the Paul Chamberland text. It's packaged and ready to be mailed back to Frank. I really like working with the Rapidograph pens.

I wrote a letter to Mike Doyle about his poems for a Seripress book. I was self-conscious about writing him; I told him all I could at this stage. Nelson read the letter and said it was fine. After I sealed it, Nelson told me that he felt a bit mean not telling me that it probably won't make any difference to Mike. He said he thought it was admirable, me writing Mike all the details of what I will do. Even if Mike doesn't know what I'm talking about, he will probably tell me to go ahead. Well, that's alright.

So now, I can think about my painting.

23 October, 1973. Tuesday

I finished the new painting today (*Colour Lock, Third Series #3*). At top centre, a green (toward blue) square shape with a blue-black at right and a purple-black at left (both are higher than wide). Below, two red square shapes: at left, a low red toward orange and at right an orange toward red. Both reds are warm like the colour of brick.

26 October, 1973. Friday

I have been looking at all four of the 5 x 5 foot paintings. I feel good about them. I like the use of "blacks," the lowest value ranges of colour. I want to go after a painting 12 feet long next. I'm reworking my sketches.

I have begun new drawings that combine pen and ink with graphite. Some good results; I find things out.

Carol came by yesterday. She saw the paintings; I don't think she liked them. She saw that I was drawing and asked where I was buying square paper. I told her I buy the same size of paper everyone else does and cut it. Once, when I was showing Milly some drawings, I said that I had drawn the shapes through stencils and she asked, "Where do you buy them?" I told her I make them. Strange.

28 October, 1973. Sunday
Frank Davey phoned this week to say he was pleased with the Chamberland piece.
He said he will give me a token payment when the issue comes out [*Open Letter.
Second Series, No. 7. Winter/Spring 1974*].

Some good things are happening with my drawings. They involve that "spatial-temporal dimension" that I worked with earlier. In these drawings I have
drawn the contour square with ink (pen line) and I've drawn the "field" with
graphite, making it active with line. By drawing the field, as opposed to leaving it
a white paper ground, I interrupt "space," or deep space (near/far relationship), and
emphasize the horizontal/vertical aspect of the plane. I have drawn pen line contours and off-set graphite contours ("alter-image") and then an activated linear
field. By changing the points of the pen, and changing the pencil weight from one
drawing to the next, I get new weights, new surfaces and almost a new "colour."
(I can't explain the appearance of colour.) Now, I'm drawing pen line contours,
each with a pen line alter-image, and a graphite linear field. This is working well,
but I'm not far enough into it to say more here.

The activity of the field gives substance to the energy of the space between
and around the contour shapes. The overlapping contours are not suspended in
"infinite" space; rather, they are *on a surface* and that surface, a web of hatched lines,
is as deliberate and finite as the contour shapes. I try to "draw" the eye back to the
surface, away from any illusion of depth [*Graphite and Ink Drawings, Series 10*. 15"
x 15"].

I have ordered canvas: forty yards of #10, 72" wide and twenty yards of #12,
54" wide. The cotton shortage has made canvas scarce and high priced.

29 October, 1973. Monday
Connie Keyser, the art consultant, called today. The people in Chicago decided to
hang prints in the room she had chosen for my painting. She will send back my
slides.

I thought I had finished with drawings yesterday, but last night, I began a new
one. It prompted a projection of two, possibly four, and now, probably six drawings. I'm working with pen line, with the "spatial-temporal dimension" as *surface* in
a new way. In the first drawing, I drew the surfaces of the square shapes with horizontal lines only; now, I am working with square shapes drawn with vertical lines
only. I think about drawing only diagonal lines. These drawings have 6 x 6 = 36
shapes; each square is drawn in the same direction. The lines of each square are
stacked; the squares are stacked on the square page. This relates to the three earlier
pencil line drawings where one large square fills the page: horizontal, vertical and

oblique. I considered doing this when I was working with graphite, but it seemed wrong; graphite lines are too varied. The drafting pen is right; the lines don't vary, but the spaces between my lines vary slightly, giving subtle variations to each shape's surface. I am drawing with the #2 point; I want to draw with the #00 point, too.

This is slow work. I must have spent seven hours on the first drawing. I have spent most of today on the second one and it is not finished yet. I'm anxious to see it complete, but that will only be achieved with slow and patient work.

My two entries to the Burnaby Print Show were rejected. I've entered three print shows this year and have had three rejections.

31 October, 1973. Wednesday
I called J. Leckie yesterday about the canvas and was told that my credit has been established and the order will be filled. I received the two slides from Connie Keyser in this morning's mail. That's finished.

I stripped the staples from the two new paintings and we rolled them. I finished the vertical line drawing and one drawn with only diagonal lines. Today, I began a drawing with the shapes drawn with horizontal lines using the #00 point.

It has rained every day this week, so I've put off going to galleries. I want to talk to Stephen Gadatsy about the show that Alan Foster is organizing.

3 November, 1973. Saturday
bp called yesterday. He'll come by tomorrow. Nelson picked up the proofs for the typeset pages for *Aleph Unit* and *Unit of Four* from Coach House Press. They look fine; I'll show them to bp.

Steve McCaffery called last night. He'll come on Wednesday to see what I've chosen for Seripress.

My canvas arrived. I expect it will cost about $240 when cutting and delivery are added.

We have stretched a piece of canvas, 12 feet long, on the easel-boards for the next painting. Right now, I'm drawing.

I'm at work on a drawing with the shapes drawn with vertical lines (#00 point) and I intend to draw another with diagonals. The #00 point is finer and the shapes are lighter and tighter than those drawn with the #2 point. When I draw the surface of the square shapes with horizontal or vertical lines, I allow the two free (or open) sides to be slightly irregular to emphasize the single lines. The diagonal line is more difficult to draw because all four sides of the square shape are free, so I hold down the irregularity.

It seemed right to move or shift the positions of the square shapes in a draw-ing in relation to the direction of the lines of the surfaces. The horizontal drawings are open and irregular; the verticals are closed with fewer irregular spaces; the diag-onal is open again, more open than the vertical and less than the horizontal and more regular than both.

5 November, 1973. Monday
bp and Ellie were here yesterday. bp is going to Florida at the end of this week. He was pleased with the proofs.

I have worked further on drawings. I'm drawing the square shapes with diag-onals now using the #00 point. This will be the final drawing for a while [*Ink Drawings, Series 11.* 15" x 15"].

8 November, 1973. Thursday
Steve McCaffery came last night. I showed him what I chose for Seripress, told him what I planned to do and he seemed satisfied for me to go ahead. I asked him if he had a title for the "Moon" pieces brought together and for someone who was so indecisive the last time we talked, he was pretty quick with the answer: *Moon. A Post-Semiotic Sequence.* I had him *spell it* for me and I wrote it down. I don't know what it means. I've looked up "semiotics" but it hasn't helped me get at "post-semiotic."

Nelson returned the proofs to Coach House; Nelson Adams will go ahead. He also took my instructions to the binder for the small portfolios for bp's two titles.

I've been working on my sketches for the next painting. This one will be 4 feet high and 11½ feet long. It will have nine colours in twelve shapes. I think about the colour energy that will pull this all together. Difficult — I'm pretty inse-cure about my decisions so far. How shall I say it?

9 November, 1973. Friday
I begin my painting. I have mixed the three reds and I'm applying the lowest now. (I write while the applications dry.) I've also mixed the blue; I hope to apply it today. The blue is the darkest colour in this painting and it will be repeated in three shapes, each a different size, each with a different position (juxtaposition). I have to see the blue now, for all the other colours will be middle to higher values. The orange and the yellow-green will be highest; the reds, although low value mixtures, will rise in value (I think).

Later: I have been working for 10 hours on this painting. I have applied three different red shapes and three shapes of the same blue — six shapes. I'm no more certain that this painting will work, for I can't "see" it until the last colour shape is applied and dry.

I made so many notes last night about how I would deal with this work. Of course, I didn't follow them, but it is somehow settling to think everything through, even to write it down. It doesn't really tell me what to do; rather, it tells me what *not* to do, so when I begin, I am focused. There are six more colours in seven shapes (a green will be repeated). I expect the green shapes (and the blue shapes I applied today) will be active with colour change because of differences in size and position. I'm very tired.

10 November, 1973. Saturday

I began to work on my painting at 11:30 this morning. It is just after 10 p.m. now and I am applying the last colour. I made some changes while mixing colours today; the green is lower in value than I intended earlier and the yellow-green is greyed which lowers it, too. The red-purple and the blue-purple shapes separate well as hues and they balance each other by their size and position. I'm pleased by this.

I can't say yet that the painting works. I mixed all of the colours in daylight hours and, once sure of them on the test sheet, I continued to work after dark. The painting is powerful and exciting to look at even now, but I want to see it in daylight. Tomorrow.

One thing: the three red shapes which lie together just left of the centre of the painting have lost some of their differences to each other. It may be because of their size, their interaction with each other or with the other colours. I don't know yet if I will need to make a change; the reds are satisfying even now.

Doug Fetherling came by this evening with some review copies for Nelson (for William Nelson Books). This is the first time anyone has come into the studio space while I have been painting. Doug was very good; he said "Hi" when he came in and "Good night" when he left. That's all. He and Nelson talked in the book room. I'm very sensitive about anyone stepping in here while a painting is happening. One word, anything, could interfere with what I have going.

11 November, 1973. Sunday

I am looking at my painting [*Colour Lock, Third Series #9.* 48" x 138"]. I'm happy with it; it works. I was afraid it would seem to have too many colours, but it pulls together. It is hugely complex. Its inner activity is still (quiet) on first viewing, but emerges as one stays with it. I discover new things happening in it. I have not *found it out* completely yet. I'll leave it on the boards for a while.

13 November, 1973. Tuesday

I've filled out and mailed the form for the exhibition that the Canadian

Committee for a Democratic Spain will have at OISE. I'll put in a framed drawing (22½" x 29"). The show is by invitation. Carol is upset because she didn't receive an invitation; Jim Gordaneer did.

I paid J. Leckie's bill for my canvas — $231. No charge for cutting or delivery.

My slides came back from the AGO with a friendly (funny) letter from Alvin Balkind. He said he is planning a Canadian show of "variations on a single theme" and wants my work in it and something from Michael Snow's series, *Walking Woman*. He ended his letter with, "You have not heard the last of me." Carol has been in touch with Balkind. She said he promised a studio visit, but made no appointment. She was quite upset. I told her that's not unusual; he will.

The four regular slide mailings are still out. So far, my little campaign has resulted in one firm exhibition date and five offers that I can follow up. At least, I am getting my work and my name out there. At best, I may hang some exhibitions over the next few years. I know that I would not have had the authority to do this without the one-man shows behind me. There's lots of promise ahead, but I'm suspicious that the public galleries are as poorly run as the private galleries. Chances seem good; I've learned to handle situations better by insisting on a clear understanding in advance and written terms.

I've been reading a lot over the past three months. I have made no note of it here.

15 November, 1973. Thursday

I stripped the staples from my painting and we rolled it last night. Today, we stretched a new piece of canvas on the boards. I have notes and sketches toward a painting that will use "blacks" and another that will use only blacks and greys.

I called Stephen Gadatsy today to ask about Alan Foster's show. Stephen said he has given Foster three of my drawings for it.

18 November, 1973. Sunday

I'm at work on the painting. I've been working for over 12 hours. I'm applying the last colour for today now. I have mixed and applied a blue-green, a blue and the four blacks — eight shapes in all. Because these shapes are dispersed on the canvas, I can't begin to "see" the painting yet. The colours look good so far.

19 November, 1973. Monday

I have mixed the two purples and I'm still mixing the grey-green. It is almost four o'clock; I have less than an hour of daylight left to determine my last colour. It seems right, now, but it's still cool-moist and I have to see it dry.

I am applying the blue-purple shapes. This colour becomes more purple, less blue, in contrast to the two blue shapes. The purples (dark) will raise in value in this painting because of their red component. I'll apply the grey shapes last. Because of the low range of the hues and the presence of four blacks (in five shapes), the chroma and value of the grey has been difficult to determine. I've added yellow (both cadmium yellow medium and yellow oxide). I have a medium grey that will be higher than middle in the painting. It leans toward green. I want to risk it high. I could lose the painting because of it.

21 November, 1973. Wednesday
I've been looking at my painting for two days now [*Colour Lock, Third Series #10.* 48" x 138"]. The grey was right; it works. This is an incredibly beautiful painting.

I'll leave this painting on the boards for a while; I have other work to do. I want to print; the stencil using larger square shapes is cut for one-colour prints (yellow). I intend to cut a stencil using the smallest square shapes to print "blue." I have Seripress work to do. I am thinking about two, maybe three more paintings.

I went to Yorkville yesterday. I saw Jared Sable's new gallery. The artist was there hanging his show — about fifteen paintings. I can't bring this artist's name to mind; he worked at the Mirvish Gallery, showed at the Dunkelman. Sable said he was "a genius" at his first show; there was much publicity.

The gallery has good space, but it is irregularly shaped with six walls in one room, four in another. There is a pillar at the centre that disturbs a partition wall. That wall is the focus for the room, so that pillar is unfortunate. There is no "signature wall"; in fact, when one enters the gallery, one sees another door in the far wall. But the long walls, even the odd shape of the place, give it good space.

I went to Marlborough-Godard Gallery and saw Gordon Smith's show. It is fine work, but there's something shallow about it. It makes me think of Richard Diebenkorn's work which also seems shallow to me. Smith's work is "tasteful" — a damning thing for me to say.

I looked in the window at Nancy Poole's Studio, but didn't go in. She's showing ceramic sculpture; the show got good reviews. The pieces look pot-like, globes with textured surfaces and slits for openings. Arthur (Mike) Handy did the last of these, the piece to end all others, when he made *Aphrodite Yawns.*

Gadatsy was showing Joe Rosenblatt. There is a lot of work hung; there have been about five sales. Joe's work is good; it has no pretensions. I was talking with Stephen when Lisl Levinsohn came in with her work so I saw her photostats of works already sold and the five original pieces she brought. Her work is very fine, but highly designed and somehow that makes it seem to lack imagination and intent. She has designed a postage stamp. She told us a horror story about a violation of her copyright, a mess that has already cost her more than she will ever receive even if she wins the case. She's sorry she ever started it.

Stephen told me that the artist's costs for a show in the gallery have risen from $100 to $200.

24 November, 1973. Saturday

Last night, we proofread the stencils for George Bowering's book [*Layers 1-13*] and for Mike Doyle's *Preparing for the Ark*. Nelson began to print and did all of Bowering's pages. Today, I began to work on the covers. The Bowering cover is ready for the printer and I have finished the lettering for bp's *Konfessions of an Elizabethan Fan Dancer*. I'm beginning the Doyle cover, but I'm not settled about it yet.

Tonight, I collated all the Bowering pages — five sheets, 400 copies — while Nelson typed the Nichol stencils. The typing will be slow; it's concrete poetry — thirty poems, about thirty-four sheets. Nelson will print on only one side of a sheet to avoid "see through."

I have put off my own printing (one-colour prints) until this Weed Flower Press work is done. These books will be the last titles from WFP; Nelson will retire the press. He has been doing this for nine years. I hate to see it stop, but four jobs are too many for Nelson. Right now, he needs to put his energy into bookselling and without WFP, he will be able to get back to his own writing.

27 November, 1973. Tuesday

bp and Ellie were here on Sunday. I showed them the cover for *Konfessions*; bp sparked when he saw it. He really likes it. He brought me his drawings for a collaboration, a new idea to merge our separate work in a way that is different from "Milt."

I spent yesterday over his notes and drawings. I can't work with them. He has drawn the block letter H and wants me to develop a series of colour prints from it. I can go nowhere with this. That volumetric H is too limiting and the complexity of its shapes give me more work than I care to do to reach an unsatisfying (and meaningless) end. I was totally frustrated by the end of the day. However, I made some sketches of my own — five images that develop from an H that is planar, not illusory. This looks like it could go somewhere and it invites the use of colour to get it there, but I'm not satisfied with it yet.

Nelson's printing is held up; the Gestetner has to be repaired, so bp's and Mike's books have to wait. We saw proofs of the covers today — one adjustment and they are fine. Big concern about paper shortages and rising prices. Gestetner paper will go up by 17% in January.

7 December, 1973. Friday
The hold-up on the WFP books is finally over. Nelson has a new rebuilt machine ($500); the old one would have cost too much to repair and the one Gestetner loaned Nelson until this one came didn't work. We lost a week and a half of work.

The Nichol book is printed and I'm collating it now. Mike's book is almost all printed; this one will go to the binder, but Nelson thinks it is too late now to have it ready for release this year. He's going to have to raise the prices for these books. All of the materials have gone up in the past few months. The covers cost $60 each; I remember that a cover cost $20 when we began doing this.

The "Art for Spain" show is on. The closing sale is tonight. Carol saw it and told me that the show is not good. It's a fundraiser. We'll see.

Alan Foster's show "Art '74" will open this weekend at the Beth Tzedec Synagogue.

17 December, 1973. Monday
Nelson is working at Marty's today. The Nichol and Bowering books are finished. Mike Doyle's book is still at the binder's, promised to be done before Christmas along with the two small portfolios for Seripress.

Nelson Adams finally finished printing the typeset pages for Seripress. Two of the pages for *Unit of Four* are the wrong size. The pages for *Aleph Unit* are okay. I will number the colophon pages and have bp sign them. I'll collate when I have the portfolios.

The folders with Nelson's poems are okay, but for the trim. Folded, they show the unevenness. I've done all the folding and tipped in my prints.

These Seripress titles will be priced at $7.50. I will use a new method for paying the author. bp told me that one-half of proceeds, after expenses, was too much; I should keep some money back so the press can do future titles. So, I am going to pay the author one-third of "anticipated sales." I will calculate the value of sales in advance (after expenses and after removing free copies from the edition) and pay the author at the same time I give him his author's copies, or from the first money received. When I am a co-author, we'll split that amount. The remaining two-thirds is for the press and for me as printer, designer, etc. (I do all the work.) If a title doesn't sell, or sells slowly, I will absorb it, or carry it.

I want to give the author *money*. This little press has been designed to make money. Nelson told me that poets don't expect money, that the author's copies are their payment. Maybe so, but if they were painters and had to watch every dollar that was paid for their work fall into someone else's pocket, they'd understand why this is important to me.

This morning, I received a letter from Christopher Youngs at Owens Art Gallery, Mount Allison University in New Brunswick, saying that he will be in Toronto on the 16th and 17th of January. He wants to visit the studio to see my work. I'll reply. My slides were not returned. I assume he will bring them with him.

I have put more work into bp's collaboration idea, but I've made no progress. I have the series I set down that starts with a planar H and moves to a Colour Lock composition, but it's too much mine, not bp's. I've considered printing it as my own title and dedicating it to bp, but I don't think I should do that. It is too far removed from bp's block letter H to be a collaboration, so I've set it aside. I don't know if we will get this collaboration off the ground. bp has given me too little (or too much?) to work with.

The "Art for Spain" show ended and my drawings were returned. It was not a very successful venture for the group. Foster's show, "Art '74," was more successful, but my works didn't sell. There is a catalogue for the show. Carol picked one up for me. I didn't get to the show.

Carol told me that Alvin Balkind told her that he has given my name and hers to the Junior Women's Committee at the AGO. They want to buy a painting by "a woman."

Balkind visited Carol's studio last Tuesday. He phoned me from there; he wanted to "drop in" because he was nearby. It was impossible because of all the books in here. Nelson was out (so I would have no help moving paintings) and Jim Gordaneer was here for a visit. I had to say no; this is just a little too informal. I am to call him in February.

It's cold in here. I'm working on sketches for the next painting.

Exhibition History

Solo Exhibitions:

1966	Gaslight Gallery, Kitchener, Ontario
1970	Aggregation Gallery, Toronto
1971	Colour Lock Series. Aggregation Gallery, Toronto
1973	Gadatsy Gallery, Toronto
1973	The Pollock Gallery, Toronto
1974	University Gallery: Ring House Number One, University of Alberta, Edmonton
1975	Colour Lock, Second Series. Owens Art Gallery, Mount Allison University, Sackville, NB
1977	Confederation Centre Art Gallery, Charlottetown, PEI
1977	Paintings 1969-1977. The Gallery/Stratford, Ontario
1979	Colour Lock, Grey Series. Agnes Etherington Art Centre, Queen's University, Kingston, Ontario
1982	Van Doesburg's Alphabet and Related Drawings. A.C.T., Toronto
1983	Colour Lock, Vertical Series. Erindale Campus Gallery, University of Toronto in Mississauga
1985	Plane Shape: Drawings 1984-85. The Manning Gallery, Toronto
1986	Small Paintings. The Manning Gallery, Toronto
1987	Paintings and Drawings. Lynnwood Arts Centre, Simcoe, Ontario (An Art Gallery of Ontario "Artists with their Work" exhibition.)
1988	Point to Line to Plane: Drawings 1973-1985. Kitchener-Waterloo Art Gallery, Ontario
1991	Primal Colour Paintings. Workscene Gallery, Toronto (With Judith Sandiford's Parallel Realities: Drawings.)
1994	Colour/Shape/Surface: small paintings and drawings 1987-88. Blackwood Gallery, Erindale Campus, University of Toronto in Mississauga
1994	Small Paintings and Drawings 1992-93. Lynnwood Arts Centre, Simcoe, Ontario (With Clive D'Oliveira's Five Year Survey.)
1996	Paintings 1990-91 and Drawings 1984 & 90. The Library and Gallery, Cambridge, Ontario
1999	Serial Works: Paintings and Drawings. Artword Gallery, Toronto
2000	Reds, Yellows, Blues, Blacks and Whites. Artword Gallery, Toronto
2002	The Alphabet Project: Part 1. Artword Gallery, Toronto
2003	The Alphabet Project and Beyond. Artword Gallery, Toronto
2004	Surfaces: drawings and paintings on paper. Artword Gallery, Toronto
2005	10 Paintings + 10 Drawings: 1989 and 1995-97. Artword Gallery, Toronto

Selected Group Exhibitions:

1964   Gran Fiera de Arte. Galería San Miguel,
         San Miguel de Allende, Gto., Mexico
1965   Painters of San Miguel. Instituto de Mexico y
         Norte Americano, Mexico City, Mexico
1966   94th Annual Exhibition. Ontario Society of Artists.
         Toronto Art Gallery
1966-67 87th Annual Exhibition. Royal Canadian Academy of Arts.
         Art Gallery of Ontario; National Gallery of Canada
1967   7th Annual Exhibition. Rodman Hall, St Catharines, Ontario
1971   Festival of Canada. Robertson Center for the Arts and Sciences,
         Binghamton, NY
1973   40th Annual Exhibition. Canadian Society of Graphic Arts.
         McIntosh Gallery, University of Western Ontario, London
1975   Festival of Women and the Arts. Art Gallery at
         Harbourfront, Toronto
1976-77 Abstractions. XXI Olympiad, Montreal, PQ;
         the Gallery/Stratford; Canadian Cultural Centre,
         Paris, France; Canada House, London, England
1977   Ontario Art Now 2. Art Gallery of Hamilton;
         Kitchener-Waterloo Art Gallery
1977-78 50 Canadian Drawings. Beaverbrook Art Gallery,
         Fredericton, NB and touring
1983   Contemporary Canadian Drawings. Agnes Etherington
         Art Centre, Queen's University
1984   Recent Acquisitions of Contemporary International
         Works on Paper. Art Gallery of Ontario
1986-87 Formalist Encounters. Woodstock Art Gallery, Ontario and touring
1991   The Empirical Presence. Optica, Montreal, PQ
2000   Regional Abstractions: Ontario. Confederation
         Centre Art Gallery, Charlottetown, PEI

Index of Persons

A

Acorn, Milton, 89
Adams, Nelson, 89, 230, 239, 247, 252
Ahvenus, Marty, 15, 21, 23, 25, 33, 61, 72, 75-77, 89, 91, 127, 131-32, 134, 191, 202, 204, 210, 215, 218
Albers, Anni, 240-41
Albers, Josef, 25, 37, 45, 59, 83, 89, 107, 111, 118, 120, 215, 217-19, 221, 243
Altwerger, Libby, 10, 17
Altwerger, Sandra, 17
Amaya, Mario, 55
Anderson, Allan, 113, 115
Andre, Carl, 84, 107
Annigoni, Pietro, 163
Appel, Karel, 71

B

Bacon, Francis, 25, 159
Balkind, Alvin, 233, 244, 249, 253
Ball, Helen, 224
Ball, Hugo, 28
Balthus, 164
Bannard, Darby, 69, 73, 75
Barbeau, Marcel, 160
Barbieri, Eugenio, 164
Barbour, Douglas, 70, 72
Barreto-Rivera, Rafael, 97
Baxter, Eve, 223, 230
Beaumont, Tib, 95
Bechtel, Jack, 19
Bennett, John, 203
Bergé, Carol, 36, 40, 42, 48, 53
Berton, Pierre, 101
Beveridge, Karl, 99
Bevington, Stan, 30, 39, 45, 64, 86-87, 89-90
Biederman, Charles, 234
Bieler, Ted, 20
Bill, Max, 210
Birkhans, Dace, 13, 17, 24-25, 30
Birney, Earle, 30-31, 33, 35, 48, 64-65, 70-71, 207
Bissett, Bill, 39, 47, 127
Blackwood, David, 103
Blake, William, 135
Bloore, Ronald, 122, 128
Bolduc, David, 87-88, 99, 101, 107, 122
Borduas, Paul-mile, 160
Bornstein, Eli, 233-34
Bowering, Angela, 71
Bowering, George, 58, 71, 79, 130, 251-52

Breeze, Claude, 29, 122
Brianski, Rita, 10
Brodzky, Anne, 75, 84, 96, 100-03, 120, 128, 131-32
Buri, Steve, 18, 21, 27-29, 31-33
Burton, Dennis, 20, 72
Bury, Pol, 122
Bush, Jack, 69, 98, 101-02, 106, 210-11

C

Cain, Jack, 9, 15, 25, 32, 35-36, 48-49, 108
Calderara, Antonio, 158
Calleja, Joseph, 202
Cameron, Dorothy, 36, 128
Caro, Anthony, 69
Carr, Emily, 217
Casson, A.J., 122
Cézanne, Paul, 122, 155
Chadwick, Lynn, 202
Chamberland, Paul, 243-45
Chambers, Jack, 36, 202, 233
Chandler, John Noel, 102
Chow, Raymond, 135, 138
Claisse, Geneviève, 162, 210
Clark, Ian, 137-38
Cleaver, Elizabeth, 145
Cliff, Dennis, 103, 112-14, 118
Cockburn, Bruce, 29, 72
Cohen, Leonard, 33, 138
Coleman, Victor, 23, 30-32, 38, 40, 44-46, 51, 56, 58, 68, 74-76, 79, 84, 86, 89-90, 102, 113, 126
Collyer, Robin, 95
Colombo, John Robert, 71, 93-94, 206, 219, 222
Colombo, Ruth, 93
Comptois, Ulysse, 20
Coughtry, Graham, 25
Creeley, Bobbie, 23
Creeley, Robert, 12, 23
Crozier, Andrew, 190
Cruz-Diez, Carlos, 132, 160
Cull, David, 14, 16, 48
Cumming, Glen, 237
Curnoe, Greg, 20, 71, 95-97, 99
Currelly, Judy, 230, 236

D

Dali, Salvador, 120, 211
Dault, Gary Michael, 96
Davey, Frank, 243-45
Davis, Ronald, 69
Deakin, Len, 201, 222
Delaunay, Robert, 91, 143, 154
Delaunay, Sonia, 154
Denny, Robyn, 89

Diao, David, 121
Dibbets, Jan, 132, 144
Dick, Gernot, 75, 78, 91, 108, 228, 232
Diebenkorn, Richard, 250
Dine, Jim, 72, 84, 106, 151
Dobbs, Kildare, 130-31, 232
Doesburg, Theo van, 143, 196, 235
Domela, César, 187-88
Dorn, Peter, 206
Downing, Robert, 63, 78, 93, 101, 114, 203, 221-22
Downing, Sally, 63, 221-22
Doyle, Mike, 117, 129-30, 132, 244, 251-52
Dubuffet, Jean, 142, 202
Duchamp, Marcel, 203
Dufy, Raoul, 122, 154
Dunlop, Alasdair, 238-39
Dürer, Albrecht, 139, 142
Dwyer, Peter, 48

E

Eastcott, Wayne, 95
Ernst, Max, 160
Eyre, Ivan, 95

F

Favro, Murray, 202
Ferron, Marcelle, 160
Fetherling, Doug, 55, 91, 93, 96, 132, 153, 215, 222, 232, 248
FitzGerald, L.L., 122
Flavin, Dan, 71
Foster, Alan, 229, 246, 249, 252-53
Foster, Doreen, 145
Fournier, Paul, 87-88, 101, 106, 119-20, 123, 215, 230
Frankenthaler, Helen, 69, 113-14, 123, 210
Fraser, Ted, 233
French, Wally, 53
French, William, 101
Frenkel, Vera, 133, 162, 205, 227, 239

G

Gadatsy, Julianne, 225-26
Gadatsy, Stephen, 225-26, 229, 231, 235, 239, 246, 249-51
Gagnon, Clarence, 217
Gagnon, Colette, 67
Gaucher, Yves, 202
Ghiberti, Lorenzo, 182-84
Gillespie, Ron, 214, 230
Godard, Barbara, 243
Godard, Mira, 223, 230
Goethe, J. W. von, 59, 146, 149